"In *Hope for W   great gift: a true-
life story filled   'e all, grace. This
is a real-life jou   sion and related
disorders, told   ess of personal
conviction that   ⌐ above more didactic
works on the sub   ..cc s lean, unsentimental style draws us in,
sits us down near a warm fire, and confidingly shares with us the soul-
secrets of a true survivor. The most profound kind of healing always
comes from those brave enough to return from battle, emotionally
undress, and show us their ugly wounds. And by allowing us into this
most private of places, *Hope for Wholeness* reflects the true face of the
healing Christ."

—JIM ROBINSON, professional recovery counselor; author of
Prodigal Song: A Memoir; founder of ProdigalSong Ministries

"As a professional counselor, I have witnessed the spiritual, emotional,
and physical devastation caused by depression. And as a survivor of
suicide, I've experienced the 'collateral damage' Sharon Fawcett
describes—the trauma sustained by those who love someone with
depression. But Sharon's words break through the darkness like a beam
of hope for those grappling with this illness. Out of her own healing,
Sharon offers a hand up to the wounded trying to find their way out
of the valley of depression. Each chapter is a trail marker, carefully
placed for journeyers willing to follow her through the rugged terrain.
Hope for Wholeness will illumine your course to freedom and empower
you to illuminate the way for others."

—DR. DAVID COX, author; counselor; speaker; coauthor of *Aftershock:
Help, Hope, and Healing in the Wake of Suicide*

"*Hope for Wholeness* gives a fresh look at the subject of depression from
a spiritual perspective. This book is more than the author's own dark
but ultimately triumphant journey through depression. It is a comprehensive look at the physical, emotional, and spiritual stranglehold
depression has on a multitude of individuals, Christians included.
Sharon Fawcett provides a voice of encouragement, understanding,

support, and hope for those languishing in the wilderness of depression. This book is a must-read for the depressed and those who love them."

"Sharon Fawcett's drama—trauma, one might say—explodes upon the mind in its opening paragraphs. *Hope for Wholeness* is no mild documentary of one woman's depression; rather, it is an excavation of the ruins of one woman's soul—and the silent movie of its reconstruction. Whether you have wrestled this enemy personally or know others who have, Sharon's warfare of hope will become your own, and you will be equipped like never before to defeat the scourge of depression. I highly commend it."

"Sharon Fawcett does an excellent job illuminating the spiritual aspects of depression without discounting the potential benefits of medical evaluation and treatment. Sharon's firsthand account of her illness, along with chapters that share perspectives from her husband and children, is both tragic and triumphant. Honest and inspiring, these pages offer a lifeline to those struggling with depression. If you or a loved one is suffering, find hope here."

"Sharon Fawcett's story of depression and anorexia is woven with the fibers of anguish and hope. Anyone who has experienced the pain of either of these disorders will recognize the conflicted emotions, confusion, and struggle. But what they will also see is the beautiful thread of God's hope woven into the tapestry of this account. This hope is not presented glibly but as a necessary and much-overlooked spiritual component to treatment and recovery."

SHARON L. FAWCETT

HOPE

for

WHOLENESS

THE SPIRITUAL PATH TO
FREEDOM FROM DEPRESSION

NAVPRESS

NavPress is the publishing ministry of The Navigators, an international Christian organization and leader in personal spiritual development. NavPress is committed to helping people grow spiritually and enjoy lives of meaning and hope through personal and group resources that are biblically rooted, culturally relevant, and highly practical.

For a free catalog go to www.NavPress.com
or call 1.800.366.7788 in the United States or 1.800.839.4769 in Canada.

© 2008 by Sharon L. Fawcett

All rights reserved. No part of this publication may be reproduced in any form without written permission from NavPress, P.O. Box 35001, Colorado Springs, CO 80935. www.navpress.com

NAVPRESS and the NAVPRESS logo are registered trademarks of NavPress. Absence of ® in connection with marks of NavPress or other parties does not indicate an absence of registration of those marks.

ISBN-13: 978-1-60006-215-5
ISBN-10: 1-60006-215-6

Cover design by Arvid Wallen
Cover image by Shutterstock

Some of the anecdotal illustrations in this book are true to life and are included with the permission of the persons involved. All other illustrations are composites of real situations, and any resemblance to people living or dead is coincidental.

Unless otherwise identified, all Scripture quotations in this publication are taken from the *HOLY BIBLE: NEW INTERNATIONAL VERSION®* (NIV®). Copyright © 1973, 1978, 1984 by International Bible Society. Used by permission of Zondervan Publishing House. All rights reserved. Other versions used include: *THE MESSAGE* (MSG). Copyright © 1993, 1994, 1995, 1996, 2000, 2001, 2002, 2005. Used by permission of NavPress Publishing Group; *The Living Bible* (TLB), Copyright © 1971, used by permission of Tyndale House Publishers, Inc., Wheaton, IL 60189, all rights reserved; *The Holy Bible, New Century Version* (NCV) copyright © 1987, 1988, 1991 by Word Publishing, Dallas, Texas 75039. Used by permission; the *Holy Bible*, New Living Translation (NLT), copyright © 1996. Used by permission of Tyndale House Publishers, Inc., Wheaton, Illinois 60189. All rights reserved; *Today's New International® Version* (TNIV)®. Copyright 2001, 2005 by International Bible Society®. All rights reserved worldwide; *GOD'S WORD* (GW) is a copyrighted work of God's Word to the Nations Bible Society. Quotations are used by permission. Copyright 1995 by God's Word to the Nations Bible Society. All rights reserved; *Holman Christian Standard Bible* (HCSB), copyright © 1999, 2000, 2002, 2003 by Holman Bible Publishers; the *Good News Translation* (GNT), second edition, copyright © 1992 by American Bible Society. Used by permission; and the *King James Version* (KJV).

Library of Congress Cataloging-in-Publication Data
Fawcett, Sharon L., 1963-
  Hope for wholeness : the spiritual path to freedom from depression /
Sharon L. Fawcett.
    p. cm.
  Includes bibliographical references (p.   ).
  ISBN-13: 978-1-60006-215-5
  ISBN-10: 1-60006-215-6
  1. Depression, Mental--Religious aspects--Christianity. 2. Depressed persons--Religious life. 3. Fawcett, Sharon L., 1963- I. Title.
  BV4910.34.F39 2008
  248.8'625--dc22
                          2008023747

Printed in the United States of America

1 2 3 4 5 6 7 8 / 12 11 10 09 08

Being deeply loved by someone gives you strength;
loving someone deeply gives you courage.

Lao Tzu, philosopher

To Tim, Lauren, and Jenna. Because you loved, I live.

CONTENTS

FOREWORD

Have you ever felt hopeless? Helpless? Despondent? Worthless? Mentally and physically exhausted? Have you ever thought that the world and, more specifically, your loved ones would be better off without you? If you have, then you are among the countless victims of the "blues" epidemic sweeping the country. The number of people seeking medical treatment for depression has more than doubled in the United States in the last ten years. What is even more alarming is that most who suffer from depression never seek any kind of help even though many treatment options are available.

Suppose you have the courage to come out of the shadows and ask for help. Where should you go? Should you see your pastor? A doctor? A therapist? A psychiatrist? Suppose your doctor correctly diagnoses your depression. What is he going to do in the ten minutes allowed by most HMOs? The doctor has only two choices: to write out a prescription for medication or make a referral. A psychiatrist is also a medical doctor and most do very little therapy work. So the psychiatrist will likely prescribe an antidepressant as well, or electroconvulsive therapy (shock treatment) in extreme cases. Licensed counselors and therapists cannot legally medicate, so they will treat depression as a psychological disorder and employ various techniques to help you think and live more responsively.

Pastoral counseling will vary greatly depending upon the pastors' education and experience. Some will not even try to provide counseling for mental and emotional problems. Godly pastors will try to help you in your relationship with your heavenly Father. Family and friends may try to jolly you up, scold you, or ignore you. It seems that friends do a lot better job of taking care of others' physical needs than of their mental and emotional needs. "How is your back doing today?" is a legitimate question, but "How is your head doing today?" isn't. That is one reason depressed people withdraw from others.

Depression is a body, soul, and spirit problem; and it requires a body, soul, and spirit answer, but seldom is such holistic help available. Most people will seek medical treatment first, and that usually takes into consideration only the physical. There certainly is a proper place for medication. Taking a pill to cure your body is commendable, but taking a pill to cure your soul is deplorable, and may the Good Lord grant us the wisdom to know the difference.

It is unlikely that the human race has undergone such radical physical changes in our brain chemistry and genes in the last ten years that would cause this increase in depression. It makes more sense to view the roots of the epidemic as being psychological and spiritual. Cognitive therapists have observed that depressed people generally have a negative view of themselves, their circumstances, and the future. Many agree that it is a sense of helplessness and hopelessness and that the precipitating cause is most often a reaction to losses in their lives.

I generally agree with this reasoning, but secular psychology can vary quite a bit from Christian psychology. God has not only defined who we are in Christ, He has also revealed in His Word adequate answers for our helplessness and hopelessness and shown how we can overcome our losses. Pastoral counselors also incorporate the reality of the spiritual world and rely upon the Holy Spirit to guide them. In *Discipleship Counseling*, I explain the role that God plays—or should play—in every counseling session.

My own counseling started to produce incredible results when I intentionally included the Wonderful Counselor in the process. There is a role that God and only God can play in our lives, and we must usurp that role. Only God can bind up the brokenhearted and set the captive free. Including the reality of the spiritual world means we must take into account Paul's warning in 1 Timothy 4:1, "The Spirit clearly says that in later times some will abandon the faith and follow deceiving spirits and things taught by demons." That is presently happening all over the world.

Sharon has written a remarkable book about her long ordeal with depression. The length of her depression was largely due to seeing her problem as only a biological and psychological disorder and seeking help only in the secular world. When she finally accepted godly counsel, she found her freedom in Christ. Her story is not unique; we have seen hundreds set free in the same way she was. I hope you read every page of this book and learn from someone who has "been there and tried that."

—DR. NEIL T. ANDERSON, founder and president emeritus of Freedom in Christ Ministries; coauthor of *Overcoming Depression* with his wife, Joanne

ACKNOWLEDGMENTS

I spent nine years in depression's wilderness and the next nine years writing a book about it. During each journey, I became lost and in need of direction and support. God provided both, often choosing to use human ambassadors.

Tim, in the darkest period of my life, your love seemed like the only thing I could count on. Though God felt far off, I now know He was there all along, wrapped in your skin. Thank you for loving me so deeply, so faithfully, and so well.

Lauren and Jenna, though you did not choose your parents, you did choose your response to a mother who failed to be all the things you needed. Thank you for offering love, forgiveness, and a second chance. You are so precious to me.

Tim, Lauren, and Jenna, I deeply appreciate your great patience in the seemingly endless process of writing this book and your willingness to allow me to share about a traumatic time in our history. Your contributions to chapter 5 were much needed; you are truly the experts on how to survive when a loved one is depressed.

To my family: They say it takes a village to raise a child. At the very least, it takes an extended family, particularly when one parent's presence is diminished by depression. Your involvement in Lauren's and Jenna's lives has not gone unnoticed, nor has the love and support you've offered me in spite of my many flaws and aggravations. I am deeply grateful. Mom and Dad, thank you for the values you instilled in me; for the hard-work ethic, honesty, and integrity you modeled; and for your love. George and Roberta, I am indebted to you for all you invested in your son — my devoted husband, a wonderful father, and a generous human being.

I'm grateful to my faith family for offering acceptance and love rather than condemnation and criticism during the years of my depression. Your response should be the model for churches everywhere.

Without the compassion and expert care I received from my psychiatrist, I would not have survived depression. Dr. C., you are a wonderful person and an extraordinary professional. I will never forget your wisdom, perseverance, and legendary patience.

When it looked as if my depression would never end, God led me to the office of a woman He would use to change my life. Berys Richardson, not only did you lead me to God's healing, you helped me develop a deeper relationship with Him. I wish it hadn't taken me nine years to find you; you are a truly gifted counselor.

Near the beginning of my writing journey, I received a phone call from a fellow writer and friend who offered some much-needed advice. Glenn MacDonald, if you hadn't suggested I attend a writers' conference, this book may never have come to fruition. Thank you for your encouragement and enthusiasm. I'm also grateful for the advice you kindly offered (and I initially spurned) to consider Christian counseling and read *The Bondage Breaker.*

I'm indebted to Marita Littauer and the staff at CLASServices for conducting top-notch speakers' and writers' conferences. Through the CLASSeminar and Glorieta Christian Writers' Conference, I met many of the people who became my mentors, encouragers, teachers, and friends — I'm grateful to you all.

Jerome Daley, I will always remember you as my first "divine appointment" at my first writers' conference. You've passionately seen this book through from its disjointed beginning to publication. Thank you for challenging me — in writing and life — as my coach and friend.

Jim Robinson, your life is a testament to the healing power of Christ and the fullness of the redemption He offers. I am so blessed to know you. Thank you for your generous spirit, your support of my writing, and your friendship. Maybe one day we *will* get to work together!

Les Stobbe, my agent, I appreciate your willingness to take a chance on an unknown first-time author. Thank you for representing me well. Thanks to Kate Epperson for championing my book at NavPress, and to the many people at this fine publishing house who committed to seeing this project through to completion.

Liz Heaney, thank you for your enthusiasm and encouragement and for enlarging my vision for this book. You really raised the bar — and gave me a boost over it! I'm grateful to have had the opportunity to work with such a gifted editor.

Dr. Neil T. Anderson, your generous endorsement brings me full circle: initially running from your teaching, finally embracing it, and now receiving your support of my work. As readers will discover, my freedom from depression is a testament to the power of your own book *The Bondage Breaker*. I am deeply indebted to you for your offer to write the foreword for *Hope for Wholeness*.

And finally, to God, the Engineer of this project and my life, I don't deserve Your grace, mercy, and love, but I accept them with gratitude. Thank You for carrying me when I was too weak to follow and for holding me close to Your heart. Though You are still writing my story, I know it will have a happy ending.

PART ONE

ILLUMINATING
THE DARKNESS

Chapter 1

CAUGHT IN THE DELUGE
of DEPRESSION

*The waves of death swirled about me; the torrents of
destruction overwhelmed me.*

2 Samuel 22:5

It should have been a day for tears, but I was no longer able to cry.
Shrouded in a damp, gray fog of apathy, I had lost the capacity for
emotion.

It was April 22, 1990, three days after my baby's first birthday. The
winter snow had finally melted on Canada's east coast, and the promise
of new life whispered in the warm, fragrant breath of spring. But my
spirit was out of touch with the seasons, still trapped in winter's long,
cold night. I walked slowly across the yard to my house, soggy brown
grass squishing beneath my feet. *How long will I be gone?* I wondered.

Hearing the door open, my daughters came looking for "Mommy."
One-year-old Jenna tottered into the entryway, still unstable with her
new skill of walking. Four-year-old Lauren followed closely behind her
sister, eyes wide, looking like a concerned little mother with arms ready
to catch Jenna should she stumble.

As they made their way toward me, my soul sighed. *How can I leave them? How can I help them understand what's happening?* Even *I* didn't understand, yet I knew I was no longer able to provide the love and attention my daughters needed and deserved.

Just one year earlier, as I lay holding my newborn daughter in the birthing room, I had been overcome by a sense of peace and contentment unlike anything I'd ever felt before. My life seemed perfect. I had a wonderful husband, Tim, and two beautiful children. So what had gone wrong?

In the past few months, it had become apparent to me that my fairy-tale life was slipping away. Instead of looking forward to each new day, I dreaded waking up. Talking to my girls, telling them stories, and listening to their chatter once delighted me; now the sound of their voices grated on my raw nerves. I no longer wanted to talk, listen, or answer anyone's questions. I craved solitude and silence.

None of my previous hobbies or activities interested me anymore. I didn't want to leave the house, or even my bed. I just wanted to sleep — eternally, if possible.

Who is this person I've turned into? I wondered. I had become an empty arrangement of bones dressed in skin — warm, breathing, and moveable but devoid of any spark of life. It seemed that my spirit had died, and as each day passed, my longing to rejoin it, wherever it had gone, grew stronger.

After I described my desire for death to my physician, he immediately referred me to a psychiatrist. Dr. Ahmed* agreed to see me the next day. He diagnosed me with major clinical depression and recommended I be hospitalized for my own protection.

As I carried my bags down the stairs and stopped in the hallway to say good-bye to my girls, I waited for the sadness to well up and spill over — but it never came. There was only a twinge of pity for these two precious children whose misfortune it was to have me as their mother.

---

* Name changed.

Holding my daughters tight, I assured them I'd be back soon. Then I walked out the door, climbed into the car, and vanished. For nine years.

Though I would return for weekend visits, or be discharged from the hospital for a few months at a time, the woman who came home was not the mother my children remembered. She would not return before they learned to live without her.

BEING ADMITTED

As I made my way down the long hallway toward the psychiatric unit, I sensed that with each reluctant step I was losing a piece of myself. As the heavy metal door clanged shut behind me, despair and confusion flooded my soul. *What's someone like me doing in a place like this?* I asked myself.

While my husband met with the psychiatrist, a nurse showed me to my room and proceeded to search through my belongings. I fought back tears as she removed the sharp items. I had always believed myself to be a responsible person; the realization that I couldn't be trusted with a disposable razor or metal coat hanger was very humbling.

After the nurse completed admission procedures and outlined the unit's rules, Tim returned and sat next to me on the small cot in my tiny curtained room. I searched his eyes for some sign of hope. Taking my hand in his, Tim told me that the doctor was confident the medication he prescribed would help. "Dr. Ahmed said you should be feeling better in a couple of weeks. Then you'll be able to come home."

Two weeks isn't such a long time, I assured myself. But the doctor was wrong.

Searching for the Missing Pieces

If I had known what lay ahead for me in my struggle with depression, I am not sure I would have persevered. But since I didn't know healing would elude me for many years, each time a new medication was prescribed, I could hope that it might be the one that would cure my brain and restore my life. Each night when I went to bed, I could imagine that tomorrow might be the day the doctor would ask the "right" question and some revelation in my counseling session might help me discover the cause of my despondency.

I am thankful that God keeps some things to Himself.

Dr. Ahmed and his colleagues seemed to believe I should know why I was depressed, but I didn't. My symptoms of depression didn't begin until eight or nine months after Jenna's birth, so postpartum depression was ruled out.[1] Other than having a baby, nothing in my life had changed in the previous year, but a painful transformation had taken place within me, a transformation as confounding as it was profound. I began to wonder if anyone could help me or if I would be left to solve this puzzle on my own.

As the days stretched into weeks, I searched for answers to a question that would turn my life upside down, a question that would take nearly a decade to solve: *Why?*

During my depression, I was an information junkie; I read everything about the illness I could get my hands on, thinking that if I learned enough, I could find my way out of the pit I'd fallen into. I tried to put into practice all the advice from each author and expert — to take my medication; change my thoughts; express my anger; make goals; visualize myself as a happy, successful person — but it seemed my efforts were in vain. *Either I'm a failure or these authors don't know what they're talking about*, I believed. I now understand that the authors did give good advice for those whose depression is emotionally or biologically sourced. It's just that I was not one of those people.

When I emerged from depression, I felt compelled to write a book that would help others, like me, who did not find complete and lasting freedom through medical or psychological treatments. *Hope for Wholeness* is that book.

HOW TO USE THIS BOOK

As you journey with me through the pages of this book, I hope you will come to understand that depression is not an enemy trying to rob you of life but rather an opportunity for self-examination and spiritual growth. I hope you will learn to identify the potential spiritual roots of depression and investigate spiritual treatments. I hope that through the deeply personal account of my battle with the illness, you will gain insight into your own depression. Most of all, I hope you will find in this book what I wish it hadn't taken me nine years to discover: the path to freedom.

Hope for Wholeness is divided into four parts:

Part One: Illuminating the Darkness investigates the complex relationship between physical, emotional, and spiritual health, and addresses the impact of depression on loved ones.

Part Two: Identifying Spiritual Roots dissects five contributing factors to spiritually rooted depression.

Part Three: Exploring Spiritual Treatments describes three powerful spiritual treatments for depression.

Part Four: Preserving and Advancing teaches how to maintain freedom from depression.

Each chapter opens with part of my story and moves into a discussion of the chapter theme, followed by "Encouragement from God's Word," a section designed to offer you hope found in Scripture. Sometimes I'll share a story from the Bible that corresponds with the chapter's topic; other times I'll use scriptural principles.

The questions in the "Self-Reflection" section are designed to help you consider what you've learned and apply it to your life. You may want to keep a journal or notebook so you can record your thoughts and answers.

Each chapter concludes with relevant quotes or Scripture verses for you to meditate on. You may want to memorize them, but if memorization is difficult for you, write them out and post them where you will see them every day. Let these positive messages nourish your spirit.

While the chapters in *Hope for Wholeness* loosely follow the chronological progression of my depression, there may be times when you feel compelled to read a certain chapter out of order. For example, if you are struggling with thoughts of suicide, skip ahead to chapter 4. This book is designed to be a manageable read for those who have difficulty concentrating due to depression. You can focus on a chapter at a time, or you may choose to read just one section of the chapter before taking a break. Do whatever works best for you.

At the end of the book, you'll find three appendixes. Appendix A lists some resources I recommend for further information, inspiration, and encouragement. If you have unresolved questions when you finish the book, check out these resources. Appendixes B and C offer help to those who have loved ones with depression (your friends and family members, for example). Please feel free to share those sections with them so they will know how to better support you as well as take care of themselves in this difficult time.

In between each of the four parts of the book, you'll find an inspirational story. During my depression, I was drawn to stories like these, though I didn't understand why at the time. Mostly I read memoirs of Nazi Holocaust survivors and in the span of a year or so had devoured more than three thousand pages in a dozen books. Every story I read was about someone who lived to tell it, who persevered through incomprehensible suffering. These documentaries helped me believe that if humans could survive such horrors, it was possible that I could endure my own emotional nightmare. These extraordinary accounts of courage fostered in me the kind of grit and determination I'd need to stay alive. They gave me hope. For that reason, I've decided to share a few of my favorites with you. If there's a day you're in desperate need of encouragement to keep going, feel free to jump ahead to a "Story of Hope."

I am grateful to the people who shared their life stories and wisdom with me over the years. God worked in my life through them. Now it's my turn to pass something on to others. It's my prayer that God will use this book to restore your hope and launch you on your own amazing path to freedom.

If you benefit from *Hope for Wholeness*, I'd love to hear about it. Send me a "postcard" from your journey by using the Contact Form on my website, SharonFawcett.com. I can't wait to find out where God leads you!

CHAPTER 2

SEEKING UNDERSTANDING

Why are you downcast, O my soul? Why so disturbed within me?

Psalm 43:5

As Dr. Ahmed, the nurses, and a social worker interviewed my husband and me and learned about our lives, they all seemed puzzled about why I was so profoundly depressed. Tim was confused about why their cure hadn't worked—why I seemed more distraught than ever.

When none of the treatments proved successful, Dr. Ahmed and the social worker began to suspect that my marriage was the culprit and that I was hiding something from them. The doctor told me that if I wouldn't reveal what was wrong, he could give me an injection of sodium amytal ("truth serum") to make me more comfortable sharing. This sounded like something pulled from the plot of a spy movie, not our lives! Though it seemed like a threat to me, I longed to know the truth and gave my permission for the injection. But the doctor did not follow through, and the drug was never mentioned again.

Next, the social worker told me that he wished to conduct a videotaped interview with my husband and me so that he could—among other things—interpret our body language and prove his theory that there was something fundamentally wrong with our relationship. When I told Tim this, he was shocked. *What are they thinking?* he wondered. Tim was concerned that someone would convince me there were problems that didn't exist, but he consented to the interview. Afterward, we were shown no tape, given no interpretation, and the issue was dropped. Thus began my husband's search for a new doctor.

At that time, most psychiatrists in our province had very long waiting lists, but an acquaintance recommended someone in another city and Tim was able to secure an appointment for me. (I have never stopped believing this was a case of divine intervention.) When my husband spoke to Dr. Ahmed about releasing me from the hospital, the doctor admitted that he and the staff had "run into a brick wall" where my case was concerned. He would welcome a second opinion.

I was discharged on July 13, 1990, almost three months after my admission. Later that day, I traveled for more than an hour to meet with Dr. Colford.* This was the first of hundreds of trips for appointments with her as well as admissions to the hospital in her city.

My first experience with a psychiatrist had not been a positive one and made me reluctant to trust another doctor, but Dr. Colford seemed different. She was pleasant, open-minded, and kindhearted—an island of compassion in the sea of my despair. I soon felt at ease in her presence. In the years to follow, I would come to know her as a consummate professional and quintessential optimist with a zest for life that I'd never before witnessed.

On this day, though, I was amazed to discover that Dr. Colford didn't expect me to know why I was depressed. Instead of challenging me, she began to explain what was happening to me, and everything she said resonated truth. I left her office that afternoon in July believing I had finally met someone who might understand me and who would be willing to help me understand myself. For the first time since the

---

* Name changed.

waves of depression had washed over me, I glimpsed a light blinking on the rocky shore: a glimmer of hope.

EXAMINING DEPRESSION

One of the first questions asked by doctors when they suspect that someone is suffering from depression is, "Do you have a family history of depression?" Not only was I unaware of any relatives who'd had depression, I didn't think I knew *anyone* who'd had the illness. I'd heard very little about depression up to the time of my diagnosis and was under the impression that I was some sort of pioneer!

Now I know how wrong that notion was; depression is not a twentieth-century phenomenon. In fact, there are several characters in the Bible who exhibit symptoms of the illness. (We'll explore some of their stories later in the chapter.) I also discovered, years after I was well, that there *were* people in my community — even in my church — fighting their own private battles with depression, while I fought a more public one.

Once I was healed, other people began coming to me — and to Tim — for advice. It quickly became obvious that we were in the midst of a virtual epidemic of depression. And as I sat with people, listening to them speak in hushed tones, seeing the look of shame on their faces, and hearing them recount the negative response that their illness had evoked in others, I realized there was a stigma associated with depression; many saw it as a character flaw or weakness.

The more I listened and the more I read, I also came to understand that the stigma was strong among Christians. You probably think I had my head in the sand during the years of my depression, but you must realize I didn't get out much. My energy was spent on surviving, not surveying the opinions of others about my illness. To me, depression was just some strange, serious sickness I'd come down with. I didn't know there were people who thought I should feel guilty about having it.

I'm thankful that no one in my church ever shamed me for having depression. I never heard a negative comment, but I think I'm in the minority.

Because of society's stigmatization of depression, you may be one of the many who suffer in silence, thinking, *No one will understand what I'm feeling. I should be able to shake it off. My faith in God is supposed to bring me joy; since I'm depressed, it must mean my faith is weak.* Perhaps you are feeling ashamed because no matter how hard you try, how much you pray, or how much confessing and repenting you do, the dark cloud hovering over your spirit refuses to lift. Believe me, you are not alone.

The World Health Organization ranks depression as the leading cause of disability worldwide and the third leading contributor to the global burden of disease,[1] following lower respiratory infections and HIV/AIDS.[2] But in high-income countries, depression ranks number one in both categories.[3]

Although millions of people are living with the illness right now, many are afraid to admit it, talk about it, or seek treatment. It's estimated that 41 percent of depressed women are too ashamed to ask for help[4] and 80 percent of all depressed persons are currently receiving no treatment.[5] Society as a whole still lacks understanding about the illness (54 percent of people believe it is a personal weakness[6]) and, for the most part, the church is no more knowledgeable.

While we all get "the blues" now and then, times when our mood is unusually sad and gloomy, this is a passing phase for most. However, when feelings of sadness persist longer than a few weeks and interfere with one's ability to function, it may be categorized as major depressive disorder (or major clinical depression), a serious but treatable mental illness that changes how a person thinks, feels, and acts. (For the signs and symptoms of depression, visit the National Institute of Mental Health's website, http://www.nimh.nih.gov/health/topics/depression/index.shtml.)

Reaching Out for Help

My heart breaks when I think of those people too afraid or ashamed to ask for help, trying to find their way out of depression on their own. If you are one of them, please believe me when I say, *You can't do it alone. There is no shame in reaching out for help.*

Few of us go through life without ever requiring counsel of some sort, whether from a pastor, financial advisor, doctor, colleague, or trusted friend. Challenges present themselves in every aspect of living and working, and those who rise above them are often those who look for the solutions outside themselves. The results of refusing to seek—or ignoring—proper counsel can be disastrous. Residents of New Orleans experienced that tragic truth when those in power chose not to act on warnings that the low-lying city's levee system was in need of serious attention. Every year officials pleaded for money to strengthen the levees, and almost every single year in the decade prior to 2005, they were turned down. On August 29, 2005, New Orleans' citizens began to pay the price when the storm surge from Hurricane Katrina overwhelmed levees and floodwalls, and the city began filling up with water. Though many escaped before the storm struck, tens of thousands stayed—trapped in attics, clinging to roofs, or as refugees in the downtown Superdome and Convention Center, where hunger, thirst, fear, exhaustion, and lawlessness reigned. Within seventy-two hours, New Orleans was transformed from modern city to Third World country.

New Orleans needed prevention projects, evacuation strategies, practical resources, and rescuers. Because there was no plan, because counsel was ignored, more than 1,570 citizens of the state of Louisiana lost their lives in Hurricane Katrina and its aftermath.[7]

CNN reporter Anderson Cooper was there. The devastation surrounding him—and the seeming inaction from those who should have been riding in for the rescue—made journalistic objectivity difficult. In his memoir *Dispatches from the Edge*, Cooper says,

Some twenty thousand people took refuge in the Superdome, told to come by the city's mayor, who called it a shelter of last resort. He'd hoped that help would arrive from the state or federal government within two days. It didn't. Hope is not a plan.[8]

If you're trying to keep your head above the floodwaters of depression, take this lesson to heart. Many hope depression will pass. They hope they'll be able to overcome it on their own by trying harder, thinking happier, praying longer. They hope God will see their suffering and choose to heal them. But *hope is not a plan*. Hope is important — it's essential to surviving the illness — but you need more. You need treatment. You need counsel. You need help.

If you want to build a solid plan for healing, acknowledging your need for objective, professional assistance is the first step. Beyond medical advice and treatment, some form of counseling or therapy is essential to help you cope with the challenges depression presents and address possible emotional or spiritual issues that may be contributing to your illness. Pursuing counseling is not an admission of failure or instability but a wise decision indicating a desire to grow to a new level of faith and well-being. And as you will learn through my story in part three of this book, pursuing spiritual counseling can be a crucial step in your journey to wholeness, one I hope you will not overlook.

The Roots of Clinical Depression

Clinical depression can be caused by physical factors (relating to brain chemistry) or by emotional issues. It can also have spiritual roots. Many cases of depression have a complex, interacting set of causes. This can make the illness difficult to treat since it is a challenge to discern whether spiritual struggles are contributing to physical symptoms and emotional pain, or the other way around.

Psychological depression can occur in someone who learned faulty coping skills as a child and does not deal with stress or difficulties in a healthy manner.[9] Poor social skills or unsupportive relationships may also contribute to depression; people who are lonely and isolated are more vulnerable.[10] Childhood trauma and loss or recent stressful life events—including loss or threatened loss of a loved one, home, job, or physical health—can trigger depression.[11] Certain personality traits (introversion, pessimism, low self-esteem, and dependence, for example) can also contribute to psychological depression,[12] though these traits may also have spiritual roots: shame, bitterness, spiritual malnourishment, low self-worth, soul weariness, or an attack by Satan.

Medication and electroconvulsive treatment (ECT, or shock treatment) are two effective methods of treating the physical component of depression. Psychotherapy and psychological counseling often work well for those whose depression is emotionally rooted. The spiritual facet of depression is not as clearly understood by the medical community in general and therefore is often overlooked in treatment.

God designed us with wonderful complexity, and science is recognizing the intricate intertwining of our emotional, physical, and spiritual health. Studies show that physical illness can affect emotional health. For example, people with heart disease are more likely to suffer from depression. Conversely, scientific evidence indicates that our emotional well-being has a measurable effect on physical health—stress, anger, hostility, and hopelessness have all been proven to contribute to physical illness.

Isn't it possible, even logical, that spiritual health can figure into this wellness equation? When our spirits suffer, our minds and bodies are more prone to illness. Nearly a decade after my battle with depression began, I discovered that until my spirit was healed, my emotions never would be. I needed a comprehensive treatment plan for depression that considered my body, mind, and spirit.

You may too.

Finding a Cure: Medicine, Miracle, or Spiritual Maturation?

Perhaps you've been made to think that it's wrong for followers of

Christ to have depression. Maybe you've been told that you just need to claim healing and, with enough faith, God will deliver you from sickness and disease.

I agree that it is right and biblical to request healing, but I also believe that God has given us the intelligence to research and discover treatments — even cures — for many of our ailments. Can God heal without medicine? Absolutely. He performs miracles. But God uses whatever He chooses to bring healing and wholeness, including medical and psychological treatments and spiritual counseling.

What if medication and psychological treatment seem to be getting you nowhere? Does that mean those people who point fingers, look down their noses, and whisper that you're spiritually defective are correct? No!

Sometimes depression is an indication there are spiritual issues that need to be addressed. But that doesn't mean you should be ashamed about it. We are constantly in the process of spiritual growth, and that growth requires that we examine ourselves — our motives, beliefs, actions, and sin. Depression can be the motivation some of us need for a period of self-inquiry and change. (We'll look at this concept more in the next chapter.) Is depression a sign of unresolved sin in a person's life? Sometimes it is. But that's not cause for humiliation. We all sin every day, but our responsibility is to repent and change as God makes us aware of our sin. The person judging you for being depressed has just sinned by doing so.

Can godly people be depressed? If you're familiar with some of the greatest stories of suffering and despair in the Bible, then you know the answer is yes.

ENCOURAGEMENT FROM GOD'S WORD

Anyone who carefully examines the the lives of some of the Bible's leading men and women can see that many godly characters suffered from what might be considered depression today. For example:

Elijah

God's prophet, Elijah, received the grim news from a messenger: Queen Jezebel was plotting his murder. Fearing for his life, Elijah fled to the desert. But the farther he trekked, the weaker his desire to live became. After a day's journey, Elijah collapsed beneath a broom tree, emotionally and physically spent. He had reached the limit of his ability to endure and pleaded for an end to his suffering. "'It's too much, Lord,' he prayed. 'Take away my life; I might as well be dead!'" (1 Kings 19:4, GNT).

Jeremiah

Known as "The Weeping Prophet," Jeremiah was primarily a prophet of doom, warning the Israelites of their coming captivity and the destruction of Jerusalem. Author Michael Card writes, "Jeremiah fulfilled a unique role by lamenting to God for the people and, at the same time, lamenting for God to the people. He was an intercessor of lament. It was a role that tore him apart."[13]

Though the writer of the book of Lamentations is anonymous, ancient Jewish and Christian traditions ascribe the authorship to Jeremiah.[14] Notice the many symptoms of depression and the thoughts that accompany the illness, revealed in this lament (I've put them in italics to make them easy for you to identify):

He has brought me into *deep darkness*, shutting out all light. And beat me again and again with merciless blows. He has left my flesh open and raw; he turned me into a scarecrow of *skin and bones*, then broke the bones. He has shut me in a prison of *misery* and *anguish*. He locked me up in *deep darkness*, like a corpse nailed inside a coffin. He has bound me in chains; I am a prisoner with *no hope* of escape. Even when I cry out and plead for help, he locks up my prayers and throws away the key — *God refuses to listen*. I stagger as I walk; stone walls block me wherever I turn; he has twisted the road before me with many detours. Like a bear lying in wait, like a lion in hiding, he dragged me from the path and mangled me and left me — *helpless* and *desolate*. He took out his bow and arrows and used me for target practice. He shot his arrows deep into my heart. I became the laughingstock of all my people; they mock me in song all day long. The Lord filled me with *misery*; he made me drunk with *suffering*. He rubbed my face in the ground and broke my teeth on rocks. I have *forgotten what health and peace and happiness are*. I do not have much longer to live; my *hope in the Lord is gone*. I'll never forget the *trouble*, the utter *lostness*, the taste of ashes, the poison I've swallowed. I remember it all — oh, how well I remember — *the feeling of hitting the bottom*. I think of it constantly, and *my spirit is depressed*. (Lamentations 3:2-20)[15]

David

The man after God's own heart was no stranger to despair. As the youngest of seven sons, in a time when the eldest was the most endeared, David knew the lonely ache of insignificance. Given the job of shepherd, he spent many years in the wilderness, physically and emotionally. But even as David grew up, achieved victory in battle, and ascended the throne as king, his life remained fraught with hardship. Death, sin, and the pursuit of enemies overshadowed him, and he poured out his anguish and despair to God. The Psalms are full of the laments of the "chosen one" (Psalm 89:3). Here are just a few:

My God, my God, why have you forsaken me? (Psalm 22:1)

I am worn out from groaning; all night long I flood my bed with weeping and drench my couch with tears. (Psalm 6:6)

My soul is full of trouble and my life draws near the grave. (Psalm 88:3)

I am losing all hope; I am paralyzed with fear. (Psalm 143:4, NLT)

Jesus

God incarnate—Jesus Christ—understands our weaknesses because He "was tempted in every way that we are" (Hebrews 4:15, NCV). He identifies with our pain. "Though a Son, He learned obedience through what he suffered" (Hebrews 5:8, HCSB). Jesus is no stranger to the anguish you have felt. The night before His crucifixion, He went to the Garden of Gethsemane to pray.

> Taking along Peter and the two sons of Zebedee, he plunged into an agonizing sorrow. Then he said, "This sorrow is crushing my life out. Stay here and keep vigil with me." (Matthew 26:37-38, MSG)

Jesus pleaded with the Father that He might be spared the agony of the cross. As our Savior sweat drops of blood, the friends He brought to support Him slumbered, of all things. Jesus knows the loneliness of depression.

I do not claim that depression is never the result of wrong choices or sin, but the fact that some of the Bible's most godly characters fell into despair proves there are other reasons one might become depressed. Whether biochemistry, emotional wounds, or spiritual matters have caused your depression, be assured that it is not a punishment. God doesn't want you to suffer from this illness or any other. Even though experiencing brokenness, sickness, and despair is part of the reality of living in a fallen world, God can use these times to change us for the better. Don't underestimate His ability or His plans for you.

If you are receiving medical treatment for depression, I encourage you to continue with that treatment for as long as it helps you. Never discontinue medication without the advice of your physician. Never feel guilty for needing it.

If you have not found help through medical treatment or psychological counseling, don't give up. As you journey with me through the pages of this book, you will begin to see that there is hope.

SELF-REFLECTION

▷ Jeremiah states, "He locked me up in deep darkness, like a corpse nailed inside a coffin" (Lamentations 3:6, MSG).

In what ways do you identify with Jeremiah's torment? How would you describe the physical, emotional, and spiritual effects of your own depression on you?

▷ In verse 21, Jeremiah's lament turns to praise and worship. (You may be encouraged by reading the rest of the chapter—Lamentations 3:21-66.) Michael Card says, "[It's] the kind of praise that only pours forth from lament. To be sure, it's a bruised and bloody praise. . . . But it's a praise that can now hope all things, having been forced to let go of everything."[16]

How might the pain of your depression draw you closer to God?

▷ Referring to his own trials, the apostle Paul wrote, "This happened that we might not rely on ourselves, but on God, who raises the dead. He has delivered us from such a deadly peril, and he will deliver us. On him we have set our hope that he will continue to deliver us" (2 Corinthians 1:9-10).

Have there been times in your life when God has delivered you from difficulty? If so, take a moment to reflect on those victories. (Record them in a journal or notebook so you can read them the next time you feel discouraged about God's seeming inactivity in your life.)

Will you set your hope on God to deliver you from depression? If your answer is yes, then you've just taken an important step of faith. If you are not yet able to believe that God can heal your depression, read on. I've been where you are now.

MEDITATION

"We have troubles all around us, but we are not defeated. We do not know what to do, but we do not give up the hope of living." (2 Corinthians 4:8, NCV)

"Fear not, for I have redeemed you; I have summoned you by name; you are mine . . . when you pass through the rivers, they will not sweep over you. When you walk through the fire, you will not be burned; the flames will not set you ablaze. For I am the LORD, your God, the Holy One of Israel, your Savior." (Isaiah 43:1-3)

"Rest in God alone, my soul, for my hope comes from Him." (Psalm 62:5, HCSB)

CHAPTER 3

GOOD NEWS
About DEPRESSION

The common response to trials is resistance, if not out-right resentment. How much better that we open the doors of our hearts and welcome God-ordained trials as honored guests for the good they do in our lives.

Charles Swindoll, author

Affliction is the best book in my library.

Martin Luther

When I began my descent into depression, I was teaching a Sunday school class of teenagers and directing the children's choir at my church. I sang in the adult choir, was a soloist as well, and served on the music committee. I took pride in being at the church whenever the doors were open; you could find me in worship services twice on Sunday and at midweek prayer meeting. It was an exhaustingly busy life, especially while trying to care for a three-year-old and a newborn.

It seemed that I was doing all the right things, performing for "the kingdom," yet I was spiritually and emotionally bankrupt. I had no joy, no peace, no energy. As I retreated to my couch, and later to a hospital bed, I realized that I no longer cared about anything. All of the things that had driven me — and defined me — for so long had become meaningless. I didn't know who I was. Was this really my life? Where had I gone so wrong?

Like the writer of Ecclesiastes, I began to wonder what it had all been for. What had I really accomplished? What was the point of going on?

> I took a good look at everything I'd done, looked at all the sweat and hard work. But when I looked, I saw nothing but smoke. Smoke and spitting into the wind. There was nothing to any of it. Nothing. (Ecclesiastes 2:11, MSG)

> So life came to mean nothing to me, because everything in it had brought me nothing but trouble. It had all been useless; I had been chasing the wind. (Ecclesiastes 2:17, GNT)

I felt trapped inside the shell of a person who no longer existed, and I knew I couldn't live like that. I had to get out. There had to be more. The instinct inside me was to run — to run and run and, I hoped, outrun the meaninglessness, the exhaustion, the fear. But I had nowhere to go. And deep down I knew that no matter where I ended up, the emptiness would find me.

While depression put the brakes on my hyper-service for the kingdom, it presented me with a spiritual dilemma. Having a devastating life crisis did not fit my perceived image of a "good" Christian — the image that I'd been trying hard to live up to for many years. My wacky theory was that only messed-up people had messy lives. The evidence to support that belief was straight from the Bible. I'd heard the stories about godly people who'd triumphed: Daniel was untouched by ravenous lions; David defeated the giant Goliath; and Noah and his family survived a flood while everyone else drowned. I guess I overlooked the rest of David's life (after his victory with the stones and the sling) and didn't connect him with the one who cried out to God for deliverance from his enemies, the one who moaned and wept and lamented. I must have missed Job's story, too. But, to give myself a bit of a break here, those aren't the things they teach kids in Sunday school, at least not in my day. We don't tell our little ones the sad stories of suffering; every tale we select has to have a happy ending, and the good guy (the God-follower) always emerges the winner.

So it's not a complete surprise that I considered it my responsibility to look like a winner, maintain the image, and try to make my life appear problem-free, as if I were a walking billboard advertising that perfect, painless lives were the product of a relationship with Christ. However, when I became depressed, this was no longer possible. (I now understand that we are meant to live triumphantly, and triumph—or victory—is demonstrated in the *midst* of pain, not in its absence.)

It's amazing how some of the darkest moments in our lives flood our souls with the brightest light of revelation. I didn't like what the spotlight revealed. It was humbling to realize that the "superior" life I'd led had truly gotten me nowhere. If I hadn't been so emotionally numb, I might even have been embarassed that I'd fallen so far. The discovery that I did not have it all together, that the paint on my billboard was badly peeling, astounded me. Whether anyone else bought my act over those years, *I had*. I'd managed to convince myself that I was who I pretended to be. My depression was like a heavy curtain falling across the stage after the final act of a Broadway musical. It was closing night for The Sharon Show.

I had been so preoccupied by the life I'd created for myself—a wild carnival ride of activity—that God had to do something drastic to get my attention, so He pulled the plug. One moment I was spinning beneath bright colored lights, then the bulbs flickered and went out.

The cheery music slowed to a haunting, creepy chorus that eventually became silent. Motion ground to a halt. Everything was still, quiet, and very dark.

But sometimes being stuck in the dark is a good thing.

SEARCHING FOR THE BRIGHT SIDE

As you read further in this book and learn how God used depression in my life, I think that you will be able to forgive me for—and maybe even agree with—the statement I am about to make. Here goes: *Depression can be good for you.* I know it's hard to fathom how something that hurts so much, that takes so much, can possibly have a bright side. I wouldn't have believed it if I hadn't experienced it myself, but I have seen depression turn other people's lives around, too.

You see, depression for me—and perhaps for you—was a wake-up call, alerting me to the fact that there was something very wrong with the way I was living my life, something I had avoided addressing for two decades. It was time to make some changes.

Although you may prefer a pill to make the pain go away, if your depression is emotional or spiritual in nature, it's going to take more than that to eradicate its roots. However, while your journey to wholeness will require much more from you than would a pill, it will also provide you with a tremendous opportunity for spiritual gain.

Opportunity. That's the key word. If you are experiencing depression, you've been given the chance to change your life by changing yourself. You may not feel you had much say in the development of your illness, but what you do now is your choice. Here are your options:

1. Try to ignore it. Paste on the happy face and pretend you are fine. Keep up the facade, driving yourself to do things you no longer have the energy or the inclination for. Hope that if you don't acknowledge the depression, it will go away. (This works as well as jogging through chest pains to stop a heart attack.)

2. Give in. Don't make any effort to seek treatment. Unplug the phone, pull down the shades, crawl into bed, and stay there. Believe that you are a victim and that there is nothing you can do to help yourself.

3. Work through it. Seek help. Get to know yourself better and do some soul-searching. Make needed changes in your thinking, behavior, or beliefs.

In my case, there were fundamental personal issues and mindsets that had to be addressed before I could be whole. And I was not a helpless observer; I could affect the outcome. Whether I would use the depression to change my life for the better was entirely up to me. You, too, can choose your response. You can choose the life you will lead.

Though it seemed as though depression had drawn me backward into a deep, dark pit, it was actually a necessary forward stride toward emotional and spiritual wholeness. If it had been up to me at the time, I wouldn't have taken that step. I'd still be spinning around on the carnival ride or performing on the stage, very far from God and very empty.

The thing about being stuck in the dark—when you don't know where the door is or how to find the light switch—is that you have a lot of time alone to think (about who you are, why you're that way, and what you may need to change). And you have time to rest. Time is a precious gift.

My brother-in-law recently earned a doctorate degree in adult education. A full-time teacher, Akaps had to squeeze his studies into summer breaks and what little spare time he could find. Partway through year four of his six-year journey, we met in a coffee shop and over hot chocolate I asked him if, looking back, he could see an easier way to have obtained this degree. Akaps sighed, slowly nodding his head, and said, "If I were to do it again, I'd plan ahead so it would be possible to take a sabbatical—a year or two to work just on my studies." In a sense, depression is an emotional sabbatical. (It's a physical and spiritual pause as well.)

My illness eventually revealed a hunger for God I'd ignored all my life, trying to quiet my spirit's grumblings with activity rather than a relationship with my Creator. God knew I would never deal with the poverty of my soul while I was attempting to fill myself up with chores, accomplishments, and things. He knew that I had much to learn and, in His wisdom, cleared my schedule so I'd be able to focus my attention where needed.

Even with my calendar wide open and nothing to distract me, I was a slow learner when it came to spiritual matters. But God was a patient teacher. One of the most important lessons I learned (and it took nearly a decade for me to get it) was that messy lives are *not* reserved for messy people. We're all broken! But there's a God who loves us, meets us, and mends us—if we let Him. And it's in that mending that we grow stronger.

ENCOURAGEMENT FROM GOD'S WORD

"Heart-shattered lives ready for love don't for a moment escape God's notice" (Psalm 51:16, MSG). Take a moment and let the truth of that verse sink deep into your soul. No matter how you might feel, you haven't for a moment escaped God's notice, or His grip. Right now, though you may be feeling alone and abandoned, He is holding you and longing to lead you on your journey to wholeness.

If you view suffering as a negative, despicable condition to be avoided at all costs, you might be having a difficult time with the idea that God allows terrible things to happen in the world, even to people who love Him. Maybe you are wondering, *If God is loving, why does He allow suffering?* I don't expect that my explanations will satisfy everyone, and I don't claim to have all the answers, but I've learned that it's okay to admit there are things we don't know. I don't completely understand God, but my experiences with Him have made it easier for me to trust Him. It wasn't always that way.

I think the confusion about God's love and goodness comes from viewing suffering as something negative. And why wouldn't we? In our news-saturated culture, we have 24/7 access to all the terrible stories of tragedy and pain in the world. We can watch unfolding devastations live through our television sets. We see houses crumbling, waves obliterating, bombs blasting, and we watch the victims standing stunned before the cameras, clamoring for their lives, or lying dismembered in the streets. Then, when the story's been captured, the suffering documented, and it seems there's nothing more to say about the matter, the cameras are packed up and the journalists move on to the next tragedy already under way.

Very rarely will the news networks allow us to revisit the victims, months or even years later, to uncover any good that might have resulted from their suffering. Good news doesn't sell. It doesn't get the adrenaline pumping. It fails to shock and awe, so we rarely hear it. But I believe that in every bad situation, a seed of goodness is planted. Some seeds take a very long time to bloom, and we may not live long enough to behold the resulting beauty. Or the blossom may be there but not obvious to us because we're preoccupied with other things, other afflictions, other tragedies. What I do know is that we will never find the treasures in suffering if we don't believe they exist or if we fail to search for them.

The apostle Paul told the church in Rome, "We know that in all things God works for the good of those who love him, who have been called according to his purpose" (Romans 8:28). "We are not necessarily doubting" C. S. Lewis writes, "that God will do the best for us; we are wondering how painful the best will turn out to be."[1] Sometimes the best things are birthed from the most painful circumstances and afflictions.

Consider some of the ways God uses suffering for good in our lives.

To Show Us Who We Really Are
It's been said that adversity introduces people to themselves. This was

true for me, and it was true for King David. He never saw it coming. Perhaps he was still on a high from slaying the giant, being anointed God's chosen one, and ascending the throne; but in the early years of his reign, David seemed to believe he was leading a stellar life. He said to God, "Don't treat me as a common sinner . . . No, I am not like that, O Lord; I try to walk a straight and narrow path of doing what is right; therefore in mercy save me" (Psalm 26:9-11, TLB).

David wanted to be rewarded on the basis of his goodness; he was blind to the fact that he, too, had flaws and sins. David wasn't ready for character change. But he was confronted with his need for it after he'd committed adultery and murder. Then David prayed for God to take away the stain of his sin and to cleanse him from guilt. "Create in me a clean heart, O God. Renew a right spirit within me" (Psalm 51:10, NLT).

He prayed: "Going through the motions doesn't please you, a flawless performance is nothing to you. *I learned God-worship* when my pride was shattered" (Psalm 51:16, MSG, emphasis added). God used adversity to demolish David's pride and wake him up to his need for repentance and character change. He used depression to do the same for me.

To Increase Our Faith and Dependency on Him

Most of us can recite the twenty-third psalm by heart, but do we really believe its message? The words flow easily off our lips — "The Lord is my shepherd. I shall not be in want" — but do we know beyond the shadow of a doubt that God will provide all we need to get us through this life?

Prior to my depression, I didn't. I believed in God, but I'd never learned to trust Him for anything besides my eternal destination. I adopted the unbiblical attitude that God helps those who help themselves. Working hard to do things on my own, I attempted to gain mastery over my universe so that everything would have a predictable, positive outcome. I presumed that waiting on God was for weaklings who couldn't manage life on their own, so I tried to take control myself and find ways to meet my own needs and desires.

But as the suffering of depression wreaked havoc on my life plans and took away my ability to help myself, I became acquainted with the God who helps the helpless and grew to understand that I could trust Him for everything.

The first sentence of Psalm 23:2, "He makes me lie down in green pastures," paints a lovely picture of little lambs lounging around in lush green fields, simply enjoying life—no worries, no cares, choosing to rest. At least that's how I envisioned it.

I've always been under the impression that the sheep were lying down because they were content with what the shepherd had provided. They didn't fret about where their next meal would come from; it was right beneath them and all around them. After meditating on this verse recently, I realized that if I'd been a lamb in this scene, I likely would not have been reclining in the pasture; I'd have been watching to see just how much the rest of the flock was eating, growing bitter about the ones who were taking more than their share, then scouting the borders to see what kind of provisions were available in the surrounding territory.

What would the shepherd do with a sheep like me—one who refused to trust? He would *make me* lie down.

My depression did just that. It forced me to lie down and knocked me off my feet for a long time. God used it to show me that even when I could do nothing, *especially* when I could do nothing, He was in control. He could take care of me—and the universe—without my help and organizational genius. Eventually, I became more comfortable with the idea of resting and waiting for God to provide. Though it's still a challenge at times, choosing to lie down proves my trust that He will not take away what He's promised to give me. As I rest and wait, He proves Himself faithful and I learn I can depend on Him.

To Make Us More Productive

In the parable of the vine and the branches (see John 15:1-2) Jesus says that His Father is the gardener who tends the vine and cuts off every branch that does not bear fruit. Those branches that do bear fruit are pruned so they will become even more fruitful.

You may read this parable and get a negative image of a displeased God hacking away at every branch that doesn't meet His expectations. But pruning isn't an act of anger; it's an act of love. Removing unhealthy branches, or trimming those that do produce, frees up energy that the plant can then use for fruit production. The plant grows healthier and its yield increases.

I was a large plant in need of some serious pruning. All of my energy went into maintaining my impressive size. I was all show and no fruit—certainly not the fruit of the Holy Spirit (see Galatians 5:22-23). My spirit was filled with bitterness instead of love, resentment rather than joy, and worry in place of peace. I believe I was kind (to most people) but generally impatient with others and myself. I was more often critical than gentle. I had strong moral values but took pride in my "goodness." I was very self-controlled, but in a sick sort of way that ultimately turned to dysfunction. Though I believed in God, I didn't trust Him, so the fruit of faith was also lacking.

Quite obviously, there was a lot of work to be done if good fruit were to grow in my life—bitter fruit to destroy, diseased limbs to cut, and branches to retrain. Getting ready for production was a painful process.

To Prepare Us for the Life God Longs to Give Us

Most of us hate broken things (toys, vows, appliances, bones). We equate brokenness with worthlessness, but God doesn't. When He looks at broken things, particularly people, he sees possibilities, potential, and promise. God delights in brokenness because it prepares us to receive His blessings. When we are unable to "fix" our lives, we are more open to stepping aside and letting Him begin to create the life He longs to give us.

Depression blessed me by closing the curtain on life as I'd known it. Caught on a merry-go-round of misguided activity, I never once considered what I was created for or what might bring me pleasure and fulfillment. I'm only now discovering that God has given me unique longings, passions, and purpose. The incredible realization is that they were there all along, but I'd buried them beneath mountains of fear and self-betrayal. It took nearly a decade of devastating suffering to put an end to my dream-sucking, life-crushing existence and release myself into the life God had created me for.

God can do the same for you. Charles Swindoll wrote, "When the sovereign God brings us to nothing, it is to reroute our lives, not to end them."[2] Depression is not a dead end on your life's journey; it's actually a pause at the beginning of a new path—the path to wholeness and freedom. Use this pause to rest, reflect, and regroup. Allow God to use it to mend what's broken, make you stronger, and change your life for the better!

SELF-REFLECTION

It's important to consider how you will spend this "sabbatical" you have been given. How might you use the weeks and months ahead for reflection and self-examination? (For example, will you seek wise counsel? Will you read books on the issues you need to address? Will you make changes in your life to allow for regular periods of rest and renewal? Will you pursue God in a deeper way? How?)

Of the four benefits of suffering explored in this chapter, which one resonates most strongly with you? Why?

Make it a priority to address the need for that particular benefit in prayer in the days, weeks, and months ahead. It doesn't have to be a complicated prayer, but be persistent. For example, you may simply ask, "God, please help me learn to depend on You. Help me see that You are trustworthy."

MEDITATION

"Show me the path where I should walk, O Lord; point out the right road for me to follow. Lead me by your truth and teach me, for you are the God who saves me. All day long I put my hope in you." (Psalm 25:4-5, NLT)

CHAPTER 4

THE BATTLE BETWEEN
LIFE *and* DEATH

To be, or not to be: That is the question.
William Shakespeare, *Hamlet* (Act III, Scene I)

Tim gripped the steering wheel with both hands, his foot crushing the accelerator. With emergency lights flashing, our minivan flew toward the city. I stole glances at my husband through my tears, trying to read his face, wondering if he'd had enough of me yet.

In the minutes that led up to our desperate departure, Tim had arranged for someone to watch our young daughters, called our pastor, then hustled me into the van. As we raced toward the emergency room, fear gripped my soul. "I'm sorry! I don't want to die!" I cried. But it was a little late for a change of heart.

It hadn't been a good day, and when Jenna toddled into the living room that evening looking for some attention from Mommy, the best I could do was hold her on my lap as I stared at the television. I'd settled for a mindless talk show—the kind that exploits the pain, drama, and dysfunction in the lives of others. Jenna sat contentedly, sucking her thumb, her body warm and full of life next to my cold, empty one. I didn't have the energy to play or read aloud, but at least I could hold her.

Then Tim walked in. He didn't see a tranquil mother-daughter moment but focused instead on the show we were staring at. "Why are you letting Jenna watch that?" he challenged.

"She's not old enough to understand what they're talking about," I said in defense. But I turned off the television and left the room. Alone in my bedroom, I wept. My soul was already filled with despair, disappointment, and my own disapproval; Tim's comment stung like salt in an open wound. But he wasn't to blame for my response. For two years I'd been digging my own grave with self-condemnation, and it was already deep enough.

Despite the medication and treatment I'd been receiving, I wasn't getting any better. All I knew for certain was that any way you chose to look at it, I was a failure. And I hated myself for it. I felt surrounded by darkness, smothered, like a thin layer of impervious film had shrink-wrapped my soul. Nothing could penetrate it and I could not escape. I wanted to see my children grow, I wanted to be a good wife to my husband, but those seemed like impossibilities to me. My pain spoke louder than my other longings, so I crossed the hall to the bathroom and opened the medicine cabinet, reached for the bottle of antidepressants I'd just had refilled, and swallowed them all. Then I returned to bed.

When Tim came up to check on me, my face was red and puffy from crying. "What's wrong?" he asked.

"Everything," was my reply. "Things will never change." I was sobbing again as my husband lay beside me and held me in his arms.

"Don't you get it?" I asked, frustrated and frantic. "I can't do this anymore."

Tim was concerned, but his voice remained calm. "We'll get through this."

If only he knew how wrong he is, I thought.

"I'm scared," I cried.

When the tears didn't stop, Tim sensed something was very wrong. "What have you done?" he asked. And I confessed. I didn't really want my life to end; I just wanted the pain to stop. I was spent. I told myself, *If the depression won't leave, I must.*

Tim immediately called my psychiatrist's answering service, and while he waited for a return call, he checked to see how many pills I'd ingested—nearly a month's worth. The doctor who phoned back instructed him to get me to the emergency room immediately; I'd taken a lethal dose.

On arrival at the hospital, I was given something to make me vomit, but the pills had already digested. We could only wait to see how my body would react. I heard whispers outside the curtain of my cubicle. "This is a dangerous medication. Your wife may have convulsions, heart failure, or lapse into a coma."

"What are the chances she'll make it?" my husband asked.

"Fifty-fifty," was the doctor's response. I was too exhausted to feel afraid anymore.

Our extended family gathered in our van in the parking lot, keeping vigil and praying, while my pastor came into the trauma unit. Standing next to me, he took my hand and squeezed it. As I fought to keep my eyes open, he said, "We love you, Sharon." Then I went to sleep.

When I awoke early the next morning, I was given a huge glass of liquid charcoal laced with laxative. The charcoal would absorb harmful chemicals in my body, the laxative eliminate them. I managed to get it down, gagging. Then the psychiatrist on call came to interview me. I was in the hospital where I'd first been admitted for depression, but my doctor practiced at a hospital in another city. The psychiatrist said she'd arrange for a sheriff to transport me there.

A sheriff? Is she kidding? All my life I'd tried to do everything right—I'd never even been to the principal's office—and someone was going to call the sheriff on me? *I'm not a criminal; I'm sick. This isn't right!* I argued silently, humiliated.

Before the morning was over, my family doctor arrived. It

comforted me to see him. I sensed no condemnation, only compassion, as he stood next to my bed wearing an expression of concern. "I took a look at your EKG. You're a very lucky lady. There's been no damage to your heart," he reported. "I guess you're being sent back to Dr. Colford."

"Do I have to go with the sheriff?" I asked.

"No. Tim can take you."

I returned that afternoon to my home away from home, the psychiatric ward. It seemed that God had given me a second chance, but I didn't receive a new life to go with it. I was still seriously depressed. The longing for a permanent end to the pain had not been undone and would revisit me many times in the years to follow.

CONSIDERING SUICIDE

Though my suicide attempt seemed to be a spur-of-the-moment decision, it wasn't. Like many who suffer from chronic depression, I'd thought about it often. I'd been dying for a long time. Because I believed depression would eventually kill me, suicide didn't seem like a choice to end my life but rather a decision to speed up the inevitable. On this day I was too weak to fight the urge anymore.

Depression brings with it a continuous barrage of negativity, hammering our spirits with perceived failure, rejection, and condemnation. We try to hold it together, but each day, with each new assault, our emotional dam gets weaker. Then, one day, a seemingly trivial comment or situation proves to be more than we can bear. The dam breaks and we drown in the

SUICIDE ON THE RISE

In the year 2000, suicide ended one life every forty seconds on our planet. That translates into approximately one million people (16 deaths per 100,000 persons).[1]

Worldwide, suicide rates have increased by 60 percent in the past forty-five years,[2] making suicide among the three leading causes of death in those aged fifteen to forty-four years (both sexes).[3] In the United States it's the third leading cause of death in children, adolescents, and young adults (ages ten to twenty-four).[4] These figures don't include suicide attempts — up to twenty-five times more frequent than completed suicide.

floodwaters: years' worth of pent-up pain.

When the pain of depression exceeds one's ability to cope, suicidal feelings may result. Everyone has different pain thresholds; what might be manageable to me may be unbearable to you. Feeling suicidal doesn't mean we are bad, weak, or insane; it means we are overwhelmed. It means that today we're carrying more than we feel we can bear.

At Risk

Up to 90 percent of people who die by suicide are suffering from a diagnosable mental illness.[5] But suicidal behavior is complex; age, gender, and ethnicity are also factors. Men are four times as likely as women to die by suicide,[6] though women attempt it two to three times as often.[7] In the U.S., suicide rates are highest in the elderly—non-Hispanic white men age eighty-five or older are at greatest risk.[8]

Other risk factors include:

- Stressful life events, in combination with other risk factors, such as depression
- Prior suicide attempt
- Family history of suicide, mental disorders, and/or substance abuse
- Family violence, including physical or sexual abuse
- Firearms in the home (the method used in more than half of suicides)
- Incarceration
- Exposure to the suicidal behavior of others (family members, peers, or media figures)
- Any type of loss (for example, relationship, job, or loved one through death)
- Divorce (a person facing divorce, recently divorced, or the children—particularly teenagers—of divorced parents)
- Disability or physical illness (terminal, painful, or debilitating)
- Social isolation (living alone, few supportive relationships)

- Being unemployed or retired
- Change in job, residence, or financial status
- A sudden, dramatic improvement during depression (possibly indicating relief after making the decision to end one's life)[9]

If a person is under psychiatric treatment, the risk is higher in:

- Those who have recently been discharged from the hospital
- Those who have made previous suicide attempts

Suicide is rarely a quick decision. There are usually clues and warning signs to alert others to someone's suicidal state, such as giving away cherished possessions or valuables, getting affairs in order (paying off debts or writing a new will), taking unnecessary risks, obtaining a weapon, or making statements like, "Everyone would be better off without me" or "You won't have to deal with me much longer."[10] If you're reading this book because someone you know is depressed and you suspect she or he may be suicidal, please visit some of the websites listed in the "Self-Reflection" section near the end of this chapter to learn of more warning signs of suicide and what you can do to intervene.

If you are feeling suicidal, please realize that your suicidal thoughts are the product of a mind that is temporarily overwhelmed. You won't always feel this way. There are other solutions to your problems and pain; allow someone to help you find them. Please use the suggested resources in the "Self-Reflection" section.

Mind Games

Suicidal thoughts are involuntary; people don't choose to think them. They come like little whispers in our heads, persistent nudges, at a time when we're emotionally drained and least able to resist them. Chemical imbalances in the brain, devastating events causing trauma or loss, or years' worth of unaddressed anguish can make us more vulnerable to suicidal thoughts. You may think life is hopeless and you are helpless to do anything about your situation. While it may seem you have good reasons to think these thoughts, a thought is not a fact. There are medications and treatments that may help restore your brain chemicals, and there are people who can help you cope with the loss and pain you may be experiencing.

Though I did not gain much noticeable benefit from antidepressant medications, when I was in my darkest periods I received electroconvulsive therapy (ECT). ECT did not eliminate my depression, but it did elevate my mood enough so that the suicidal thoughts vanished for a period of time, my mind cleared, and I could resume counseling with my psychiatrist.

In our society, we often learn to avoid dealing with feelings and unpleasant life issues. We're told to suck it up, sweep it under the rug, get over it. When we ignore important matters such as bitterness, feelings of worthlessness, and unresolved conflict, it can result in depression and cause us to fall prey to any of several lies that can lead to suicide, including:

- *I'm a burden to others.* Depressed people become the center of attention in their families (though not intentionally), as the illness generates much worry, concern, and frustration in others. While aware of this, we feel powerless to change it or ourselves. Sometimes the guilt is so overwhelming that we believe our loved ones — and the world — would be better off without us.
- *Things will never get better. There's no hope.* Author Greg Garrett refers to his own depression as "the spiritual cancer that had metastasized into my heart and brain and bones."[11] This malignant melancholy causes us to believe we'll never feel alive again, overwhelming us with hopelessness.
- *I don't deserve to live.* Like depression, suicidal thoughts are often triggered by feelings of failure and shame. Sometimes these feelings are so intense we believe we're unworthy of life. Because I measured my worth by my achievements

(and depression greatly inhibited my ability to accomplish anything), I believed I was useless and I couldn't justify my existence.

- *Death will solve my problems.* Suicidal people believe they've exhausted all options for relief from their pain. Death seems like the only way out. There were times when I struggled with this "solution" because I knew that in ending my life, I'd be leaving a legacy of pain for my family. Often, this realization was the only thing that kept me going. But many times, pain obliterates rationality.

Thirty-six years after his own father's suicide, Dr. David Cox says he still thinks about it daily. David was nine years old when it happened. He states, "On that day my perfect world was shattered; my life was forever changed."[12] David was not encouraged to talk about his father's death, or his own pain, further compounding the devastating fallout of suicide. He writes about its impact:

> By the age of thirteen, my feelings of anger and guilt were so great I was almost dysfunctional. I missed fifty-four days of the seventh grade, locked in my room, sleeping and watching TV. . . . To go along with my anger was an overwhelming sense of guilt for being angry with a parent I longed to have alive.[13]

Suicide solves no problems. It just passes them on.

Sometimes deceptive thoughts come from the Deceiver. Satan loves to grieve God by destroying what's most precious to Him. Your life is precious. You are God's treasure, created in His image (see Genesis 1:27), made in an amazing and wonderful way (see Psalm 139:14). Your life is full of purpose, meaning, and value.

The Bible teaches that Satan "prowls around like a roaring lion looking for someone to devour" (1 Peter 5:8). He's "a liar and the father of lies" (John 8:44). John records Jesus' warning about Satan and a promise about Himself: "The thief comes only to steal and kill and destroy; I have come that they may have life, and have it to the full" (10:10). When we believe we're worthless and unforgivable and that life is hopeless, we believe lies whispered by the enemy of our souls—lies intended to destroy us and others.

Though suicide may seem like a way to end your pain, it will cause great trauma and distress to others (your family, your friends, the person who discovers your body, or the medical team who tries to save you). The psychological aftershock of your death will shake the foundations of many other lives to the core as they are left with haunting questions and feelings of guilt, anger, and betrayal. Your death may prove so devastating to those who knew you that some may decide to end their lives as a result; many families bear a dark genealogy, a painful legacy of suicide.

If you think your situation is hopeless and that depression will destroy your life, then it very well may. But if you choose to believe you are not helpless and that God still has a future full of hope awaiting you, then you will take a huge step toward healing.

ENCOURAGEMENT FROM GOD'S WORD

If anyone had a reason to feel hopeless it was Job. The attack Satan launched against him was fierce, and Job's losses and suffering became legendary. Even though Job was one of the most righteous men of his time (see Job 1:1,8), he was not immune from despair, depression, or a death wish.

Prior to becoming Satan's target, Job was a man who had it all: children, livestock, land, and servants. The Lord had blessed the work of his hands, and he was very wealthy. Satan told God that good fortune was the reason for Job's faithfulness and challenged, "Stretch out your hand and strike everything he has, and he will surely curse you to your face" (Job 1:11). God granted Satan permission to do what he wished with all Job had but not to harm him physically.

It took only a few moments for Job to lose what he had spent a lifetime gathering. Four messengers arrived, one after another, with heartbreaking reports. They spoke of enemy attacks, lightning, raiding parties, and a devastating tornado. Death. Destruction. Destitution.

When that didn't cause Job to curse his Creator, Satan returned to God in an attempt to further undermine Job's integrity. This time he gained permission to afflict Job physically, as long as he spared his life. After Satan attacked God's servant with painful sores that covered his body, Job felt that death would have been a gift of mercy. And he cursed the day he was born:

> Cursed be the day of my birth, and cursed be the night when I was conceived. Curse it for its failure to shut my mother's womb, for letting me be born to all this trouble. (Job 3:3,10, NLT)

He questioned his Creator:

> Why is light given to those in misery, and life to the bitter of soul, to those who long for death that does not come, who search for it more than for hidden treasure? (Job 3:20-21)

He became despondent and despaired of life itself:

> I have no peace, no quietness; I have no rest, but only turmoil.[14] And now my heart is broken. Depression haunts my days.[15] I have no concern for myself; I despise my own life;[16] I loathe my very life.[17]

But Job did not choose to end his life. He endured it. Yes, he railed at God, he pleaded, he lamented, and then he listened. God told Job, "Brace yourself like a man; I will question you, and you shall answer me" (Job 40:7). Then God explained to Job the limits of his human understanding compared to the limitless wisdom of the Creator. And as Job listened, he had a spiritual awakening. He realized that the same God who laid the earth's foundations, caused the sun to rise and set, dispersed lightning bolts, and watered the deserts so they bloomed with life had a plan for his life that could not be thwarted (see Job 42:2). Job recognized that even though he did not understand the reason for his suffering, he could trust that his Creator had a purpose for it.

Job repented for the accusations he'd made against God and for the presumptuous words he'd spoken, and God once again blessed him with health, wealth, and more children. In fact, Job lived another 140 years—long enough to cradle his great-great-grandchildren. He'd have missed all that had he chosen suicide as a solution to his temporary suffering.

I'm sure that during the worst of his suffering, as Job sat among the ashes scraping his sores with a shard of broken pottery, he never anticipated that God would restore everything he'd lost. Job could not have imagined that people would once again call him "blessed," but God had not abandoned the one who had honored Him. Even as Job lamented his ruin, God was planning his restoration. Don't underestimate His plans for you.

CHOOSE LIFE

God created us for life, but the Enemy is bent on our destruction. Instead of listening to the lies of the Deceiver, why not trust in the One who is infinitely more powerful? Ask God for His strength. Stop trying to fix things on your own; allow God to guide you. He can use others to help you through this time of crisis. Talk with someone about your feelings and be sure to mention if you are feeling suicidal. If you're uncomfortable speaking with someone in person, there are many confidential help lines available, operated by trained volunteers who want to help you and will listen without judging. I called one once. I'm still alive, and life has never looked better. Please use the resources listed in the "Self-Reflection" section so that you, too, can have a chance to live a full, rich life.

Though I don't know your story, I know that suicidal feelings are generally temporary or intermittent. Don't make a choice to end your life when you're in an emotionally weakened state, unable to think rationally and consider other options. If it seems life hasn't been fair to you, why not break that cycle by being fair to yourself and not acting on your impulses until your emotions subside and you're able to think clearly?

You don't have to let your pain destroy you; you can choose to let God use it for healing. In chapter 3, we looked at the many ways God uses suffering for our ultimate benefit. He truly can work all things together for good (see Romans 8:28), even when all seems hopeless. Give God time to work, to turn this painful experience into something of great value and beauty as He transforms you and your life.

Self-improvement expert Dale Carnegie writes, "Most of the important things in the world have been accomplished by people who have kept on trying when there seemed to be no hope at all."[18] During my depression, I had every reason to feel hopeless, and much of the time I did. It was a grueling journey, and it often seemed that I was moving backward rather than forward. I'd stumble and fall, but each time I hauled myself back up, I took another step toward healing.

I didn't do anything you can't also do. If you persevere and continue to believe that there is hope for wholeness, I believe you'll find it.

SELF-REFLECTION

As I considered the impact my death would have on my family, I thought of all the milestones in my daughters' lives that they would face without a mother to share them: birthdays, graduations, weddings, and births. What would your loved ones want to experience with you? What would you like to live to do and see?

▷ God has a good plan for your life that you can't know right now. If you are suicidal, will you make a decision not to act on that urge today?

▷ Using the following resources, make a plan to get help.

Information, resources, and conversations to help you choose life can be found at:
- Metanoia: http://www.metanoia.org/suicide
- Life Link: http://www.lifelink.org.uk/pages/feeling_suicidal .htm

To talk with someone who cares, call one of these help lines:
United States
- National Hopeline Network: 1-800-SUICIDE (1-800-784-2433)
- National Suicide Prevention Lifeline: 1-800-273-TALK (1-800-273-8255)

Canada
- Centre for Suicide Prevention: http://www.suicideinfo.ca/csp/ go.aspx?tabid=77 (find the phone number of a crisis center near you on this website, or call 911 and say that you are in suicidal danger)

International
- Befrienders Worldwide: http://www.befrienders.org (find help lines in almost forty countries)

Help and support for those who suspect someone is suicidal, or for those coping with the loss of a loved one through suicide, can be found at:
- Stop a Suicide Today: http://www.stopasuicide.org
- Befrienders Worldwide: http://www.befrienders.org

- American Foundation for Suicide Prevention: http://www.afsp .org

Or read:

- David Cox and Candy Arrington, *Aftershock: Help, Hope, and Healing in the Wake of Suicide* (Nashville: B&H Publishing, 2003).

MEDITATION

"For I know the plans I have for you," declares the LORD, "plans to prosper you and not to harm you, plans to give you hope and a future." (Jeremiah 29:11)

"I am still confident of this: I will see the goodness of the LORD in the land of the living. Wait for the LORD; be strong and take heart and wait for the LORD." (Psalm 27:13-14)

CHAPTER 5

WIFE *and* MOTHER GONE AWOL

Love does not begin and end the way we seem to think it does. Love is a battle, love is a war; love is a growing up.

James Baldwin, author

W hen Tim and I started our family, I was grateful to be a stay-at-home mom: I wanted to devote all my energy to caring for our children and home. Our first five years of marriage—and my first four as a mother—were wonderful. I loved spending time with Lauren and being there for everything. Later, Jenna's birth was one of the highlights of my life. But depression ended my dream of being a perfect mother. It transformed me from a loving nurturer to someone distant, fragile, and sometimes frightening.

My illness took a huge toll on my family, and as year seven of my depression rolled into year eight, Tim seemed to have reached a breaking point as well. The stress of caring for—and worrying about—me had worn him to a nub of his former self. He became weary and depressed. We had no idea how far he might fall and were afraid of what would happen to our daughters if we were both incapacitated. Who would care for them?

After several months of avoiding treatment, Tim finally began taking medication prescribed by his physician and talked with a psychologist on a few occasions. The doctor seemed in awe of what Tim had endured and that he'd put up with me for so long. I don't know if he was trying to commend Tim or give him permission to quit.

I felt extremely guilty and responsible for Tim's depression. *If I've done this to my husband, what am I doing to my kids?* I wondered with dread. I'm grateful that this dark phase didn't last long and that Tim soon began feeling stronger and more like himself again. My children's trauma was yet to unfold.

Dealing with my perceived failure as a wife and mother was difficult, and I questioned God about it at length: *Why would You give me these children and then not let me take care of them?* Battling depression was all-consuming. I exhausted my energy just trying to stay alive. My family had to accept whatever was left, and it usually wasn't much. Though they longed to have me present, my presence was often painful, and there was always the looming uncertainty of how long I'd be home.

During a particularly long hospitalization, when Jenna was two years old and Lauren almost six, Tim announced to the girls one morning that the doctor was letting me come home that day. They were very excited. As I cuddled on the couch with them that evening, Jenna, full of innocence and not yet understanding the relentlessness of my illness, looked hopefully into my face and said, "You not sick anymore, Mommy?" Lauren was quiet and pensive. "What are you thinking?" I asked. She responded sadly, "I wish you could come home forever." Lauren was beginning to learn that "coming home" was always followed by "going back."

Depression wounds families. It crushes the spirit, steals joy, and causes confusion. As the family becomes fractured, home is no longer a haven to retreat to for comfort but a wounded place filled with uncertainty and turmoil. Sometimes called *silent victims*, those who love someone with depression suffer every bit as much as the one with the illness but in different ways.

In this chapter, we'll look at how your depression may affect your children and your spouse and what you can do to help them.

DEPRESSION'S IMPACT ON CHILDREN

As you read about parental depression's impact on children, realize that shining a light on it has nothing to do with blaming you and everything to do with making the future brighter for you and your children.

Acknowledging the Fallout
Here are some of the things children of a depressed parent often grapple with:

Confusion. When a child's once happy and involved parent becomes withdrawn and irritable, spending all her days in bed, it is deeply confusing. Rather than being warm and selfless, the depressed parent becomes impatient, distant, and self-centered. Anger, criticism, and constant dissatisfaction are also characteristic in people with depression. Children are keenly aware that something is wrong, though they may not understand it.

Dysfunction. Rates of anxiety, disruptive disorders, and depressive disorders are all higher in children of depressed parents. The disorders begin early, often continue into adulthood, and are impairing.[1] (Rates of depression are more than three times higher in children with a depressed parent than in children with non-depressed parents.[2]) Kids from families enduring depression are less skilled in their interactions with people and, as a result, may be rejected by others more often. This may cause them to become withdrawn and may delay their social and emotional development.

Loneliness. When depression strikes their parent, children become lonely. During my depression, I was frequently in the hospital for weeks—even months—at a time. When I was at home, I was still often unable to do much to ease my children's longing for my attention. My daughter Lauren explains,

> When she wasn't in the hospital, Mom slept all the time. She was ethereal, intangible, elusive. I could look at her and touch her, but I was only glimpsing and feeling a body. Seeing her asleep in bed or on the couch was like seeing her in a coffin every day. Her spirit was missing. My mother was gone.

Guilt. Children often fear they are the cause of their depressed parent's change in mood and think that if they behave well, they can make their parent happy again. My daughters tried that tactic for years, attempting to be perfect little girls, denying their own needs, silencing their "voices."

Low self-worth. The first person children turn to for validation is their mother, but if she suffers from depression, she may not be able to offer it.[3] The critical nature that accompanies depression has a destructive impact on children when criticism is directed toward them. Sooner or later, children come to believe the negative messages they hear about themselves from their mothers. This results in low self-worth, impacting the child's social life, academic performance,[4] and who he or she becomes.

Depression. Tim attempted to give our daughters enough affection and attention to make up for what I couldn't offer. He tried very hard in every way, and they knew it. But he couldn't completely protect our girls from the impact of my illness. Three years after my depression ended, theirs began. Lauren was sixteen and Jenna thirteen when they each began to withdraw from their friends and eventually became unable to attend school. Both received counseling and medical treatment, with varying levels of success. Jenna spent two weeks in a children's psychiatric ward. As I write this, she is nineteen and Lauren twenty-two. I believe they're both on the road to recovery and pray their restoration will be complete. Though frightening, frustrating, and painful, my daughters' illnesses allowed me to experience depression from a different vantage point and offered me a second chance to be the mother I'd wanted to be all along.

Helping Children Cope

If you have depression, the best thing you can do for your children is seek immediate treatment for yourself. Here are ten more steps you can take to help your children cope during this difficult time.

1. Provide accurate, honest information. Lauren says that one of the most difficult aspects of having a parent with depression was feeling left out of what was going on — not having enough information. She was confused about what was happening to me and what would happen in the future. Match the amount of information you give to your children's level of understanding and what they want to know.

Some key messages children need to hear are:

- This is an illness.
- They did not cause this illness and they cannot make it go away.
- With treatment and support their parent will eventually get better.

Depression temporarily changes people, affecting the way they think, feel, and behave. If the depressed parent seems harsh or unaffectionate, it's because of her illness, not because she's a bad parent or because the child is a bad child.

2. Let them share how they feel. Children may repress feelings in order to keep peace in the family, or they may not understand that it's okay to be angry or afraid. Be sure they know that what they feel is important to you. Gently encourage them to open up and share what's on their minds. You can do this in quiet times spent with each child. Bear in mind that your children may not want to be completely honest, for fear of hurting you. For this reason, it's important that the other parent also set aside relaxed time to allow each child to share his or her feelings.

This is a challenge that Tim and I didn't do very well on. Our daughters were concerned that if they weren't extraordinarily good, they might upset me to the point of a return to the hospital. They were also sensitive to their father's stress and didn't want to cause him any more problems. As a result, now they are having to learn as young adults how to deal with conflict and freely express their feelings.

3. Reassure them they are loved. During stressful times when attention is drawn away from the children, they may feel uncared for. Let them know, through words and actions, that they are loved and important to you and the family. Tell them you understand that your moods can be upsetting for everyone, that none of them is the cause, and apologize.

4. Spend time with them each day. Try to spend time alone with each child. Give focused attention to each one, even if it's for only a few minutes each day. Go to a movie or watch a favorite television show together, and talk about it afterward. Spend five or ten minutes each day in conversation about something of interest to your child. Even though you may not take pleasure in things right now, help your child do whatever he or she enjoys and is good at.[5]

5. Involve others in supporting them. One of the things that Lauren says helped her most during my depression was spending time with extended family, particularly her grandparents. They often invited our girls over to spend the night or go on fun outings. Enlist the support of other family members and close friends in bringing some enjoyment and much-needed special attention into your children's lives.

6. Aim for predictability. Children thrive when life is predictable and structured, but depression invites chaos and uncertainty into the home. Try to maintain normal routines as much as possible and set reasonable rules and limits for your children. If the stress that accompanies disciplining is too much for you to cope with now, ask your spouse to take up the slack in this area.

7. Inform their teachers. Dealing with the depression of a parent can make everything else more challenging. It's difficult for children to concentrate at school when they are worried about their parent. They may also struggle to complete homework assignments and study for tests if you are unable to help them or keep them on task. This can contribute to monumental stress for children.

Take advantage of parent-teacher meetings to monitor your children's performance and behavior at school. If they are having difficulties or acting out, inform teachers of the challenges being faced with your depression. Again, if this is too much for you to do at this time, ask your spouse or a close relative to speak to the teachers for you and your children.

8. Allow them to be children. Don't rely on your children for emotional support. If you need additional support, seek it through friends, adult family members, a professional counselor, or a support group. Encourage your children to be involved in things they enjoy, whether sports, music, or other extracurricular activities, and make every effort to encourage and support your children's friendships.

9. Monitor them for symptoms of depression. Your illness increases your children's risk for depression, so it's important to keep a close watch for symptoms. Jenna struggled with depression for two years before we recognized it.

Because many of the symptoms of childhood and adolescent depression are different from adult depression, they're easy to dismiss as something else. For symptoms of depression in children and adolescents, visit the "Recommended Resources" page on my website, SharonFawcett.com, or read *Psychology Today*'s article "Depression in Children and Adolescents" at http://www.psychologytoday.com/conditions/childdep.html#Symptoms.

10. Consider counseling. If you and your spouse are unable to help your children cope with the challenges they are facing (social, behavioral, educational, or emotional), it may be wise to seek the input of a psychologist or counselor. Having someone to talk with is important for your children's emotional health and well-being.

DEPRESSION'S IMPACT ON MARRIAGE

Depression fallout is Anne Sheffield's term for what happens to those caught in the midst of a loved one's battle with depression, one person's automatic response to someone else's despair.[6] Those on the sidelines experience a range of emotions from confusion to anger and ultimately a desire to escape.[7]

Sheffield describes why depression causes such turmoil in a marriage:

> Keeping a marriage solidly intact and mutually rewarding is virtually impossible when a partner of either sex suffers from [depression]. Not only do they no longer behave as expected; they appear to have undergone a personality change for the worse. All their good qualities — patience, reasonableness, affectionate cheerfulness, and responsiveness — have flown out the window, to be replaced by an array of bad spirits.[8]

The drastic change in my personality and behavior affected my husband as well. While I battled my illness, he fought the fallout.

Acknowledging the Fallout on Spouses
Here are some of the things the spouse of a depressed person has to wrestle with:

Confusion. In the beginning, Tim thought my moodiness was a nasty case of premenstrual syndrome, and — with jaw clenched — waited for it to pass. But when it lingered for several months, he wasn't sure what was happening to me. When my doctor told Tim the antidepressant medication should make me feel better in two weeks and I ended up more distraught than ever, Tim was confused and worried for our future. This confusion returned often as treatment after treatment failed to restore me.

Demoralization. The dictionary definition of *demoralize* is "to deprive a person of spirit and courage; to destroy his or her morale; to throw him or her into disorder and confusion; and to bewilder."[9] That's an accurate description of how my depression affected Tim. He states, "Every man wants his wife to be happy, but in spite of the sympathy, support, and love I offered, I came home day after day to a woman who was miserable. Sharon remained distant and critical, and I was discouraged and bewildered."

The normal balance of our previously healthy relationship was completely off. Tim received no positive reinforcement, no compliments, and no encouragement from me; there was no give-and-take. No matter what he wanted, my needs and desires dictated the course of our lives. My husband yearned for the loving relationship others seemed to have. "As I'd see couples holding hands, walking down the street," he explains, "I'd wonder, *Why can't I have a wife like that—someone who smiles?* Several years later, when I eventually lost hope that Sharon would ever recover, I gave up the dreams I had for my marriage and began telling myself that she was no longer my soul mate; she was now my ministry."

Anger. A year or two into my depression, Tim began to think that despondency must be part of my identity—a part he'd failed to detect prior to our marriage. (But I had never been depressed or despondent before.) He suspected I was satisfied with the continuous gloom that enveloped me.

A lot of his frustration came from the unpredictable roller-coaster ride he endured. I could be feeling well for a few days or weeks and he'd begin to get hopeful that maybe I was finally "coming out of it." Then suddenly I'd be back in the hospital. Tim never knew what was around the corner and found that maddening, discouraging, and emotionally exhausting.

The desire to escape. Though Tim says he never considered abandoning me, he can relate to the yearning to flee that many depression fallout sufferers experience. One of his brothers used to urge him to take a vacation or do things for himself. Though Tim now believes he would have benefited from heeding this advice, he couldn't bring himself to do so at the time. *How can I go out and enjoy myself,* he wondered, *when my wife is in so much pain?*

Tim dreaded coming home from work each day because he didn't know what state he'd find me in. Would I be dead or alive? He just hoped *he* was the one who found me, rather than our daughters. My husband's "escape" came when I returned to the hospital. He says,

> Then I didn't have to lock the dead bolts on our doors and hide the keys each night for fear that she'd leave while I was asleep and end up on the railway tracks or over a cliff. I didn't have to stash her medication under the mattress and dole out the pills to prevent a lethal overdose. I was relieved when Sharon would leave, because I knew she was safer at the hospital and I was a lot less stressed. But the relief brought with it a huge burden of guilt for not mourning her absence.

Helping Your Spouse Cope

As a depressed individual, you may feel that you're doing all you can to keep yourself together and that you have no energy—or ability—to help your spouse cope with your illness. But there are some fairly simple things you can do, and others you can attempt, to make a difference. Here are Tim's suggestions:

- *Accept that you need help and seek it.* If your spouse doesn't see you making any effort to get better, it may cause an escalation of resentment in the relationship.
- *Reduce negativity.* Try not to be critical or judgmental.
- *Try to contribute something to the running of the household.*

Resentment builds when one partner does everything while the other sits and watches.

- *Encourage your spouse to have outside interests that offer a break from caring for you and the family.*
- *Don't expect your spouse to be present 24/7.* If you need constant support, enlist the help and companionship of a friend or family member while your spouse is away.
- *Encourage your spouse to get support.* It would be helpful for your spouse to attend a support group for people who love someone with depression or to get counseling early on to learn how to cope with your illness, how to support you, and what to expect.
- *Invite your spouse to meet with you and your counselor periodically.* Your spouse may wonder if what you are experiencing is normal and may welcome another person's point of view.
- *Don't allow your mood to control your family's activities.* If you make plans to go somewhere together and you change your mind because you aren't feeling up to it, don't require your spouse and children to cancel too. They need a break, a change of scenery, and the companionship of others and will only be disappointed and resentful if they have to stay home. Find someone to stay with you or check in on you while your family is away.

I suggest that you ask your spouse to read this book to gain a better understanding of how depression impacts the person experiencing it. Be sure to refer him or her to Appendix B: "How to Help a Loved One Who Is Depressed" and Appendix C: "How to Help Yourself When Caring for a Depressed Loved One."

ENCOURAGEMENT FROM GOD'S WORD

God can heal wounded families. The Bible's story of Jacob's family is proof. As a father, Jacob made a lot of mistakes. His blatant partiality for Joseph, his favorite wife's firstborn son, provoked bitterness in his other children. When beloved Joseph was seventeen, his brothers plotted his murder, but the eldest, Reuben, tried to rescue him and talked the others into sparing his life. Instead, Joseph was sold to a caravan of merchants en route to Egypt, where he became the servant of Potiphar, one of Pharaoh's officials.

Joseph's years in Egypt were most unusual. God was with him and he prospered in all he did—whether servant or prisoner. But Joseph's life changed drastically when he gained Pharaoh's favor by interpreting his cryptic dreams, warning of a famine that would strike Egypt. He was able to advise Pharaoh on how to prepare so the Egyptians wouldn't starve. As a result, Pharaoh placed Joseph in charge over the palace and the whole land of Egypt, second in command to Pharaoh himself.

Not only was Egypt spared the disastrous effects of the famine under Joseph's guidance but through divine intervention, his estranged family (in another country) was provided for as well. After many years of separation, God reunited them when aging Jacob sent his sons to Egypt in search of food.

Joseph had every right to be bitter and vengeful, but he forgave his brothers, recognizing God's great provision for his family—and many others—through the seemingly evil events that transpired years earlier. In a stirring speech, Joseph reassured them, "Do not be distressed and do not be angry with yourselves for selling me here, because it was to save lives that God sent me ahead of you. . . . You intended to harm me, but God intended it for good" (Genesis 45:5; 50:20).

Pharaoh gave Joseph's family a choice parcel of land to raise their sheep and live on, and when Jacob brought the entire clan from Canaan to Egypt, he finally got to see the son he'd given up for dead.

Let's face it: This was a dysfunctional family if ever there was one. Their resentment and animosity separated them and nearly cost one member his life. But God had chosen to bless Jacob's family, and nothing could prevent Him from doing so—not jealousy, not bitterness, not deception, not even hatred. God's timing seems slow by our standards, but in His timing, He restored the family of Jacob and Joseph and prospered them in spite of—even through—the pain and difficulties they endured.

God wants to do the same for all who love and follow Him. Depression may be an enemy attack on your family, threatening to break and even separate you. But, as I have so clearly learned in my own life, God can use depression for good. He can use it for your growth, but—imagine this—He can even use it to refine love, strengthen commitment, and draw families closer. Tragic events in our lives are often God's launching pad for blessings. One day you may look back and see, as Joseph did, that what the Enemy intended for your family's destruction, God has worked for good.

SELF-REFLECTION

In his book *Soul Space*, Jerome Daley writes about true intimacy in relationships that have endured hardship: "In these moments we discover, perhaps to our surprise, who is committed to us with a love beyond affection and who lives for our good when the cost is high. Trust is the sweet fruit that falls from the branches of a relationship shaken by storm."[10]

What future benefits might be harvested in your relationships with your spouse and children as a result of this experience with depression?

If you are a parent struggling with depression, what will you do to help your children through this difficult time? If you are married, what will you do to help your spouse?

Make a list of people you and your spouse might seek out (relatives, friends, members of your church) to help support your family.

MEDITATION

"The God of all grace, who called you to his eternal glory in Christ, after you have suffered a little while, will himself restore you and make you strong, firm and steadfast." (1 Peter 5:10)

"Many waters cannot quench love; rivers cannot wash it away." (Song of Songs 8:7)

"The art of love . . . is largely the art of persistence.[11] (Albert Ellis)

JOHN BUL DAU: THE POWER *of* HOPE

Hope is never lost.

John Bul Dau, humanitarian, survivor

To see him today, a six-foot-eight-inch tall man, one would never believe that John Bul Dau spent fourteen years of his adolescence and young adulthood existing on survival rations and fasting when the food ran out. His life in arid refugee camps was worlds apart from his happy childhood tending cattle in the lush grasslands of southern Sudan.

In the 1950s, as the British ended their colonization of northern Africa, they cobbled together two separate territories into one Sudan, Africa's largest nation. The new government, headquartered in Sudan's Arab north, minimized the voice of the southern tribes, ignored the south's Christian heritage, and coveted the oil that lay beneath their land. A violent civil war erupted.

In 1974, John Bul Dau was born to a Dinka family in the southern village of Duk Payuel, during a tenuous season of peace that lasted a decade. During John's tenth year, tensions between the north and south exploded again, and the government ordered the extermination of all Christian males (women and girls would be raped and enslaved). When John was twelve, war landed on his doorstep.

It was summer and the adults slept outside to allow children and the elderly indoor refuge from the biting insects. John and his siblings were stretched out inside a shelter specially built for them when the Muslim government troops attacked Duk Payuel. As he stumbled out of the sleeping hut, John saw that the tall grasses surrounding the village were on fire. Some of the neighbors' huts, and a cattle shed, were also burning. As he searched for his parents, "shells landed in showers of dirt, smoke, and thunder," John recalls. "Bullets zipped through the air like angry bees."[1]

In the confusion, John was separated from his family but followed a neighbor, Abraham, into the forest, where they began a four-month odyssey to safety. Though Abraham's wife and children were killed in the raid, Abraham kept John's hope alive by assuring him his parents were on their way and they would meet soon, somewhere to the east.

John ended up in Pinyudu refugee camp in Ethiopia, where up to a hundred boys and young men—walking skeletons—trickled in each day.[2] En route, they had been pursued by armed soldiers; hunted by wild animals; and weakened by starvation, dehydration, and disease. Western journalists and aid workers named them "Lost Boys" after the boys in *Peter Pan* who had no families and never grew up.

John spent three years at Pinyudu, leading a makeshift family of 1,200 boys, before civil war broke out in Ethiopia and forced them to flee once again, back through Sudan to Kenya. More than twenty thousand children walked about a thousand miles, half of them dying along the way, before finding safety in a United Nations refugee camp in Kakuma, Kenya.[3] One psychologist described the boys as "one of the most traumatized groups of children I have ever met."[4]

In his memoir, John describes his five-year exodus:

> I have witnessed my share of death and despair. I have seen the hyenas come at dusk to feed on the bodies of my friends.

I have been so hungry and thirsty in the dusty plains of Africa that I consumed things I would rather forget. I have crossed a crocodile-infested river while being shelled and shot at. I have walked until I thought I could walk no more. I have wondered, more times than I can count, if my friends or I would live to see a new day. Those were the times I thought God had grown tired of us.[5]

At the Kakuma camp, the United Nations provided the boys with survival rations, used clothing, and a basic education. John began first grade at the age of eighteen in an outdoor class held in the shade of a tree. He was eager to learn. "If I studied, I thought . . . I could do good things for myself and for my people."[6] In 2000, at the age of twenty-six, John earned his high school diploma.

With little hope of finding their families, the United States agreed to relocate some of the boys to America. By the time John's name appeared on the list of those accepted for resettlement, Kakuma camp had swelled to 86,000 residents. A church in Syracuse, New York, volunteered to sponsor several Sudanese refugees — one of them would be John Dau. He boarded a plane for the United States in August 2001, after lingering nine years in Kakuma.

The refugees were given ninety days to become self-sufficient, and while John embraced his new life in America, it was not an easy life. Adapting to a foreign culture, sometimes working three jobs to make ends meet, and dealing with loneliness and isolation were difficult.[7]

But John made a good life for himself and shared it with his friends in Kakuma, frequently sending financial support. Seven years after his arrival, John has earned an associate's degree in public policy at Syracuse University. He's founded three nonprofit organizations to benefit the people of Sudan and its refugees in America. Through funds raised, he built a medical clinic in his home county in Sudan, and plans are in the works for six additional clinics and integrated schoolrooms.

John has written a memoir and starred in a documentary film, both titled *God Grew Tired of Us.* He's been the recipient of numerous national and international awards and speaks at universities, colleges, and corporations, informing and inspiring others. He is using his education and experiences to make life better in Africa and America. John says, "I know I have been blessed and that I have been kept alive for a purpose. They call me a Lost Boy, but let me assure you, God has found me."[8]

God also helped John's family find him! Though he had been searching for them from the moment he arrived in Kakuma, writing approximately seventy letters he gave to the Red Cross, his efforts proved unfruitful. John didn't know that on the night Duk Payuel was attacked, his family fled in another direction, settling on the Sudan-Uganda border. Two days after arriving in New York, John wrote letters to his friends in Kakuma to tell them how wonderful life in America was. One of those young men took the letter he received on a trip to Uganda where he told others about the Lost Boys in America, and John Dau.

Word spread from person to person, and one of John's brothers heard the story. He peppered the friend with questions about the Lost Boy in New York, and realized it had to be his brother. The eldest brother wrote to the return address on John's letter. Fourteen months after John's arrival in America, he received that letter from Uganda, with photos of his parents tucked inside. John learned that three uncles and their families were killed in the shelling so many years ago, but John's mother, father, brothers, and sisters were all alive, including another sister born after John had last seen his family.

After being separated from them for two decades, John was able to return to Africa for a joyful reunion. His mother and youngest sister now live with him in New York. But the good news doesn't end there. John also found love. He located his girlfriend from Kakuma, who had settled in Seattle. They married in 2005 and had their first child the following year.

Hope carried John through a long, dark period of existence to the life of peace and joy he now embraces. Through his neighbor and companion Abraham, the hope that he would see his family again was kept alive. The education John received at the Kakuma refugee camp birthed a hope that he would have a role in building a brighter future for his people. The opportunity to emigrate to America gave him hope for a new life and an escape from his violent past.

"There have been many impossible situations in my life, but I keep trying," John says. "My family in Sudan thought I was dead and I feared they were dead, but 20 years later we were reunited. You can't give up. . . . Hope must not be lost. All those miles in the desert, I always said maybe tomorrow will not be like this."[9]

You may feel lost with no chance for a better future, but maybe tomorrow will not be like this. John's story proves that there is *always* hope, and if you choose to take hold, its power can change your life.

PART TWO

IDENTIFYING SPIRITUAL ROOTS

CHAPTER 6

SPIRITUAL MALNOURISHMENT

Blessed are those who hunger and thirst for God's approval. They will be satisfied.

Jesus (Matthew 5:6, GW)

During my first hospitalization for depression, I developed the eating disorder anorexia nervosa, a perplexing and potentially life-threatening illness characterized by self-starvation and excessive weight loss.[1] The recipe for an eating disorder is complex. A mysterious mix of personality characteristics, family dynamics, biochemistry, and social influences converge upon those who fall prey to anorexia.[2] The physical wasting, obsessiveness, and self-denial are obvious, but most fail to understand that these are symptoms of a deep soul-hunger.

My anorexia was initially triggered by at least three coinciding factors: rapid weight loss from my depression, a desperate desire for control, and a lifelong yearning to be thin. In my case, depression was accompanied by a loss of appetite (a common symptom of the illness). I had no interest in food, and the medication initially prescribed to treat my depression intensified this problem. (One of this medication's most commonly reported side effects is loss of appetite.) It's no wonder I dropped so many pounds in such a short time, but the doctor never addressed this issue. When I failed to respond to the first antidepressant, he changed my medication to another with the same problematic effect, and something inside me snapped.

I had been big all my life. It's never hard to pick me out in school pictures: always positioned in the middle of the back row to make the grouping symmetrical, my head forming the tip of the class pyramid. And because I was much taller than everyone else for many years, I felt conspicuously large. I saw myself not as "bigger-boned" but as fatter than the girls my age with petite builds and pencil-thin legs.

So there grew a longing within me for thin thighs—dainty appendages, instead of the weightier, clumsy ones I possessed. I never had dieted to extreme, but in my teen years I was always trying to shed a few pounds, without much success.

When, during my depression, I realized I was losing weight so easily, I felt a sense of satisfaction bordering on euphoria (if euphoria is possible in depressives). *This is the one good thing to come from this miserable experience*, I thought. Finally, I was achieving what I had always dreamed of. But not everyone shared my excitement.

By the time I was transferred to Dr. Colford's care, the eating disorder was well entrenched. Physical neglect had caused me to become weak, dehydrated, and dizzy. I was advised to stay close to bed, was given intravenous fluids, and started on a behavior-modification program to try to get me to resume eating. But it wasn't easy.

I believed that if I gave in and ate, my weight would skyrocket and I'd become obese. I was terrified of gaining weight and, as a result, became terrified of food. I'd lost control of everything, except what I put in my mouth and how much I weighed. I clung to this last bastion of control as if my very existence depended on it and, in so doing, nearly lost my life. It would take three years of consistent, patient, expert medical care before I was free from this horrifying illness. But even when the anorexia was dealt with, the depression remained.

I now see my eating disorder as a haunting metaphor for the malnourishment that was causing my spirit to wither. I was deeply engaged in religion before I became depressed, but my level of involvement was not the product of a healthy relationship with God. In many ways, it was a cheap substitute. In chapter 3, you read about my being a whirling dervish of "spiritual" activity, resulting in a bad case of burnout. Though I was a believer in Jesus Christ, I didn't really know the One I thought I was serving. I attended church faithfully, listened attentively to sermons, taught biblical truths to teenagers in my Sunday school class, and tried to teach my own children about the Lord. I read my Bible, devotional books, and books by other Christian authors, but all I acquired was head knowledge of God, Jesus, and the Holy Spirit. I did not know how to apply that knowledge to my heart or how to allow God and His Word to transform me. I didn't understand that I could have an intimate relationship with my Creator—that He could be as active and alive in my life as He was in the lives of those characters I read about in the Bible. I thought it was enough to know, and teach others, about Him, and I did all that with little true comprehension of Him.

I might compare it to being married to the most wonderful man in the world and living on a different continent than he. Each night I would dine alone and retire to a cold, empty bed while my husband would faithfully wait for me to return home so that he could lavish his love on me. That's how it was between God and me. Even though I devoted my time to telling others about Him, singing songs about Him, and reading stories about Him, I never *experienced* Him.

Because I failed to make myself available to God, He was not able to fill me with His love, peace, and acceptance. I chose, instead, to settle for the praise of humans (who seemed more easily accessible), believing that's what would fulfill me. I was wrong. My spirit was hungry for nourishment, and I was feeding it garbage. Spiritually, I was starving myself to death.

PATHWAY TO MISERY

God offers food for the spirit—love, acceptance, peace, joy, hope, strength, and passion—and we are born with an instinctive longing for this spiritual provision. But it's easy to overlook that longing when we're distracted by pain or fear. In our efforts to numb the ache of our emotional wounds or quell the raging anxiety within, we often eliminate spiritual food from our diets and fill ourselves with worldly offerings, or "anesthetics." Trying to fulfill our longings and ease our pain with sex, shopping, success, drugs, alcohol, and countless other things, we end up caught in dysfunctional relationships, trapped in addictions, defeated by our circumstances. And we remain empty.

Often our energies are focused on pursuing things we think—and society affirms—we need in an attempt to appease a hunger only God can satisfy. We gorge ourselves on power, possessions, prestige, praise, education, and entertainment. In the midst of this incredible feeding frenzy that is our lives, we fail to notice the still, small voice of our Shepherd, calling us to greener pastures.

For me, praise, people pleasing, and the pursuit of achievements were the things I focused most of my energies on prior to depression, the worldly "food" I ate. Receiving the instant gratification of human approval allowed me to ignore my need for something deeper and more fulfilling from God. This spiritual malnourishment—failure to receive the love, words of affirmation, wisdom, and truth God wanted to give me—made me vulnerable to shame, low self-worth, fear, and unforgiveness (the other roots of my depression). Because my relationship with God was not a priority, I didn't try to hear His voice or understand how He felt about me, and consequently I developed a distorted view of my worth. Because I was so busy performing in my own power and trying to control my life, I failed to experience God's trustworthiness. Because I didn't grasp His grace and mercy, I was unable to offer it to others.

An Important Reminder

It is possible to nourish one's spirit and still become depressed. Sometimes God allows depression to teach, or accomplish, something specific in the lives of even the most spiritually well fed. We are constantly growing in our journey of faith, and even though we may be spiritually nourished, there are still lessons to learn and deeper levels of intimacy with God to attain.

St. John of the Cross (1542–1591) described a "dark night of the soul" that sounds like what we would call depression today. In *Celebration of Discipline*, Richard Foster sheds some light on the purpose of the dark night that St. John of the Cross wrote about:

> The "dark night" to which [God] calls us is not something bad or destructive. On the contrary, it is an experience to be welcomed much as a sick person might welcome a surgery that promises health and well-being. The purpose of the darkness is not to punish or afflict us. It is to set us free. It is a divine appointment, a privileged opportunity to draw close to the divine Center. . . . The dark night is one of the ways God brings us into a hush, a stillness so that he may work an inner transformation upon the soul.[3]

Job's losses, suffering, and depression caused him to ultimately draw closer to God and experience Him in a deeper way. At the end of his journey through the valley of despair, he tells God, "My ears had heard of you but now my eyes have seen you" (Job 42:5).

It is possible that God allows depression in even those who are in good spiritual health to draw them even closer to Himself and further transform them in Christlikeness.

Rejecting God's Provision

While it requires time and commitment to nourish our spirits, God offers all that we need. The story of the Israelites' exodus from slavery in Egypt is a wonderful symbol of this divine provision. As they fled their Egyptian oppressors, God miraculously afforded them safe passage between the walls of a sea that submerged and drowned the pursuing enemy (see Exodus 14).

Three days later, when God heard the Israelites grumble, "So what are we supposed to drink?" (Exodus15:24, MSG), He poured out water from the desert. When they moaned about their hunger and the full stewpots they had left behind in the land of their bondage, the Lord sent down bread and meat from heaven (see Exodus 16:11-14).

God supplied His children's every need during their forty-year wilderness experience. Food, water, and clothing that never wore out (see Deuteronomy 29:5). Direction, protection, and His holy presence among them. But in spite of all He did for them, the Israelites were never satisfied. They were compelled by what they wanted, not what they needed. Consequently, God's people became rebellious, disobedient, and unfaithful (see Deuteronomy 9:7,24; Jeremiah 7:24-26; Psalm 78:10,17,32,40,56).

Thousands of years later, much remains unchanged. We continue to pursue our own desires. And God still longs to meet our needs, our *real* need as only a Creator can know.

It was I, the LORD your God, who rescued you from the land of Egypt. Open your mouth wide, and I will fill it with good things. (Psalm 81:10, NLT)

PATHWAY TO HEALING

During my treatment for anorexia nervosa, I loathed those involved in the daily ritual of coercing me to eat—the nurses most of all. I saw them as jealous enemies trying to interfere with my "success." I believed that everyone wanted what I had—willpower—and I was determined that no one would sabotage me. But my strong people-pleasing streak made me long for the approval of my doctor and psychologist, so I managed to follow the behavior-modification program and gain the required weight to be deemed healthy enough to go home. There the disorder took over again and I'd quickly revert to starvation mode. It wouldn't be long before I was back in the hospital on another program to save my life.

Though doctors could reason with me, remove privileges to make me want to comply, or even force-feed me through a tube if necessary, when I was out of their supervision I was left to make my own choices about how I would care for myself and what I would eat. The same is true with our spiritual nourishment: We choose what and how often we will eat.

God does not feed His children against their will. When the Israelites obstinately turned against the One who wanted to give them everything, the Father "let them follow their blind and stubborn way, living according to their own desires" (Psalm 81:12, NLT). God provides for all of our needs, but we must open our "mouths" and accept His provision.

Why do we sometimes reject the spiritual food God offers? It has much to do with our appetites. During one period home from the hospital, I was leaving my daughter's music lesson when another mother questioned me about my eating disorder. She was not critical—rather incredulous. Wondering how I could eat so little, she asked, "Don't you ever get hungry?"

I didn't. During the development of the disorder, I learned to ignore the pains in my stomach, and in time they disappeared. Trying to convince my psychiatrist that I didn't *need* more food, I explained, "I must be getting enough to eat because I'm never hungry."

Dr. Colford didn't buy my theory. Instead, she explained how the appetite functions and told me that if the hunger signal is repeatedly ignored, the brain stops sending it.

Is it possible that spiritual cravings are similarly regulated? Why else would we continuously disregard our spirits' needs? Have you ignored the "signal" so many times that you no longer yearn for God? Some of the hunger pangs, or signals, you may experience are a desire to know more of God and spend time with Him, to be unconditionally loved and accepted, to understand your purpose in this world, to hear God's voice and receive His direction, and to feel as though your life has significance and value. An intimate, spiritually nourishing relationship with God fulfills those desires as you come to know the truth about Him, your worth, and your life's purpose.

If we do not hunger for God, He will not fill us. If we don't accept His provisions, we become vulnerable to spiritual starvation and its consequences. This is a tough lesson to learn. Only God could feed the deep poverty of my soul, but as you'll discover, many more years would pass before I opened my mouth.

ENCOURAGEMENT FROM GOD'S WORD

God urged the Israelites to reject the culture of spiritual malnourishment that had caused them to turn away from Him and landed them in exile. Through the prophet Isaiah, God invited His people back to feast on spiritual food, to satisfy their thirst and hunger with Him.

> The Lord says, "Is anyone thirsty? Come and drink—even if you have no money! Come, take your choice of wine or milk—it's all free! Why do you spend your money on junk food, your hard-earned cash on cotton candy? Why spend your wages and still be hungry? Why pay for food that doesn't give you strength; that does you no good? Listen, and I will tell you where to get food that is good for the soul, the richest of fare!
>
> "Come to me; hear me, the life of your soul is at stake. Listen carefully to my life-giving, life-nourishing words. I am ready to make an everlasting covenant with you. I will give you all the mercies and unfailing love that I promised to David" (Isaiah 55:1-3).[4]

Humankind hasn't changed much since the days of Israel's exile in Babylon. We still waste our money—and our lives—on "food" that does nothing for us. But God hasn't changed either, and He continues to offer us good food that nourishes our spirits and truly satisfies our spiritual hunger. When we are willing to accept our Creator's provision, He meets our needs through His Word, His voice, and our relationship with Him. These essential elements of a diet that produces spiritual wholeness will be discussed further in part 4 of this book.

God said that if His people would just listen to Him and follow Him, He'd subdue their enemies and nourish them: "I would feed you with the finest wheat and satisfy you with wild honey" (Psalm 81:16, GNT). God wants to meet the needs of your spirit with the finest food, and there's no cost to those who accept it, only to those who don't. Feast on what God offers and receive His blessings: a future full of mercy and unfailing love.

SELF-REFLECTION

▶ Though depression probably makes it difficult for you to feed your spirit, think about your level of spiritual nourishment prior to becoming depressed. What did you fill yourself with? (You can answer this question by considering where you invested the bulk of your time, what motivated you, and what you were working toward in life.)

As your depression lifts, you'll feel like reengaging in life. Make sure you have your priorities in order and make spiritual nourishment part of your plan for lasting freedom. (I'll explain how to do this in chapter 14.)

▶ Depression may affect your ability to pray, study the Bible, or even feel connected with God. For now, meditate on the verses at the end of each chapter (and other hope-filled verses). Recite and memorize them if possible.

Music can be therapeutic. It penetrates the silent isolation of your depression and can elevate your spirit or give expression to unspoken longings. When you can, fill your home (or car) with music that is encouraging and uplifting.

MEDITATION

"The LORD is my shepherd, I shall not be in want. He makes me lie down in green pastures, he leads me beside quiet waters, he restores my soul." (Psalm 23:1-3)

"Like newborn babies, crave pure spiritual milk, so that by it you may grow up in your salvation, now that you have tasted that the Lord is good." (1 Peter 2:2-3)

"I will refresh those who are weary and will satisfy with food everyone who is weak from hunger." (Jeremiah 31:25, GNT)

CHAPTER 7

LOW SELF-WORTH

*Remove those "I want you to like me" stickers from
your forehead and, instead, place them where they
truly will do the most good—on your mirror!*

Susan Jeffers, author

It was a typically noisy noon hour with shouting and laughter filling the hallways of my high school. Students lined the length of the main hall, bordered on one side with wire-mesh-covered windows overlooking the gymnasium—appropriate because life at my school revolved around sports, particularly basketball.

It was tryout day for the girls' team, and the coach left a clipboard in the gym for those interested to sign up. Groups of girls gathered around it, but I waited until the crowd dispersed. Then I picked up the clipboard, wrote my name halfway down the page, and quickly exited the gym.

In the minutes that followed, I tried to envision what the tryout might entail and began to grow uneasy. At five-foot-eleven, I looked like a basketball player, but I wasn't particularly athletic or coordinated.

I'm not sure why I decided to try out for basketball. In my high school, those most revered were the ones who played the sport. Never mind being intelligent, kind, or honorable. None of that was as important as being on the team (though there were some players who managed to have those other admirable qualities as well).

I never had a longing to fit in or be "cool," but I certainly wanted to be admired, so it's possible that my need for affirmation fueled my momentary interest in the sport. But it's also possible that I thought it might be fun—something I've always had a tendency to neglect.

Though I fail to recall precisely what prompted me to try out for the basketball team, I vividly remember why I changed my mind. After stewing about it for much of my lunch hour, I snuck back into the gym, picked up the clipboard, and crossed my name off the list. I realized that even though the coach herself had asked me to try out, there was a very real possibility that I might not make the team—that there might be fifteen people better than me. That was a frighteningly big number.

Fear of failure was a driving force in my life, leading me to demand much of myself. I knew from gym class that I wasn't great at basketball (though apparently I'd managed to hide that from my teacher, who was also the team coach). For me, running and dribbling a ball at the same time required enormous amounts of concentration. I doubted my ability to perform well and decided it would be safer if I didn't even attempt it.

I knew that if I didn't try out, I couldn't be on the team, but it would be the result of my own choice, not someone else's rejection. I could always maintain that I didn't play basketball because I wasn't interested in the sport, not because I wasn't good enough. That fear of being perceived as less than adequate drove me to work hard to prove otherwise. Though it wasn't until depression hit that I consciously realized what little regard I had for myself, I spent most of my life trying to keep the world from discovering the loser I subconsciously believed I was.

PATHWAY TO MISERY

Looking back, from the other side of depression, I'm able to better understand how the pieces of my personality fit together to make me a perfect candidate for the illness. One of the roots of my depression was a low sense of self-worth, which affected almost every aspect of my being, behavior, and relationships.

Before you read any further, I would ask that you take some time to write a description of yourself, which you'll use in the "Self-Reflection" section at the end of this chapter. Focus on your personality, character, values, and abilities. It's important that you do this now so you're not influenced by what you read later in the chapter. Write from the perspective of someone who knows and understands you well and is describing you to others. Write in the third person, using "he" or "she" rather than "I" or "me."[1] When you're finished, keep the description somewhere you can easily access for reference when you reach the end of the chapter.

Self-worth is a measure of how much we value ourselves. True self-worth is not dependent on external factors, such as physical appearance, intelligence, performance, popularity, or achievements. Self-worth is unconditional self-love.[2] Low self-worth is a symptom of depression, but it can also be a root cause of the illness. Developing low self-worth is a slow process that can begin in early childhood. How much you value yourself can be influenced by other people's treatment of you (including physical, emotional, or sexual abuse); the kind of home you were raised in; experiences in school, sports, or work; culture, race, or religion; and your status in society.[3]

So how is self-worth different from self-esteem? Author Tom G. Stevens suggests,

> Think of self-esteem as composed of two parts — the *unconditional* part, and the *conditional* part. The unconditional

self-valuing part is our *self-worth*. The conditional self-valuing part is our *self-confidence*.[4]

In my earlier years, I had lots of self-confidence (at least in those areas where I performed well) but very little self-worth. I followed a pattern of choosing to do only things I knew I could do well and giving them everything I had. To most, I'm sure I seemed self-assured and confident, but no one saw the tyrant within, always demanding more than I could deliver.

Low self-worth changes the way we think about others, the world, and ourselves. The distorted views we adopt affect our developing personalities and our behavior. Low self-worth may make us crave approval, fear rejection, avoid conflict, lack assertiveness, struggle with problem solving, avoid intimacy, or become domineering and manipulative.

James J. Messina, PhD, and Constance M. Messina, PhD, authors of the Tools for Coping series at Coping.org, describe nine personalities, or unhealthy behavioral patterns, that result from low self-esteem: non-feeling, acting out, pulling in, entertaining, enabling, people pleasing, troubled person, looking good, and rescuing. You can read more about each behavioral pattern on the website http://www.coping.org/lowesteem/content.htm, but in this chapter, I'll focus on the three that impacted me: Non-Feeling, People Pleasing, and Looking Good.[5]

Non-Feeling

Some of the many characteristics of the Non-Feeling personality include feeling ashamed or afraid to show emotion, trying to remain calm and collected in all situations, having difficulty expressing affection, and being threatened by discussions about emotions.[6] My earliest remembrance of consciously repressing my emotions was during my maternal grandmother's funeral when I was seven years old. Seated with my family in the mourners' pew, I fought hard to hold back my tears and made it through the service dry-eyed. But as I followed my grandmother's casket out of the chapel, grasping my father's hand, the dam that had been holding back my emotions broke, and I began to sob.

Later, at the cemetery, my sister and I waited somberly in the car while Mom and Dad went to the grave site, but the sadness penetrated our steel and glass cocoon. As mourners filed past on their way to my grandmother's grave, I felt very small. And *ashamed*. Though it seems an unlikely emotion for a seven-year-old grieving child, it was completely appropriate, given my beliefs. Even at that young age, I'd come to the conclusion that showing "negative" emotion (sorrow, anger, fear, disappointment) was a sign of weakness; strong people kept their feelings in check and *never* cried in public! From that moment on, I worked very hard to avoid ever feeling that kind of shame again. One year later, I was back in the mourner's pew at the funeral of my other grandmother. Even though I loved her dearly and would miss her greatly, this time I managed not to shed a single tear.

As I grew older, I would tease my sister for crying at sad movies, feeling superior to her because I could control my emotions. When my parents would discipline us, my sister would wail; I would steel my soul, grit my teeth, and give nothing. I think I ended up getting worse punishments because I showed no remorse. I believed that if I allowed others to see that they could affect me emotionally, they might take advantage of that and cause me pain, so I became "strong," stoic, and even-tempered, burying any pain, fear, or anger deep within me. I became so good at it that by the time I was a teenager, I didn't even have to think about it. Emotional repression became a subconscious part of my everyday existence.

As a psychiatric patient, I was told many times that depression is anger turned inward. I think there's some truth to that. I internalized so much pain and anger in my life that by the age of twenty-six, my spirit couldn't hold anymore. Emotional repression literally shut me down.

People Pleasing

No was not a word I used much prior to depression. I don't recall feeling an overwhelming need to please my parents or siblings, but everyone outside the door of my home was in a different category. At school I was a model student. Returning home from parent-teacher conferences, my mother often reported at least one teacher using some variation of the statement, "If all my students were like Sharon, my job would be a lot easier!" I always felt a tingle of satisfaction when I heard that— *Yes! She likes me!*

Being liked was extremely important to me. I subconsciously believed that if I could make people like me, my value would increase; if people didn't like me, it would prove that I was worthless. So I worked hard to gain people's approval, being careful to avoid conflict, not offend others, always be kind and agreeable, and never say no when asked to do something. As a result, I was asked to do a lot of things; I took on project after project until I became overwhelmed. My mouth couldn't say no, but my weary soul and spirit eventually did by making me unavailable due to depression.

Many People Pleasers feel as though they're being taken advantage of and become exhausted by their efforts to be all things to all people, longing to flee the resulting stress.[7] Perhaps depression was partly my weary soul's attempt to run away.

Looking Good

I lived with the unspoken fear that people would reject me if they knew who I really was, and I subconsciously believed that I could hide the ugly truth of my worthlessness by working hard to look good. So I gave it my all. I said "please" and "thank you," kept quiet so others could speak, always got to school on time, and kept my clothes on hangers rather than on the floor. I tried to follow every rule and obey every law that I knew existed, never crossed on the "Don't Walk" signal, and brushed my teeth after every meal. I put my used towels in the hamper and resisted the urge to cut across the lawn of the house on the corner near my school. I stuck to the sidewalk, stepping over the cracks — most of the time. (I wasn't totally without a sense of adventure!)

The Looking Good personality shares many similarities with the People Pleaser. The world sees Looking Good people as responsible, hardworking, achievement-oriented, and successful in many things.[8] They appear to have good self-esteem and seem to have it all together.[9] That's exactly what I wanted people to think — in fact, I even believed it! But deep within me was a person who never felt "good enough," couldn't enjoy her success, and felt a compulsion to work harder and accomplish more.

Not only were my personal standards extraordinarily high, I expected a lot from others, too, and was often angry and disappointed when they failed to meet my expectations. For this reason, I always preferred to work alone on school projects. I also took leadership positions in anything I was involved in and then did the work myself rather than delegate.

Because I felt that so much was riding on my performance I feared taking risks — the reason why I changed my mind about trying out for the basketball team. I believed I had to do extraordinarily well at everything I set my hands to or else it proved I was no good. There was no room for mediocrity. My goal was perfection, but I could never achieve it.

In her article "The Pitfalls of Perfectionism," Jennifer Drapkin points to findings from decades of personality research indicating that while perfectionists are often high achievers, they are also at risk for eating disorders, obsessive-compulsive disorder, sexual dysfunction, depression, divorce, and even suicide. "They lead a life of continual anxiety and fear of failure. Even when they succeed . . . perfectionists never feel satisfied with themselves."[10] How true!

Author Jerome Daley sounds this warning about perfectionism:

To take on the identity of a perfectionist is to willfully cast yourself into a pit of torturous examination. As a perfectionist, you are forced to constantly evaluate your own performance (and the performance of others) with devastating results: Either you fail your own evaluation and succumb to consequential guilt and condemnation, or you pass your own evaluation and evolve into consequential pride and judgmentalism. It's a lose-lose proposition.[11]

For me, sometimes the "devastating result" was my private judgment and criticism of others. If I could identify others' flaws and weaknesses, I felt better about myself. The regular monologue in my mind went something like this: *I may not be good at sports like she is, but I'm smarter. He may make better grades than I do, but he's kind of a nerd. She may be pretty and popular, but she has loose morals; I would never do some of the things she's done.*

Tearing people down to build myself up. It was an ugly way to live. But I now recognize the fears that fueled those critical, nasty thoughts. What my soul was really saying was, *If you don't get top grades, people will realize they're better than you. If you don't get elected for this position, people will know you're a loser. If it's not perfect, people will see you're worthless.*

An ugly consequence of conditional self-worth is pride, and I did not escape this pitfall. When we're successful at the things we base our conditional worth on, we may begin to consider ourselves better than those who haven't achieved the same measure of success in those areas. I was guilty of this. I actually had a lot in common with the Pharisees of Jesus' day. In Matthew 23, Jesus denounces their superficiality and hypocrisy:

Woe to you teachers of the law and Pharisees, you hypocrites! You are like whitewashed tombs, which look beautiful on the outside but on the inside are full of dead men's bones and everything unclean. In the same way, on the outside you appear to people as righteous but on the inside you are full of hypocrisy and wickedness. (verses 27-28)

The Message translates verse 28 as, "People look at you and think you're saints, but beneath the skin you're total frauds."

I was the whitewashed tomb, surrounded by manicured lawns and pretty flowers. I looked good on the outside, but inside I was full of stench, rot, and decay. I had a season of even greater hypocrisy in my late teens when I left home for university. I gave up my quest to look good and became someone else, turning my back on rules and morals and much that I'd once stood for. Maybe it wasn't hypocrisy; maybe it was the most *honest* time of my life to that point, as my outward behavior was reflecting my inward confusion, vulnerability, and neediness. The door of my tomb was ripped off its hinges, and everyone could peer inside. Some didn't like what they saw. I didn't either. So when I returned home, I returned to what was familiar, safe, and seemed in my control: pretending.

As a result of living to please others, trying to become someone I thought would be admired, and carefully controlling all emotional expression, I lost myself. I wasn't sure who I was or what I wanted, and the people I shared my life with had no idea what lay beneath my facade. As author Brennan Manning explains, "Living out of the false self creates a compulsive desire to present a perfect image to the public so that everybody will admire us and nobody will know us."[12] Not even ourselves.

PATHWAY TO HEALING

Maybe you're not a people pleaser or a perfectionist. You may be very emotionally expressive and never worry about making others happy, but you still may be suffering from low self-worth. There are other indications of destructive personality patterns rooted in low self-worth, and I'd encourage you to visit Coping.org (mentioned earlier in the chapter) and explore them.

Psychology offers many approaches to healing low self-worth, but most involve a slow, gradual process of identifying the contributing irrational beliefs (lies) and replacing them with positive self statements. There is even a twelve-step program called Self-Esteem Seekers Anonymous. However, this program does not "dwell on the sources of low self-esteem"[13] but on the impact it has had on one's life. For me, identifying the *source* of my negative feelings was one of the keys to being set free.

In my experience, believing lies about one's worth is not something that can be changed in the mind. Though believing those lies was a process that began in my mind—as I reflected on hurtful words spoken to me, things I'd failed at, and what these things indicated about who I was—the false belief that was formed became a lie anchored deep in my spirit. For that reason, psychological treatments focusing on changing my mind and thoughts were unsuccessful for me.

It wasn't until I submitted to spiritual counseling that God showed me the lie that was the spiritual root of my longing to look good, my penchant for people pleasing, and my emotional repression: *I'm not good enough.* As part of my healing journey, I had to identify the wounding events that triggered belief in the lie, accept God's truth about my value, and forgive those who had caused me pain. I'll share more about this process of truth discovery in chapter 13.

I don't claim that low self-worth is a contributing factor to every case of depression, but it's likely that if you didn't feel worthless before your depression, you do now. It's a natural product of an illness that strips us of all positivity and light and forces us to see everything— every situation, every person, and even ourselves—in shades of gray and black. For some of you reading this book, your sense of low self-worth will lift with the clouds of your depression. Others of you will have to address its roots on a spiritual battlefront. But believe me when I tell you it's a battle you'll be glad you fought! The reward is a "new," beautiful, gifted, loveable you—the person you've always been but just didn't recognize.

ENCOURAGEMENT FROM GOD'S WORD

You may have heard it said that the Bible is God's love letter to human-kind. It's full of history and parables, laws and instruction, but woven throughout its pages is the thread of love—God creating us in love, longing for us to experience the fullness of His love, and constantly trying to woo His beloved back to Himself. Here is part of the story; I encourage you to read it as a prayer and a declaration of God's immeasurable love for you.

O God, long before you laid down the earth's foundations, you had us in mind, you had settled on us as the focus of your love, to be made whole and holy by your love. Long, long ago you decided to adopt us into your family through Jesus Christ. (And you took great pleasure in planning this!)[14]

You delight in your people. You allow us to be called your children, and we really are! Like a Shepherd gently tends his flock, so you care for us—feeding us, carrying us close to your heart. You have pity on us when we suffer and you comfort us. You heal the brokenhearted and bandage their wounds.

You've written our names on the palms of your hands and you're always thinking about us. You demonstrated your love for us by sending your one and only Son into the world so that we might live through Him, even though it meant He would have to die for us! Then you poured your love into our hearts through the gift of your Holy Spirit. You have made us your temple; you live within us! With you on our side, how can we lose?

Give me the power to understand how wide, how long, how high, and how deep your love is, O Lord! You said that even if the mountains crumble, your love for us would never end. Your love endures forever and your faithfulness continues through all generations.[15]

SELF-REFLECTION

▶ Review the self-description you wrote as you began to read this chapter. Do your statements about yourself reflect self-love and acceptance, or are they condemning and belittling? Do they point out the positive qualities you possess? After reading this chapter, do you see any statements about you that now seem unfair or untrue? Which ones?

▶ If you suspect you're suffering from low self-worth, I encourage you to seek spiritual counsel to explore solutions. (Chapter 11 focuses on the powerful role Christian counseling can play in your treatment.) Also, there are things you can do now to address your feelings of low self-worth:

- Tell God that you are willing to have His truth replace the lies you have believed about yourself.
- Find verses in Scripture that convey the truth you need to hear, whether about God's love for you, His acceptance of you, or His forgiveness of your sins. Here are a few suggested passages to get you started:

Truth About God's Love and Delight
Psalms 149:4; 100:5; 130:7; Isaiah 54:10; Romans 5:5,8; 8:31-39; Ephesians 3:16-19; 1 John 4:9

Truth About God's Care
Psalms 139:1-4; 147:3; Isaiah 40:11; 49:13,16

Truth About Who You Are
Romans 8:16; 2 Corinthians 6:16; 1 Peter 2:9; 1 John 3:1

- Write down a few of these verses and post them somewhere you will see them each day. Recite them, reflect on them, and remember them. Ask God to help you believe His words.

MEDITATION

"Low self-esteem is like driving through life with your hand-break on." (Maxwell Maltz)

"Having a low opinion of yourself is not 'modesty.' It's self-destruction." (Bobbe Sommer)

"The thing that is really hard, and really amazing, is giving up on being perfect and beginning the work of becoming yourself." (Anna Quindlen)

"People are like stained-glass windows. They sparkle and shine when the sun is out, but when the darkness sets in, their true beauty is revealed only if there is a light from within." (Elisabeth Kübler-Ross)

CHAPTER 8

SHAME

*I can bear scorpion's stings, tread fields of fire, in frozen
gulfs of cold eternal lie, be tossed aloft through tracts of
endless void, but cannot live in shame.*

Joanna Baillie, Scottish poet and dramatist

It was one of the worst nights of my young life. Seated on the stage
with a hundred of my senior classmates, I waited for my name to be
called. Highest Achievement awards were being given for each subject,
and while I realized I didn't have the highest grades in the graduating
class (and had no hope to win the Governor General's Award bestowed
on that person), I believed I'd done the best in at least one subject:
communications.

As the ceremony progressed, I mentally rehearsed walking across
the platform to receive my award: reaching for it in my left hand while
shaking the principal's hand with my right, pivoting and walking away
with just a slight smile so I wouldn't look too excited. My thoughts
were interrupted with the announcement I'd been waiting for: "Highest
Achievement in 12-2 Communications goes to . . . Marla Kent*."

---

* Name changed.

Who? I felt a knot in my stomach and was slightly queasy with emotion. *I made better marks than Marla! I know I did. How could the award go to her? There has to be some mistake.* I liked Marla, she was intelligent and capable (*and* played basketball), but I'd been following our grades and believed I had been making top marks all along in this course. I felt angry and humiliated but made sure not to show it as I smiled and applauded for Marla.

Double Whammy

As the remaining achievement awards were announced, I stewed about this snub I'd received and tried to comfort myself with the thought that there was still one more prize I was qualified for: the Birk's Medal, awarded to the graduate who had shown the most leadership in student affairs. I'd served as senior class president, yearbook editor, and president of our Inter-school Christian Fellowship Group this year. Surely there was no one more qualified than I was for the prestigious award.

As the big moment neared, the principal explained what a big deal the Birk's Medal was and that the teachers' votes determined who would receive it. I had butterflies in my stomach as I anticipated hearing my name and walking across the stage in front of my classmates and most of our community who had gathered to watch the ceremony.

"This year's recipient of the Birk's Medal for leadership is . . . David Bunden.* The crowd broke into applause as my heart sank. David had worked with me as vice president of the senior class and yearbook photographer. He was a nice young man, highly intelligent, with a great deal of integrity, but all of his wonderful attributes did nothing to temper the turmoil within me.

The Birk's Medal was the highlight of the ceremony, the last honor of the evening, and I was going home empty-handed. Not a single award. Not even a pat on the back. After all that I'd done for my classmates and my school, I would receive nothing. *Why did the teachers pick*

---

* Name changed.

David? I wondered. *What do they have against me?*

As the graduates rose to leave the stage, I couldn't wait for the night to be over. I couldn't wait for my association with this school to end. I couldn't wait to get out of there and as far away from the village as I could. I left the building sensing that everyone now knew there was something not right with Sharon Gillies; my deep flaws and unworthiness had been exposed for the whole community to gawk at and gossip about. I was so ashamed.

In the days that followed, I rehashed the repercussions of that evening. *I'm such a loser,* I thought. *The town will be talking about this for years — "Oh, look, here comes the Gillies girl — the one who never won anything!" What did I do to make the teachers reject me like that? I thought they liked me. What a fool I was to think that hard work would pay off.* I dreaded going out in public and was glad when I didn't have to. I spent the summer at home, taking care of my younger brother while my mom worked. In the fall, I left my small town for a large university several provinces away, where no one knew my horrible history — no one except Birk's Medal winner David Bunden, who'd set his sights on the same school.

Unable to Shake the Shame

Though I managed, for a time, to escape the place that fed the embarrassment associated with my academic "failure" in high school, I didn't escape my shame. It had been shadowing me for years. I never consciously acknowledged its presence, but I now see that I lived my life attempting to silence the secret bully without success. I tried to be the best at everything I did, perhaps still hoping to capture the elusive award that would prove to the world that I wasn't the worthless person shame said I was.

Then depression hit and knocked me off course and out of the running for best homemaker, best mother, and best volunteer. I felt useless.

PATHWAY TO MISERY

Deep shame is often instilled at a young age as a reaction to wounding events in our lives: the belittling of a parent, the taunting of our peers, or being shunned, for example. When these events occur, we interpret them, translating how others have treated us into a statement about who we are. *I'm weak. I'm incompetent. I'm bad. I'm lazy. I'm unwanted. I'm unattractive. I'm a disappointment.*

Shame is "a painful emotion caused by a strong sense of guilt, embarrassment, unworthiness, or disgrace."[1] At some level (conscious or subconscious), shamed people believe they are unworthy of life — that they are worthless and defective. This subconscious feeling became painfully obvious during my depression. I felt stained, diseased, and vile, for no explicable reason.

I was unhappy with my weight and also believed I was a useless mother and an unsatisfactory wife. I felt guilty about the thoughts I had — judgmental, belittling, critical thoughts of others — and believed I must be a disappointment to God; in no way did I resemble the image of Christ. Busyness helped to ease my shame, but never for long. Six years into my depression, during a reprieve from the hospital, I wrote this prayer in my journal:

I've always been a dirty, worthless person. . . . I know if people really got to know my thoughts and feelings, they would agree that I'm a poor excuse for a human being.

It's interesting that I'm writing this description of myself today, because for the past two days I've been feeling fairly good. I've gotten the girls off to school and started an exercise program, biking thirty minutes each morning. My days have been filled with work; I've been very productive and have accomplished a number of things I'd been putting off for some time.

I now realize that I was feeling good because I was so efficient and was accomplishing so much, working hard and being productive. If I stop the frenzied pace and sit quietly reading or doing nothing, it doesn't take long for guilt to set in. Guilt about what? Guilt for not doing anything to make myself useful and to justify my existence. Guilt for just being worthless after all.

Deep down, unless I can prove otherwise, I am a worthless human being. The way I try to counter this feeling is by working obsessively. (August 29, 1996)

You may have noticed that I did not mention feeling shame but rather guilt. While my doctor identified my shame early on, I didn't acknowledge or understand it until much later. Some people use the terms *guilt* and *shame* interchangeably, but though it's not unusual for these emotions to exist simultaneously, they are very different. Guilt is based on what we have done—an offense or sin our conscience convicts us of—and is linked to what's wrong with our actions; shame emphasizes what's wrong with ourselves.

We don't have to do anything wrong to feel shame; it can be triggered through negative internal self-talk. While guilty people fear punishment, shamed people fear abandonment:[2] *If people know who I really am, they won't want anything to do with me.*

Symptoms of Shame

There are physical signs evident in some people grappling with shame: avoiding eye contact, looking down or away from people, blushing, pounding heart, inability to speak or think, desire to flee, and even nausea.[3] These occur when the shamed person is around others he or she doesn't feel at ease with. I now see that my own uncomfortable "shyness" was really rooted in shame.

Some people build defenses to protect themselves from being overwhelmed by shame. Here are some examples:

- *Escape*—a pattern of seeking out private, safe places where one can be alone.
- *Emotional withdrawal*—living behind masks that hide the real self. These masks may be smiling, people pleasing, appearing self-confident, and pretending to be comfortable.
- *Perfectionism*—demanding much of themselves so they will never make a mistake and, thus, will avoid feeling shame.
- *Criticism*—trying to give their shame away by dragging others down through criticism.
- *Rage*—attacking those they believe are attacking them enables shamed people to fight against humiliation.[4]

I now understand that shame sank its roots in my spirit through an experience very early in my childhood that left me feeling as though I wasn't special or loved. My shame and low self-worth were closely linked, and I spent my first three decades fighting the subconscious, unbearable belief that I was of no value. I did so through emotional withdrawal, perfectionism, and criticism.

Shame and Depression

In chapter 3, I shared a belief I adopted in my early years as a follower of Jesus: *Only messed-up people have messy lives.* I thought that followers of Christ are supposed to live like walking billboards, advertising perfect, painless lives as the product of a relationship with Christ. I gave all I had to projecting the victorious image, but the truth was that deep inside I was one of the messy ones. Almost everything I did was birthed from pain and shame.

You see, it's not impossible for Christians to carry the baggage of shame. The term *born again* does not mean we receive new and improved lives, free from the problems of our pasts; it means we are liberated from the penalty of our sinfulness and given access to the power of Christ and to the Holy Spirit as our Comforter and Guide. We're offered everything required for living out a future full of hope and victory, but when we don't use it, we find ourselves being defeated by the same difficulties we had before our rebirth. Some continue to accumulate baggage until they're buried beneath its weight. That's what happened to me.

I had all the shame-filled misbeliefs related to depression that William Backus outlines in his book *Telling the Truth to Troubled People*:[5]

- *I'm no good.* There are many variations of this lie, but the belief in personal worthlessness is "universally present" in depression.
- *My life is no good.* People who are depressed almost always feel dissatisfied with their lives.
- *My future is hopeless.* Many with depression reach a point where they can't fathom ever feeling differently and believe they'll never get well. When hope is lost, it's easy to slip into despair and even long for death.

Depression isn't always rooted in shame, but it can be. Psychologist and noted journalist Robert Karen documents the impact of shame on today's Western society:

> Current research identifies shame as an important element in aggression (including the violence of wife-beaters), in addictions, obsessions, narcissism, depression, and numerous other psychiatric syndromes. . . . Psychologists now believe that shame is the preeminent cause of emotional distress in our time.[6]

For many, shame lurks beneath the reaches of our conscious thought. Robert Karen says shame that's hidden can "stalk one's being inflicting an unconscious self-loathing."[7] This repressed but unrelenting torment drives people to extraordinary measures to relieve it. When it becomes too painful to live in our own skin, we may try to medicate the pain with alcohol, drugs, or other numbing addictions.

Reinforced by the Enemy

Whether Satan plants these lies within us or we do it ourselves, I believe he works to reinforce them, entrenching them deep in our souls until we live as if they were true; we behave in ways that are destructive to others and ourselves, and our shame grows. Shame is alive. It feeds on the negative events of our lives, swelling and spreading.

Our emotions are based on what we believe. If we think a thought enough times, it becomes a belief and then it has the power to control us. That's why Satan invests so much energy into influencing what we think, because he knows that's the way to manipulate our beliefs and actions, ultimately for our destruction.

Satan begins his shaming work by leading us to believe that we are uniquely deformed, that no one else feels this way or will understand. He makes us fear discovery and disclosure by assuring us we'll be rejected and abhorred. And then, when he has us effectively isolated from all who might be able to offer support, he tries to convince us that even God is disgusted or that we are so horrible, we are beyond His grace. Through deception, Satan intimidates us so that we are so bruised and weary and overcome, it's easier to curl up and die than it is to reach up for help. I remember the feeling well.

In the fifth month of my first hospitalization, Dr. Colford went on vacation and left me in the care of a colleague, Dr. Krakow.* I was having suicidal thoughts and Dr. Krakow was not sympathetic. When he expressed exasperation with me, shame reared its ugly head. I wrote these grim words in my journal:

> I felt pretty small and quite misunderstood after he finished with me. Dr. Krakow's reaction to my suicidal thoughts was a mixture of shock and repulsion. His "How dare you?" and

---

* Name changed.

"How could you think of doing such a thing to your daughter; what has she ever done to make you want to hurt her so much?" just convinced me that I am a terrible mother, a lousy wife, and a horrible person. I deserve to be severely punished for the things I have been doing and thinking. Someone should do the world a favor and bludgeon me to death. (August 25, 1990)

Instead of seeing suicide as an escape from a torturous depression, I began to consider it an acceptable punishment for being worthless.

THE PATHWAY TO HEALING

Because shame is so deeply rooted and the shamed person believes his or her worthlessness is unquestionable, it often remains unrecognized as the source of pain and dysfunction. Healing shame requires the courage to uncover the wounding events that planted it.[8] (I'll explain how I did this in chapter 13.) It also requires an awareness of Satan's involvement.

The idea that Satan can have a real and powerful influence over your life — even as a believer in Jesus Christ — may be a foreign concept to you. For many years, I assumed that because I was Christ's, Satan couldn't touch me, so I lived unaware and unable to defend myself.

I've come to understand that although Satan can wreak havoc in our lives, he can do so only if we allow him to. Christ's power is infinitely greater, and as followers of Jesus, we have access to that power. But it takes a conscious decision to use it in order for it to work in our lives. We must defend ourselves against Satan's attacks by asking Jesus to help us recognize the lies we believe and then to replace them with His truth. You may need the help of a Christian counselor, but you can do this. Don't let the "father of lies" (see John 8:44) convince you that nothing can ever change. Don't let him rob you of the freedom that can be yours.

As long as we carry around our bags of shame and lies, Satan can reach into them and fling accusing, condemning, disturbing thoughts at us. But as we're healed from the wounds of our past and the lies we believe, our bags grow lighter and Satan loses his ammunition. When the bags are emptied, we release our grip on them and walk into emotional freedom.[9]

I've experienced this miraculous transformation, though it was a long process and I needed a lot of help. It took the insight of a trained Christian counselor—and divine illumination from the Holy Spirit—for me to identify and renounce the lies that had held me in bondage for three decades. Be encouraged that if I can lose my baggage, you can too.

ENCOURAGEMENT FROM GOD'S WORD

Lest you feel overwhelmed and disheartened at the idea that Satan may be intensifying your feelings of shame, I want to point out that Jesus' power to heal and His power over Satan are well documented in the New Testament. While He lived among us, Jesus healed lepers, restored sight, even breathed new life into those who were dead. But His power was not restricted to miracles of a physical nature. In the book of Luke, we read about a spiritual showdown between the powers of Darkness and Light as Jesus steps in and sets a demon-possessed man free.

Luke tells us that Jesus met the tormented man in the wilderness of Gerasenes. Driven by some madness that raged within him, he lived in the graves of dead men. Because he was crazed and violent, the villagers had shackled the man for their own protection, but that seemed to feed his fury, making him even wilder and stronger, and he shattered his bonds.

Day and night he wandered among the rocky hills that cradled the bones of the dead. At times he was so tormented and lonely, he longed for the eternal sleep of those who rested in the tombs. In anguish he ripped off his clothes and slashed his skin with jagged stones. His agonized cries echoed in the wilderness along Galilee's shores.

Then one afternoon, as the rocks baked and the lake shimmered under a hot sun, a boat dropped anchor and several men waded toward the beach. It had been months since anyone had dared pass near the area, and the wild man eyed them suspiciously. As the intruders drew closer, he screamed and ran—first away and then toward them. The faces of a dozen men betrayed their fear, but one looked at peace and, strangely, near tears. As the outcast fell at the gentle man's feet, he cried out—in a voice that was not his own—"What do you want with me, Jesus, Son of the Most High God? I beg you, don't torture me!" (Luke 8:28). God's Son asked who the shrieking voice belonged to, and it replied, "Legion," because the man was filled by a mob of demons. They begged Jesus not to send them into the depths of the earth, imploring instead for permission to enter a herd of pigs feeding on the mountain. He granted their request, and as the demons entered the pigs, the entire herd rushed down the steep bank and drowned in the lake.

When the villagers heard about the swine's stampede, they hurried into the wilderness to see what had happened and found the once-crazed man dressed and sitting peacefully at Jesus' feet. As you might imagine, the man wanted to stay with Jesus and go wherever He was going, but the Lord sent him home to tell others how much God had done for him. Obediently, he returned to the town that had driven him out, to the people who'd chained him, and testified to the power and goodness of the One who set his spirit free (see Luke 8:39).

We don't have to be possessed by demons to find ourselves cut off from the world and isolated, but the most painful isolation is experienced when we're cut off from ourselves—when we've been listening for so many years to the tape of negativity playing in our heads that we've lost all sense of who we truly are. We no longer believe we were created for a glorious purpose. We lose the hope that God can use us or that we can ever be of any good to anyone. We feel as if there's no point to our existence; we're just taking up space, using up oxygen, and don't deserve to be here. We find ourselves wandering in an emotional and spiritual wilderness: crying out in anguish, lashing out in anger, helpless to stop the negative thoughts from slicing deeper into our souls.

Jesus' truth is infinitely more powerful than the lies that may be causing you to live as an outcast, but you have to receive it. In chapter 12, I'll share more about how to use God's power to defeat your spiritual enemy. And in chapter 13, you'll learn how to replace Satan's lies with God's truth. Your Shepherd knows where you are, and He wants to lead you out of that dark and lonely place. He wants to bring you peace. Believe that what He did for the man of the tombs He can do for you. Perhaps this will be the day you'll see a boat on the horizon, coming to anchor on the shore of your soul.

SELF-REFLECTION

▶ Which, if any, of the symptoms of shame do you have?
▶ Which of the shame-filled lies commonly believed by depressed people resonates with you? (*I'm no good. My life is no good. My future is hopeless.*) Ask God to help you learn and receive the truth to replace those lies.
▶ If you're carrying a suitcase of shame, what will you do to get help?

MEDITATION

"Now that we know what we have—Jesus, this great High Priest with ready access to God—let's not let it slip through our fingers. We don't have a priest who is out of touch with our reality. He's been through weakness and testing, experienced it all—all but the sin. So let's walk right up to him and get what he is so ready to give. Take the mercy, accept the help." (Hebrews 4:14-16, MSG)

CHAPTER 9

FEAR

*The one who doubts is like a wave of the sea, blown
and tossed by the wind.*

James 1:6, TNIV

I never really trusted God, but I didn't realize this until years of anxiety and doubt had caused me much misery. I believed *in* God and His Son, Jesus, but that wasn't enough to make me depend on Him or to keep my fears at bay.

I believed that God watched us from heaven, considered our prayers, and made His decisions about whether to answer them as we wished based on a complex formula that I didn't have the mathematical genius to understand. Something like this: $(PRAYER + SINCERITY) \times (WORRY + EFFORT) \times (DEGREE\ OF\ MAINTAINING\ "IMAGE" + GOODNESS)^2 = Y$. So I tried to increase my chances of having life "work out" for me by repetitive prayers, constant worry, continuous effort, emotional repression, and exemplary—though obsessive—behavior.

Obsessive Worry

Looking back, I see lots of evidence that I didn't have much confidence in God's ability—or desire—to direct my life and take care of me.

Fear and worry was a thread that ran through my existence, the cord that helped me hold it all together. At least I *thought* I was holding it together. Isn't that what all worriers believe? *If I worry enough and imagine the worst, it won't happen* or *If I conceive of the catastrophe in my mind, it won't come true in my life—and if it does, after repeatedly rehearsing it in my brain, at least I'll be prepared to handle it.*

I worried about what the teacher would say or the look of scorn I might receive if I were late for class. I worried I hadn't studied enough for a test and sometimes faked being sick so I could stay home and have one more day to prepare. (Sorry, Mom.) I worried about what to say to people; I was so shy that I would cross the street to avoid having to greet someone. As a teenager, I worried that the pastor would think my family was heathen, so I made sure the Bible was "casually" in full view on the coffee table when he came to visit. (No, Reverend MacDonald, we didn't really gather 'round on the good furniture to read the Good Book every day.)

As a teenager I sang in church quite often and always felt nauseous beforehand. I was worried I might forget the words or sing when I was supposed to pause or make any of a zillion other potentially embarrassing mistakes. I might trip on the stairs leading up to the stage or slip and fall behind the piano on my way back down—actually, it was my friend Glenn (Reverend MacDonald's son) who did that, but it *could have* been me.

Fear's Painful Beginnings

Even though I wasn't conscious of it at the time, a few childhood losses triggered a fear that bullied my life for decades: a long battle with breast cancer ended my maternal grandmother's life when I was seven years old, and one year later, my other grandmother died of uterine cancer. In my tenth year, I experienced another profound loss when my family moved halfway across the country. It broke my heart to leave the home I'd lived in all my life, and this pain was compounded by having to say good-bye to my best friend, Heather, and her parents. Though we wrote letters regularly after I moved away, and I returned to Toronto a few times to visit, I never got over the trauma of losing them.

I adjusted to my new life on a farm in rural New Brunswick alone, fearing that if I opened myself up to another relationship, I'd be hurt again. There was one special family who tried to reach out to me, but I essentially lived my life sheltered from the pain of loss by refusing to connect with another soul. My future husband, Tim, was the exception, eight years later.

When my grandmothers fell ill, I prayed — and worried — sincerely and religiously. Either I'd gotten something wrong in the equation or God wasn't listening. He didn't intervene in my parents' decision to relocate our family, either. It seemed that God had "checked out" and left me to my own devices. These childhood wounds left an ugly scar — a lie that caused me to be afraid to love: Relationships seemed hazardous and unpredictable, and since God had not protected me from pain in the past, I decided it was up to me to do so as far as the future was concerned.

Losing so many people I loved at such a young age was perplexing and painful. I didn't want to be hurt like that ever again. I didn't want to need anyone ever again. Because the wounding events were real, I believed that the assumption they provoked in me was valid: *I would not experience the agony of loss if I kept people at a distance.* I can't bear to consider how much I've truly lost because of this belief. In the past several years, I've been healed from a number of wounding events and corresponding lies, and though I've overcome the fear of allowing others to truly know me, I still don't pursue close friendships. I guess I've learned to live without them; old habits die hard. Perhaps there is still some healing to be done.

THE PATHWAY TO MISERY

Fear, which at its core is a lack of trust in God, can hold us hostage, preventing us from experiencing the lives we were created for. It caused me to live a very cautious, controlled existence without spontaneity or room for God's plans for my life.

When Core Needs Are Not Met

In *Fear No Evil*, Brad Jersak explains how fear can control us. Every person has the need to live life fully; to be known and loved; and to live in peace, safety, and security. When these core needs go unmet, primal—or foundational—anxieties and phobias may develop. Jersak points out that in order for these primal fears to take root, we must first adopt foundational lies about ourselves, others (people or God), and life. These lies become beliefs that are the basis for a fear-filled existence. They direct our choices about the way we live, and they give birth to all kinds of other fears.

When the core need of living life fully is unmet, we may believe one or more of the lies: *Life has no meaning. There's no hope. I can't go on. I am not safe. I am going to die.* We may fail to trust that God gives our lives meaning and will take care of us. These lies can lead to feelings of hopelessness and meaninglessness as well as the fear of pain and death. If we feel that life is meaningless, we may try to numb our pain and disillusionment through addictive and self-destructive behaviors. When we fear pain and death, we become overly restrictive of the activities in which we participate and overly cautious of whom we trust. Because I feared that God wouldn't protect me from the pain of lost relationships, I became cautious about my level of involvement with people, restricting close friendships.

When the core need to feel loved is unmet and we don't receive a healthy amount of affection and nurturing, we may believe, *There's something wrong with me. I'm unlovable. I'm worthless. I'm alone in the world.* Because we fail to trust that God loves and accepts us as we are (and that His love and acceptance are truly all we need), we end up fearing abandonment and rejection and may do whatever is necessary to earn the approval and acceptance of others. We may become people pleasers or perfectionists (as I did), or we may become involved in codependent, dysfunctional, or abusive relationships.

In the midst of a life that is lacking peace and security (other core needs), we may come to believe, *My life's a mess. I can't be sure of anything. I have no control over what happens to me.* We may fail to trust that God is in control and that He is steadfast and dependable. As a result, we may fear chaos, powerlessness, and the unknown. Such fears may launch us into a desperate attempt to gain control, carefully ordering our universe by focusing on every detail, demanding much of ourselves, and trying to be in command of our relationships. We may become controlling and manipulative and risk developing a host of other fears, including: the unknown, the future, change, or anything different from what we are accustomed to.[1]

When Fear Looms Larger Than Faith

As I worked through my depression and all that contributed to it, I discovered other lies that changed the course of my life and who I became. I now see that all the lies I have confronted throughout my recovery share one thing in common: fear. When lies overshadow truth, and our fear looms larger than our faith, there are consequences. I've found that they fall into three categories:

1. When we fear rather than trust, we suffer. I didn't recognize the relationship between my lack of faith in God's care and my depression until shortly after I was set free. Author Mike Yaconelli also reaped the negative repercussions of fear, spending much of his life suffering because he failed to trust in God's infinite love. In *Messy Spirituality*, Mike tells about the day, when he was eleven years old, a lie was planted in his soul that led him to doubt God's goodness.

Mike fell in love with a conga drum he saw in the window of a local store. After purchasing it with money from his savings, he brought it home and excitedly showed it to his father. Mike attributes his dad's reaction to his being a very practical man who'd lived through the Depression. He asked Mike how much he paid for the drum and then demanded, "Take it back!"

Mike was stunned but obedient, and when he took the drum back to the store the next morning, he walked away carrying something else: a very heavy burden and a lie. He explains:

> For reasons I don't really understand, the trauma of that experience burned itself deep into my soul. Emotionally, I was crushed, and every good experience since has been shadowed by the words "Take it back." Buried in the back of my mind is the gnawing worry that my grace credit card is going to be cancelled. Parked somewhere in my subconscious is the belief that grace and forgiveness are lavish, unconditional, and *limited*.
>
> Cross Jesus one too many times, fail too often, sin too much, and God will decide to take his love back. It is so bizarre, because I know Christ loves me, but I'm not sure he likes me, and I continually worry that God's love will simply wear out.[2]

Many years after the wounding event, through an intervention by his own son, Mike learned the truth about the limitless love of God. But he'd suffered extensively with the pain of believing a lie and living in faithless fear.

2. When we fear rather than trust, we fail to live up to our potential. We might have been robbed of some of the most beautiful paintings of all time had one artist not resisted fear. Claude Monet was an aspiring caricature artist and skeptical when Eugene Boudin, a friend of his drawing teacher, invited him to paint out-of-doors. Monet might well have feared failure or being unable to make a living at the new art form Boudin proposed, but if he did, he managed to summon something within him greater than his fears. As a result, Monet became a pioneer of the French Impressionist movement, one of the most sweeping revolutions in the history of art. He later recalled, "It was like a veil had suddenly been lifted from my eyes and I knew I could be a painter."[3]

Monet had to venture out *into the light* to discover his real potential as an artist. Though a talented caricaturist, it's obvious that he was gifted for more. He fulfilled that potential even though many in his day failed to appreciate his style of painting. Monet followed his new passion, persevered, and ultimately achieved great things.

I was not as bold as Claude Monet. Rather than seeking what I was created for, I spent many years doing the things I thought would please others and gain their praise and approval. I missed the thrill of purposeful living, as Monet expressed: "Every day I discover still more beautiful things. It's enough to drive one mad, I've got such a desire to do everything my head explodes."[4] Certainly, there were times I nearly went mad trying to do everything, but my motivation was not passion and desire but fear and duty.

I tried to do everything through gritted teeth. Intimidated, I chose not to step out into the light—God's light—to see what He wanted me to be, choosing instead to be guided by my dark fears. For many years, I failed to find God's purpose for me and the joy that comes from living to fulfill it.

3. *When we fear rather than trust, we have no peace.* I subconsciously feared that God wouldn't deliver the things I most wanted: love, acceptance, and security. After all, I'd been disappointed more than once in my young life. Where was the proof that God was on my side, looking out for me? If I couldn't rely on Him, I had to depend on my own abilities and devices to get my needs met.

Isaiah delivers this message from God to the Israelites, but it's also a warning for people like me:

> If you are walking in darkness, without a ray of light, trust in the LORD and rely on your God. But watch out, you who live in your own light and warm yourselves by your own fires. This is the reward you will receive from me: You will soon lie down in great torment. (Isaiah 50:10-11, NLT)

Why do we sometimes choose to step out of the healing, guiding brightness of God's light? And what happens when we do? Author Charles Swindoll explains:

> When times are tough, the Lord is our only security. When days are dark, the Lord is our only light. Yet, I have observed that we frequently have trouble believing that God is our only hope, security, light, and strength because we are so prone to try everything else. We automatically depend on everything except the Lord. Yet still He waits there for us—patiently waiting to show Himself strong.[5]

My need for control led me to try everything but trusting God. As a result, my obsessive-compulsive behavior, impossible expectations, isolation, and ultimately depression overwhelmed me with the torment Isaiah warns of. Yet God was there, waiting to help me, protecting my life until I was ready to trust Him.

One of the contributing factors to my lasting freedom from depression has been learning to trust that my heavenly Father will take care of me. It may be hard to believe, but throughout my life and the years of my depression, I never realized that I *didn't* trust Him. God revealed my lack of faith (and the reason for it) in a powerful prayer session shortly after He set me free from depression. That's one of the stories I'll share in chapter 13. But even though my new faith in God's trustworthiness brings me peace, I still encounter difficulties. The difference is that I don't face challenges alone and I'm no longer afraid. Being at peace doesn't mean we live life problem free; it means we confront life's problems with hope that we can overcome them, trusting God to give us the strength we need and show us the way to go while we fumble in the dark.

Bible teacher Dr. Charles F. Stanley offers this recipe for peace in the midst of life's difficulties:

We, too, can learn to be at peace while the storms of life rage around us. The first step is believing that the power of God is within us through the presence of His Spirit. We then must accept that God's priority for us is transformation into Christ's image, and not necessarily comfortable circumstances.[6]

If we believe that God truly can—and does—work all things together for the good of those who love Him (as Paul writes in Romans 8:28), then we can accept life's pain, sorrow, and discomfort with peace and hopeful anticipation of the promising end result.

ENCOURAGEMENT FROM GOD'S WORD

When God called Moses to pack his bags, grab his shepherd's staff, and head back to Egypt to confront Pharaoh and lead the Israelites out of bondage, Moses was full of fear. Had he understood the pivotal role he would play in Israel's history and that his fame would endure for millennia, surely the hillsides would have echoed with his excitement. "Woo-hoo! I'm gonna be a leader. A LEADER! I've hit the big time now. Just wait 'til Pharaoh sees me coming; he won't know what hit him." But Moses wasn't thrilled or bold. Instead, he was overwhelmed by thoughts of all that could go wrong. Moses was afraid because he didn't trust God yet.

He feared the mission: "Why me? What makes you think that I could ever go to Pharaoh and lead the children of Israel out of Egypt?" (Exodus 3:11, MSG).

He feared rejection: "Suppose I go to the People of Israel and I tell them, 'The God of your fathers sent me to you'; and they ask me, 'What is his name?' What do I tell them?" (Exodus 3:13, MSG). "They won't trust me. They won't listen to a word I say. They're going to say, 'GOD? Appear to him? Hardly!'" (Exodus 4:1, MSG).

He feared his inadequacies: "Master, please, I don't talk well. I've never been good with words, neither before nor after you spoke to me. I stutter and stammer" (Exodus 4:10, MSG). When God refused to change His mind about Moses' mission, the future leader of the Israelite nation was reduced to desperate pleading: "Oh, Master, please. Send somebody else" (Exodus 4:13, MSG).

I relate to Moses' misery. I've done a little pleading on more than one occasion, when I felt small and God's task looked big.

Fear is fundamentally a failure to trust that there is Someone who can meet all of our needs and care for us no matter what situation we're facing. Even those who believe in God experience times of fear. The good news is that even though God can use us when we are afraid, He relentlessly works to remove our fear by proving Himself faithful—like He did to Moses.

God provided Moses with a spokesperson in his brother, Aaron, so that his inadequacy in speech (and fear of public speaking) would not hinder him. When Moses and Aaron met with the leaders of the Israelites and told them everything the Lord had said to Moses about delivering them from bondage and leading them to a new land, they didn't question as Moses feared they might. They believed what they heard and bowed down and worshipped God because of His concern for them. Each time God told Moses what would happen next, it came true. He foretold each plague, Pharaoh's decisions, the parting of the Red Sea, the safe passage of the Israelites, and the drowning of Pharaoh and his army in the receding waters.

As the Israelites wandered in the desert and complained about being hungry, God told Moses He would send them food each morning and evening. The promise was kept with meat at night and manna at daybreak. When the Israelites were thirsty, God told Moses that if he struck a particular rock with his staff, water would flow from it. It did. As God continued to prove Himself trustworthy, Moses' fear was transformed into faith. Forty years later, in a full-circle experience, Moses found himself at the end of his mission as the Israelites' leader, ready to send them on their own journey of faith across the Jordan River to take possession of the Promised Land. Though Moses could not go with them, he assured the Israelites they wouldn't go alone. "Be strong and courageous. . . . The LORD himself goes before you and will be with you; he will never leave you nor forsake you. Do not be afraid; do not be discouraged" (Deuteronomy 31:6,8).

In the years since my depression ended, I have come to know the God who keeps His word. It seems that He's constantly testing my faith by giving me assignments I feel unqualified for or allowing difficulties I don't believe I have the ability to face. But He's also proving Himself faithful by providing all I need to accomplish His will and the strength to endure all things. Now that I know I don't have to do things in my own power, I no longer fear my inadequacies or making a fool of myself. Now that I know God can carry me through any painful circumstance, I no longer fear loss. Now that I've seen God use my experience with depression and eating disorders to help others—and transform me—I know that He can make miracles out of life's misery and I no longer fear difficulties. Now that I know I can trust God, I have peace.

The next time you feel afraid, don't beat yourself up about it. Ask God to help you overcome fear by proving Himself to you. He's patiently waiting for the opportunity.

SELF-REFLECTION

In the gospel of Mark, we read about a man who brought his demon-possessed son to Jesus for healing. As the boy convulsed on the ground, foaming at the mouth, his father said to Jesus,

"If you can do anything, take pity on us and help us."

"'If you can'?" said Jesus. "Everything is possible for him who believes."

Immediately the boy's father exclaimed, "I do believe; help me overcome my unbelief!" Jesus commanded the evil spirit to leave and the boy was healed. (see Mark 9:22-24)

If you relate to this mixture of faith and doubt, the next time doubt arises, ask God to make your faith stronger than your fear. While you're waiting for Him to do so, reflect on the ways He's proved Himself faithful to you in the past.

▶ Charles Haddon Spurgeon said, "Anxiety does not empty tomorrow of its sorrows but only empties today of its strength."[7]

Identify an area of your life in which you struggle with fear or anxiety. How is that fear robbing you of strength?

If you're ready to release your fear to God, consider praying a prayer such as this one:

I believe in You, Lord. Help my unbelief. Heal me of the wound that caused me to fear_____. Help me to remember that You are in control and to put my trust in You. Amen.

MEDITATION

"There is no one like the God of Israel, who rides through the skies to help you, who rides on the clouds in his majesty. The everlasting God is your place of safety, and his arms will hold you up forever." (Deuteronomy 33:26-27, NCV)

"Will you rely on him for his great strength? Will you leave your heavy work to him?" (Job 39:11)

"Surely I am with you always, to the very end of the age." (Jesus, Matthew 28:20)

CHAPTER 10

UNFORGIVENESS

*Resentment is like drinking poison and waiting for the
other person to die.*

Carrie Fisher, author, movie actress

*Forgiveness is the fragrance that the flower leaves on
the heel of the one who crushed it.*

Mark Twain

I was only three desks away from the door. I thought I might escape in one grand leap, but running away would only draw more attention to myself and the terrible transgression I'd just committed. The class had never been my favorite, and my teacher had just succeeded in making it traumatic as well.

After instructing us, he'd sat down to read the newspaper and told us to work on our next assignment. I dutifully obliged and finished the task two minutes before the end of class. Rather than continuing on to the next unit, I closed my book and waited quietly for the bell. Then it happened.

This particular teacher was a bit of a mixed bag when it came to personality. He could be kind and amusing but had a temper that was legendary. It was difficult to know what to expect from him, though it never was much of an issue for me, a conscientious, well-behaved student. But on this day, he had it in for "Goody Two-Shoes." When he observed me observing the clock, he decided to make an issue of it.

"Miss Gillies, I didn't hear the bell. Why is your book closed?" His booming voice filled the small portable classroom, jarring me out of my daydream. I was in eleventh grade and had never been reprimanded by a teacher. I think my classmates were in as much shock as I, and they all turned to see how I would respond. The teacher's words were like a heavy weight on my chest, forcing the air from my lungs. I felt nauseous and mortified, and within moments, fury took over. But I dutifully opened my textbook, picked up my pencil, and pretended to get back to work for the remaining thirty-odd seconds of class time until the bell released me.

The teacher had humiliated me and I never forgot it, nor did I intend to let him forget. From that day forward, it was war. I worked my passive-aggressive magic on my teacher, looking the other way when I passed him in the hall, refusing to contribute to class discussions or laugh at his jokes, and speaking only when asked a direct question. I recall my satisfaction when, at parent-teacher conferences a while later, he expressed to my mother that I seemed "aloof." He had noticed! I graduated high school without making amends or forgiving him.

Though this seems like a minor incident, it illustrates how petty I was when it came to resentment. I was always one to hold a grudge, whether the wound was shallow or deep. I've been stubborn about forgiveness, both asking for and offering, most of my life. My bitterness has infected my family, ruined relationships, and wounded people in ways I may never know. Even when I began exploring spiritual treatments for my depression and, on my counselor's advice, chose to forgive those who had hurt me, there was a small group of people I didn't think deserved forgiveness.

Their offenses against me weren't huge (and some would argue they were imagined), but I'd been dealing with their subtle harassment for years and I was sick of it—and them. So even though I made a statement that I'd forgiven these people, my heart was not in agreement and the bitterness was tucked away in a secret corner no one was allowed to touch.

I would sneak into that corner daily and feed my resentment with negative thoughts, constant ruminations about the latest sins committed against me. It managed to numb my pain—for a time. Then Bitterness began demanding more, so I found another means of satisfaction. I became more vocal and freely spoke my criticisms and judgments of my enemies—in the privacy of my home. I spewed negativity all over my family so I could feel that sense of superiority that kept Bitterness content. When I'd encounter someone who expressed a similar dislike of these people, I'd indulge in the rush that came from talking about them behind their backs, and Bitterness squealed with delight.

I denied I had a problem, though it was obvious to others. The Bible teaches, "If someone says, 'I love God,' but hates a Christian brother or sister, that person is a liar; for if we don't love people we can see, how can we love God, whom we have not seen?" (1 John 4:20, NLT). In light of this verse and others with a similar message, I refused to consider the possibility that I hated anyone. That would be calling my love for God into question. So when my husband would raise the issue, I denied hatred, trying to make my feelings more acceptable by using terms like *disdain, strong dislike,* and *can't stand.*

Then, one day, as my daughter and I were driving home in the car and I was muttering about the latest transgression by one of the perpetrators, Jenna interrupted with a question that stopped me mid-sentence: "Mom, why do you hate her so much?" Up to this point, Tim had been the audience for most of my rants and had been the only one who had brought up the "H" word. But now it was apparent that my twelve-year-old saw it too. The Holy Spirit used her words to convict me, and though I didn't admit to it at that moment, I knew Jenna was right: I was filled with hatred.

That realization spawned a long journey to get rid of this newly named sin. It was a gradual process that began with a futile attempt to will hatred away and ultimately led me to pray for the desire to love my enemies, not with human love (I couldn't summon that up) but with God's sacrificial *agape* love. I prayed that prayer every morning and, ever so gradually, the hatred turned to ambivalence, and ambivalence finally gave way to love. This was a process that took six years, and it wasn't easy, but it has changed my life in a profound way. For the first time ever, I feel at peace with others. Where I once would have delighted in the difficulties faced by my offenders, I now find myself praying for them. I'm no longer a slave to angry, spiteful, or critical thoughts. I've moved on and kicked the beast of Bitterness out of the basement of my soul.

I still pray for *agape* love every day, but it's no longer for the people I hate, because hatred is gone. I hope it stays that way.

THE PATHWAY TO MISERY

I carried around the emotional and spiritual baggage of unforgiveness all my life, namely, a lack of peace and an inability to experience an intimate relationship with God. Reliving, over and over, the offenses committed against me, I ruminated about retribution. I believed being angry and bitter was the right response to those who hurt me—that my resentment would somehow punish the perpetrators. But I was the one who suffered. I was carrying a lifetime of unresolved, internalized anger that infected my mind and spirit and contributed to depression.

Like me, many people struggle with forgiveness. One survey reported that 94 percent of Americans believed it was important to forgive but only 48 percent said they usually try to forgive others.[1] Why don't more people try? Do we think forgiveness is beyond our ability, a quality possessed only by saints?

Ignoring the Benefits

Perhaps it's because we don't realize the benefits forgiving offers: reducing the severity of heart disease,[2] prolonging the lives of cancer patients,[3] reducing back pain,[4] easing depression,[5] and even preventing wrinkles,[6] not to mention the spiritual benefits. Social scientists believe that forgiveness education can help reduce the number of crimes committed as vengeful acts and heal troubled marriages.[7]

Dr. Neil Anderson defines forgiveness as "an act of the will whereby we give up our claim to seek revenge for an offense against us."[8] In our society, "giving up" anything isn't popular. We're taught to fight for our rights, demand justice, never surrender. To some, forgiveness is for weaklings. But the truth is quite the opposite: It takes strength to forgive—the kind of strength that often can only come from God.

Believing Lies

It took me so long to forgive partly because I was spiteful, but also because I believed a lie about forgiveness: *You don't have to forgive those who don't apologize.* Many myths cause confusion about forgiveness and keep us bound by bitterness. Let's look at a few common ones:

I have to heal before I can forgive. Healing is not a prerequisite to forgiveness; forgiveness actually promotes emotional, spiritual, and physical healing. We can never be emotionally and spiritually whole until we release bitterness through forgiveness.

Forgiving means forgetting. We can't, by an act of will, remove memories from our minds, but we can control what we do with them, refusing to dwell on past hurts or use them against our offenders. If we continually bring up what others have done to us, then we're still living in bitterness.

Forgiving means you excuse the act. Forgiveness does not condone hurtful behavior. God forgives, but He doesn't tolerate sin. While forgiveness means God doesn't punish us for sin, He doesn't remove its consequences. When Jesus forgave, He said, "Go and sin no more"

(John 8:11, KJV). You can refuse to tolerate your offender's hurtful behavior and set boundaries to protect yourself from further abuse. To learn how to do that, consider reading one or more of the books in Dr. Henry Cloud and Dr. John Townsend's BOUNDARIES series.

I have to feel forgiving to forgive. Forgiveness is a decision, not a feeling. You can feel offended, angry, and betrayed and still forgive the person who hurt you. The "feeling" (peace and love) comes after the decision has been made to let go of bitterness and get on with your life.

Refusing to forgive those who have wounded you can lead to a lifetime of physical, emotional, and spiritual misery. You won't be losing anything of value when you release bitterness and open the door for God to do a work of forgiveness in your spirit.

THE PATHWAY TO HEALING

Choosing to forgive is an important step in the pathway to healing. In this section you will learn how to take that step. You'll also discover that forgiving others is never impossible with God's help, and it's an action that will change your life for the better.

Recognize the Benefits

Forgiving others can release us from the bitterness that contributes to physical and emotional illness. But there are other good incentives to forgive:

Forgiving frees us to live the life God wants for us. If anyone ever had reason to resent, Reverend Majed El-Shafie did. After converting from Islam to Christianity, he was confined in the torture section of an Egyptian prison and sentenced to death. Majed was burned with cigarettes, assaulted with attack dogs, and even crucified, with a mixture of salt and lemon used to anoint his wounds.

A daring escape brought him from Egypt to Israel and then to

Canada, where he now resides and operates a human rights organization defending persecuted Christians. In speaking about the decision to forgive his own persecutors, Majed explained that in ancient times, the punishment for a killer was to carry the victim's body on his back. After three days, it would be in such a state of decay that the dead body would kill the live body carrying it. Majed said he carried the "dead bodies" of his persecutors for three years, and during that period of unforgiveness, he was unable to preach the gospel. Finally, he threw off the burden by choosing to forgive.[9]

The Greek word most often used in the New Testament for forgive is *aphiemi*, meaning "to let go from one's power, possession, to let go free, let escape."[10] Forgiveness is the act of cutting free the bodies bound to our backs. It won't undo the pain from the past, but it will release us from a future of misery.

As Majed learned, it's impossible to live the life God wants to give us, and to do the work He's called us to, when we're burdened with resentment and unforgiveness. When we choose to carry heavy loads—scores of bodies of those who've hurt us—we're the ones who suffer.

Forgiving hinders Satan. Unforgiveness leads to bitterness, a spiritual disease that grows and spreads through our souls. Satan loves to keep us preoccupied with bitterness—our energies focused on licking our wounds and nursing our grudges—so we're unavailable to do God's work and unable to receive the peace, joy, and freedom He longs to give us.

Our bitterness can also spread to those around us, destroying families, churches, and communities. For that reason, the Bible instructs, "See to it that no one misses the grace of God and that no bitter root grows up to cause trouble and defile many" (Hebrews 12:15). Bitterness is like a nasty weed and "a thistle or two gone to seed can ruin a whole garden in no time" (Hebrews 12:15, MSG). Only forgiveness can halt the spread of bitterness and restore peace to the soul of the one who's been wounded.

Forgiving makes us more like Christ. Just as Jesus agreed to pay the penalty for our sin, forgiveness means we agree to accept the consequences of another's sin and not seek revenge. As Neil Anderson writes, "You pay the price of the evil you forgive."[11] Though forgiveness isn't popular, it's possible. The divine power we receive through our relationship with Christ enables us to live differently than the world does. As followers of Jesus, we share in His divine nature (see 2 Peter 1:1-4), and it's His nature to sacrificially forgive.

Forgiveness is grace—giving someone something he doesn't deserve. And the gift of godly forgiveness is love. We can't love without forgiving because love "keeps no record of wrongs" (1 Corinthians 13:5). Jesus said, "All people will know that you are my followers if you love each other" (John 13:35, NCV).

Target Mercy

Two of the people most often overlooked when forgiving are God and oneself. A perfect and loving God cannot actually wound us, but when He doesn't answer prayers the way we'd like or allows suffering for reasons we don't understand, we may grow bitter toward Him.

Sometimes we even blame God for the injuries we receive from others or for the things we *think* they've done to us. (We may perceive actions committed against us that aren't based in reality.) "Forgiving God" isn't placing blame on Him but making a choice to let go of the bitterness we hold toward Him for things that have happened to us.[12]

Sometimes we're angry with ourselves. We hold the blame for unfortunate life circumstances, bad decisions, and even the way others have treated us. Learning to forgive oneself is a crucial step in being able to forgive others. We can't give away what we don't possess, and if we don't have self-love, acceptance, and forgiveness, we won't be able to offer them to others. Ask God to help you accept that you're not perfect and to embrace the gift that Jesus Christ gives: His life in exchange for your messes, mistakes, and sins. Continuing to punish yourself for things Jesus died to atone for is not honoring to Him nor helpful to you.

Though I did not struggle with unforgiveness toward God or myself, I know that many do. If you're one of them, you may benefit from the help of a godly counselor to guide you in this area. Once you've allowed God to deal with any bitterness you may harbor against Him or yourself, you'll be more effective at forgiving others.

The Bible teaches that there is no one unworthy of our forgiveness. On the night before His crucifixion, Jesus washed the feet of the one who would soon betray Him (see John 13:1-12) and then shared a meal with him. Jesus knew what Judas was about to do (see Matthew 26:20-25), but I believe He'd already forgiven him. If we've experienced the love and forgiveness of Christ, we are required to act accordingly toward others, regardless of their offenses.

Take the Steps to Forgive

Once you have decided to forgive, there are steps you can take to achieve it. Ask God to give you His power to accomplish each step.

1. Acknowledge the hurt. Denial doesn't make an injury go away. Ignoring our wounds causes them to become infected, inflamed, and irritated, which delays healing. You can't forgive someone until you acknowledge they've hurt you.

It isn't necessary to confront your offender; you can communicate your pain to God through prayer.

2. Remember how God forgives you. Too often we are like the unforgiving servant in Jesus' parable (see Matthew 18:23-25) who was shown compassion when it came time to settle his large debt to the king. By not considering the king's mercy toward him, he failed to be merciful to a fellow servant and, as a result, was imprisoned and tortured. When you're tempted to rehash another's offenses, ask God to remind you of the forgiveness you've received.

3. Release the hurt. It was difficult to let go of the hurts from my past; my obsessive nature made me more inclined to revisit them over and over. But when I became consumed by those thoughts, I finally asked God to change me. You can too. Decide not to dwell on the past and to give up any ridicule, resentment, or reproach toward your offender. Avoid criticizing that person verbally or in your mind. Ask God to replace your thoughts about your offender with thoughts of Him and His goodness.

4. *Cancel the debt.* Once you have acknowledged and released the hurt, you must release the one who wounded you, as God does:

> The LORD is compassionate, merciful, patient, and always ready to forgive. He will not always accuse us of wrong or be angry [with us] forever. He has not treated us as we deserve for our sins or paid us back for our wrongs. As high as the heavens are above the earth—that is how vast his mercy is toward those who fear him. As far as the east is from the west—that is how far he has removed our rebellious acts from himself. (Psalm 103:8-12, GW)

God tells the prophet Jeremiah about a new promise He will make with the people of Israel and Judah. He will write His teachings on their hearts. He will be their God and they His people. "I will forgive their wickedness and I will no longer hold their sins against them" (Jeremiah 31:34, GW). That's the kind of mercy and grace we are to emulate—one that cancels the debt.

God would not command us to forgive others if it weren't possible to do so. Even if you're unable to forgive in your own power, God's Holy Spirit can provide the power. Ask God to give you the desire to release those who've hurt you and then to supply the forgiveness and the love.

ENCOURAGEMENT FROM GOD'S WORD

An extraordinary example of forgiveness is found in the first book of the Bible, with a battle between two brothers. The rivalry began early for Jacob and Esau, wrestling in their mother's womb. At birth, they jockeyed for position as firstborn; the younger baby emerged grasping his brother's heel. But the prize was named during the barter for a meal when they were grown men, and a hungry Esau agreed to give Jacob his birthright in exchange for a bowl of stew.

Many years later, when their father, Isaac, was very old and believed he wouldn't live much longer, Jacob sealed the deal with Esau in an act of deception. Taking advantage of his brother's absence and his father's blindness, Jacob impersonated Esau and received the blessing his father intended for the firstborn son. When Esau learned of his brother's betrayal, he wept bitterly and vowed to kill Jacob after his father's death. But the deceiver ran away.

Twenty years passed before Jacob returned to his homeland, sending messengers ahead to announce his coming and tell Esau that he was hoping to "find favor" (Genesis 32:5) in his eyes. While Jacob feared his brother's retribution, Esau welcomed his former rival home. "Esau ran to meet Jacob and embraced him; he threw his arms around his neck and kissed him. And they wept" (Genesis 33:4).

Though there's no record of what happened to Esau during the two decades following his decision to kill Jacob, a great inward transformation had taken place, quite possibly a work of divine grace. Now Esau offered love instead of hate, reconciliation instead of retribution. Jacob tried to purchase peace (with a gift of livestock), but Esau offered it freely, saying, "I already have plenty, my brother. Keep what you have for yourself" (Genesis 33:9).

But the story doesn't have a perfect ending. I'd like to think that this great act of forgiveness on Esau's part would have changed Jacob. But he remained a deceiver, telling his brother one thing and then doing another. There are many stories of forgiveness in the Bible that are left unresolved to the reader. The parable of the prodigal son ends with the father welcoming his wayward boy home and preparing to throw a feast in his honor (see Luke 15:11-32). I wonder, *What impact did forgiveness have on this foolish young man? Was he grateful? Did he turn his life around?*

I believe that the stories are left unresolved because forgiveness is not ultimately about the guilty party; it's about freedom for the innocent, the ones who have been wounded. It's apparent Esau claimed that freedom before Jacob headed for home. He was gracious even though his brother acknowledged no wrongdoing.

Sometimes forgiveness does transform the life of the one who receives it, as a burden of guilt is lifted, but that's not why we offer it. Forgiveness is an act of obedience to God. When we love others and forgive their transgressions, our lives are changed as we're set free from the burden of bitterness.

Forgiving those who have wounded us is a crucial step toward wholeness and lasting peace and is perhaps one of the most difficult things we are called to do in life. Sometimes it's impossible to forgive in our own power, but the story of my journey to forgiveness proves that all things are possible with God. All you need is a spirit that recognizes your need to forgive. If you ask, God will supply the rest.

SELF-REFLECTION

> Borrowing Majed El-Shafie's illustration, let me ask you this: Whose body are you carrying around on your back?

> Have you ever sought God's help in forgiving? Why or why not?

> Make a commitment to yourself and God to address the issue of forgiveness — if not today, then before you finish this book.

Ask God to bring to mind the names of people whom you need to forgive. Write them down, including the things they've done that hurt you. As you ponder each name, you can pray a prayer such as this:

Lord, I choose to forgive (name offender) for (name offense) because it made me feel (unloved, rejected, stupid, worthless). Please heal my damaged emotions and spirit and bless this person.

MEDITATION

"Love your enemies, do good to those who hate you, bless those who curse you, pray for those who mistreat you. . . . Do to others as you would have them do to you. . . . Then your reward will be great, and you will be sons of the Most High, because he is kind to the ungrateful and wicked. Be merciful, just as your Father is merciful." (Luke 6:27-28,31,35-36)

"Be kind and loving to each other, and forgive each other just as God forgave you in Christ." (Ephesians 4:32, NCV)

"To forgive is setting the captive free, and finding the captive was you." (Lewis B. Smedes)

IMMACULÉE ILIBAGIZA: THE POWER *of* FORGIVENESS

Impossible things are the things you refuse to do.

John Bul Dau, humanitarian, survivor

"**I**mmaculée, I saw them, I saw the killers. . . . They have a list of names of all the Tutsi families in the area, and our names are on it! It's a death list! They are planning to start killing everyone on the list tonight!"[1] Immaculée Ilibagiza and her family were relaxing in their living room after a lovely meal together on Easter Sunday in 1994 when her brother Damascene broke the horrifying news. She was a twenty-two-year-old student home on a break from her studies at the National University of Rwanda when her nation of Rwanda erupted in a bloody genocide. Her family, members of the Tutsi tribe, became targets of the Hutu extremist killers and those they terrorized into joining their death squads—people who had been their neighbors, teachers, and friends.

Immaculée's father sent her to seek shelter at the home of a moderate Hutu pastor, where she hid with seven other women in a tiny three-foot-by-four-foot bathroom. Terrified, Immaculée spent up to thirteen hours a day in silent prayer. She often heard gangs of killers in the yard screaming their murderous slogans and calling her name. She grew to hate them.

One day Immaculée heard a voice in her head that asked, "How can you love God but hate so many of his creations?"[2] She heard God say, "You are *all* my children."[3] It was a transformational moment when Immaculée realized that she couldn't ask God to love her if she were unwilling to love His children, so at that moment, she prayed for *their* sins to be forgiven. And for the first time since she'd entered the bathroom, Immaculée slept in peace.

When she finally emerged after ninety-one days, she learned the tragic fate of her family. One brother, who was studying out of the country, was safe. Her mother, father, and other two brothers had all met violent deaths; Immaculée was not spared the details. Grandparents, aunts, uncles, and cousins were also dead. When the killing ended, one hundred days after it began, 80 percent of the Tutsi population in her area—and nearly 800,000 of her countrymen—had been massacred.[4]

As the prisons filled with those who'd perpetrated the genocide, Immaculée asked to be taken to meet the man who had led the gang that killed one of her brothers. She recognized the gaunt, bruised, and broken prisoner as Felicien, a prominent businessman whose children she had played with in primary school. She also recognized his voice as one she'd heard calling her name as she hid in the bathroom. He had hunted her.

But Immaculée no longer hated him; instead she was overwhelmed with pity. In her memoir, *Left to Tell*, Immaculée writes, "Felicien had let the devil enter his heart, and the evil had ruined his life like a cancer in his soul. He was now the victim of his victims, destined to live in torment and regret."[5]

As they both wept, Felicien's shame-filled eyes met Immaculée's for a brief moment before he looked away. She reached out, touched his trembling hands, and softly spoke the words she had come to say: "I forgive you."[6]

The guard was enraged. "That was the man who murdered your family. . . . Why did you forgive him?" he demanded.[7]

Immaculée writes, "I answered with the truth: 'Forgiveness is all I have to offer.'"[8]

Immaculée was reunited with her surviving brother Aimable a year after the genocide. Today, he is a doctor in Kigali, Rwanda, and she lives in the United States with her American husband and children. Immaculée works at the United Nations in New York and lectures around the country on the radical power of forgiveness. A portion of the proceeds from her lectures go to the Left to Tell Charitable Fund she founded to help Rwandan orphans. Those who have met Immaculée in recent years describe her as a "transcendentally spiritual woman [who] always . . . shines a light that captures everyone within its boundaries."[9] She "emanates peace and light."[10]

That peace would not have been possible had Immaculée not chosen to forgive. During the months she spent in hiding, she realized that the tiny bathroom was not her prison; the bitterness she held in her heart was. God showed her how her hatred prevented her from knowing Him and knowing peace. Without forgiving, Immaculée would spend the rest of her days in a prison of her own making. She made a decision to guard against that possibility:

> I knew that my heart and mind would always be tempted to feel anger—to find blame and hate. But I resolved that when the negative feelings came upon me, I wouldn't wait for them to grow or fester. I would always turn immediately to the source of all true power: I would turn to God and let His love and forgiveness protect and save me.[11]

Immaculée's story of emotional and spiritual survival through one of history's most horrifying events is proof there is no act that's unforgivable. Her painful past will always be a part of the woman Immaculée has become, but she no longer carries the burden of bitterness, and her future is gloriously bright.

PART THREE

EXPLORING SPIRITUAL TREATMENTS

CHAPTER 11

SPIRITUAL COUNSELING

The world is full of broken people who think they're surrounded by whole people.

Greg Garrett, author

Healing is a process, but progress is not restricted to forward movement. There were times I believed I had finally discovered the cure to my despondency only to find myself back in the dark—floundering, fearful, dismayed. In my ninth year of depression, it seemed as if I had exhausted every avenue for healing and was faced with having to resign myself to a painful existence. Though my depression was merciless, at least I'd learned what to expect by now. But in recent weeks, the familiar illness had joined forces with a brutal bully—anxiety—and all the rules had changed.

I had always been a loner, and depression had induced my even deeper retreat from the world. But with anxiety's invasion, I feared even solitude. Once my husband was at work and my daughters at school, I was taken captive by a voice that taunted and terrified me: *You'll never make it through this long day. You're all alone. There's no one to help you.*

The killing beast was closing in, its heavy paws crashing through the dense thickets surrounding me, frosty billows of heaving breath lingering in the frigid air of my soul. As Death stalked, I craved the companionship of living beings and began seeking people out, searching for safe havens to hunker down in while my family was away. I went to my parents' house just to listen to their voices. I stopped at my pastor's home to watch his wife making tea. Those who knew me probably took my interaction as a sign that I was getting better, but the truth was that I'd never felt worse.

The new terror seemed to coincide with my latest antidepressant treatment. *It's not working*, my mind screamed at me. During my next session with Dr. Colford, she decided to discontinue the drug. At that point, we'd tried nearly twenty antidepressants and combinations and more than a hundred electroconvulsive treatments. It was time for a reevaluation.

"I'm considering changing your diagnosis," the doctor said, "from major clinical depression to refractory depression." She explained that this was essentially depression that did not respond to most forms of treatment. Surely she'd tried them all.

I felt as if someone had just sucked the hope, tiny fragment that it was, right out of me and handed me a death sentence.

"I'm going to refer you to a specialist in Toronto," Dr. Colford continued.

Toronto is a thousand miles away. How long will I be gone? How do they treat someone who doesn't respond to treatment? My mind was full of questions. Then the doctor said something about a waiting list. I was not optimistic.

I left her office dazed and, not surprisingly, was readmitted to the hospital shortly afterward, depressed enough to require another round of ECT. My discharge came nearly a full month later, following the final shock treatment on my thirty-fifth birthday. I'd spent *eighty weeks* of the last nine years in the surreal world of psychiatric wards, surrounded by other wounded, bleeding souls — many seemingly broken beyond repair. *Was I one of them?*

I returned home to await the call from Toronto, but the terror was still there. Desperation forced me to disregard my penchant for privacy: I decided it was time to visit my pastor. After I'd shared my suicidal fantasies, he made a suggestion that showed great discernment: "Have you considered seeing a Christian counselor?"

It had been proposed before, but no, I hadn't really given it consideration. I believed I'd been a "good" Christian, living a moral life and being the super-servant. I took pride in my level of religiosity. It never dawned on me that my depression might have anything to do with spiritual matters.

For nearly nine years, I'd been educated about the physical and emotional causes of depression and assumed my own resulted from a biochemical imbalance or unresolved emotional issues. I was receiving excellent medical treatment, yet after all these years I remained seriously depressed. Now I believed I was incurable. *What could a Christian counselor possibly do that hasn't already been done?* I wondered.

But as I sat across from my pastor, it became clear to me that I was at the end of my rope, or—more specifically—the edge of the ledge, as a leap from a very tall building was beginning to seem like a good idea. I knew if something didn't change, I'd soon be dead, so I decided to give the Christian counselor a shot.

"Her name is Berys Richardson" (pronounced "Berry"), he said while jotting down the phone number of the counseling center where she worked. I went home, swallowed my pride, and with lingering cynicism made the call. It turned out to be a decision that would both change my life and ultimately save it. But I would not see improvement immediately. I'd soon discover that spiritual inquiry invites opposition from spiritual enemies. I had just made myself a big target in a spiritual battle that threatened to kill me. Things would get worse before they got better.

GODLY COUNSEL

I wish it hadn't taken me nearly nine years to realize that depression can have spiritual roots. Had I known sooner, I might have sought the guidance I needed from a Christian counselor. I might have saved myself—and my family—years of suffering and grief.

I now understand that an important step toward wholeness is to accept godly counsel. Sadly, for me, Christian spiritual counseling was the treatment of last resort. It's puzzling how so many followers of Christ seek care for only the body and mind, through medicine and secular psychological therapy. Those types of therapies can offer relief if your depression is biochemical or emotional, but they don't address or heal the potential spiritual roots of the illness.

Secular counseling emphasizes reason, scientific inquiry, and human fulfillment in the natural world. Most often it seeks to help a person adapt to difficult circumstances.[1] In contrast, Christian spiritual counseling is grounded in the truths found in God's Word. It employs the most current psychological insight for healing and growth but also utilizes spiritual resources: biblical principles, prayer, and God's Holy Spirit. Christian counseling teaches that we don't have to adapt to life's circumstances; we can transcend them through the peace God offers. But there's more. Beyond transcendence of the unavoidable messiness that accompanies human existence, God grants transformation— healing from the deeper wounds that derail our lives.

Counselor Jim Robinson explains the process this way: "Together, the client and the counselor embark on a journey . . . with Christ leading the way."[2] In my own experience with Christian counseling, Christ was invited into each session, through the Holy Spirit. My counselor guided me in prayer to God, and through prayer—asking and listening—He directed me to issues and beliefs that needed to be addressed if I were to find healing. Berys offered her direction and insight, but we took our leading from the Holy Spirit, and God provided the power for the great work of restoration that took place.

Finding the Counselor for You

Being a Christian doesn't automatically make someone a gifted counselor, any more than it might make another person an exceptional teacher or mechanic. And not all Christians who have counseling practices address the spirit's needs, incorporate biblical principles into counseling, and involve God in the process. If you want someone who can offer you spiritual care, this is an important consideration.

Ask those who have had positive experiences with Christian counselors for references. Phone several churches in your area and ask whom they refer people to. If one or two names continue to come up, follow up on those leads. Above all, invite God to guide and direct your search and give you discernment as you meet with potential counselors.

What to Look For

Once you have considered the spiritual factors important to you in a counselor, there are other things to take into account: training, accreditation, specialization, and personality. Trust is essential to a successful therapeutic relationship, so seek out a person with whom you feel comfortable. As you meet with a potential counselor, ask yourself:

- Do we connect?
- Does this person reflect the love and acceptance of Jesus Christ?
- Is this someone who is willing to offer more than just answers and advice and can actually join me on this journey toward wholeness?

A good counselor will help you learn more about yourself, your abilities, and your potential. Sometimes the counseling process is uncomfortable as you revisit painful moments from your past, but addressing those events is part of the healing journey.

For the counseling process to be its most effective, your core values and those of your therapist should match. Your counselor's own spiritual journey is important; someone who is unable to stand on spiritual truth and walk in the freedom Christ gives cannot guide you in how to do so. Always weigh what the counselor says against the Word of God. If he or she suggests you do something contrary to Scripture, then you have the wrong counselor.

Professional credentials are important, indicating a counselor's qualifications, education, and commitment to excellence. Requirements for licensure or certification vary from state to state and from country to country, so make sure to ask questions concerning this.

But there's something even more important than certificates and degrees, and it's not as easy to find: giftedness. Those who come highly recommended by others likely possess this extraordinary quality.

Financial Obstacles

If the cost of counseling seems prohibitive to you, ask yourself what the cost of not receiving counseling will be. Has your depression caused you to lose time from work, drop out of school, or jeopardize precious relationships? What emotional toll has it taken on your spouse or children? How much money do you spend on cigarettes, alcohol, food, or "shopping therapy" to calm your nerves, ease your pain, or self-medicate? Can you anticipate the cost of your depression to you (and those who love you) in the years to come?

Many company health plans will pay a portion of the counseling fees or for a certain number of sessions. Qualified Christian counselors are sometimes willing to reduce their fees for individuals with limited financial resources and no health insurance. Some churches allocate funds to contribute to the cost of counseling for those in need; others offer pastoral counseling at no cost. Remember that God wants you to be well, and He can overcome all obstacles to treatment. Ask Him to provide the solution.

What to Ask Potential Counselors

Keeping the spiritual, professional, and practical considerations in mind, you may want to consider asking potential counselors some of the following questions:

- Are you a follower of Jesus Christ?
- Do you incorporate biblical truth into your counseling practice? If so, how?
- Do you pray with your clients?
- What degrees do you hold? Do you specialize in any areas?
- Are you licensed? Certified? If so, by whom?
- How many clients have you treated with my types of issues?
- How do you define successful treatment?
- What is your hourly rate? Do insurance companies typically reimburse your services?
- How often should we meet?[3]

Measuring Success

Counseling is an interactive process between counselor and client, so it's impossible for anyone to guarantee improvement. Initially, you should set measurable goals that will help you evaluate your experience later on. Licensed professional counselor Rob Jackson suggests that a good goal is: To get healthier and overcome any personal problems you may be facing. A better goal is: To learn to help others with what you've learned from your own experiences. And the best goal is: To know and enjoy God.[4] "It is here, in our intimacy with God, that Christ becomes the *Wonderful Counselor* and *Great Physician* who makes us whole."[5]

My primary goal was certainly to regain my mental health—to no longer be depressed. I measured progress toward that goal with smaller goals: Stay out of the hospital. Be more involved in my children's lives and activities. Stop hating myself. Be able to be home alone without feeling afraid. Sleep peacefully. Want to *live* more than die.

My counselor directed me toward a few other things that I should focus on in order to gain freedom from depression: Choose to bless rather than be bitter toward certain people in my life. Forgive those who had hurt me.

But the best goal was one I think my counselor set for me without telling me outright. She knew, as Rob Jackson states, that intimacy with God would be what would help me maintain freedom from depression and empower me in facing all future difficulties. With her guidance and through many homework assignments, I did achieve a greater level of intimacy; I began to hear God's voice and eventually learned how to consult Him when my spirit needed counsel and when I needed direction. Though there have been a few times in the not so distant past when I've sought Berys' advice, she essentially worked her way out of a job where this client was concerned! But I expect that's the goal of every good counselor, the measure of his or her success.

As you work with your own counselor, assess your progress. After several months, ask yourself if you are better able to cope with the symptoms of your depression or if you're symptom free. For example, do you still feel sad, anxious, or empty? Have you regained any interest in activities you enjoyed before you became depressed? Have your sleep patterns returned to normal? Do you feel more energetic and able to concentrate? Have feelings of hopelessness, worthlessness, and helplessness diminished?

Review the goals you set in the beginning of your counseling experience. Have you made progress in each objective?

For some, healing is a miraculous, instantaneous event, but for many, it's a process. Your wholehearted effort, combined with godly counsel and divine participation, will launch you on a healing journey that, whether long or short, will make a miraculous change in your life.

ENCOURAGEMENT FROM GOD'S WORD

The Bible offers examples of wise counselors — people in tune to God's direction who work to educate, encourage, and empower others.

Nehemiah was one of them. When we're introduced to him, he's serving as a cupbearer to King Artaxerxes, 150 years after the Israelites were banished to Babylon and Jerusalem had been plundered and torched. A remnant that survived the exile has returned to the province of Judah, where the Holy City still lay in ruins and they are living in great trouble and disgrace (see Nehemiah 1:3). With the city walls destroyed and the gates burned down, Jerusalem is defenseless, but the exiles seem willing to accept a life of defeat.

This grieves Nehemiah and prompts him to mourn, fast, and pray. He confesses the sins he and his people have committed against God, and asks for His direction and help. God plants a desire in Nehemiah's heart to rebuild the city walls and provides the means to do so. With the permission and cooperation of Babylon's king, Nehemiah journeys to Jerusalem to assess the damage. Then, assuring the city officials that God is with them on this project, he rallies them to rebuild the walls and gates.

When I read this story, I can't help but see parallels between my situation and that of the Israelites. When my life lay in ruins, it took the insight of an objective observer—a Christian counselor—to motivate me and direct me in the rebuilding. My psychiatrist was wise and had used her knowledge and insight to offer me the best in medical treatment to help me overcome my eating disorder, to make me aware of aspects of my disordered personality that needed to be addressed, and to keep me alive. She worked tirelessly with me for years on many issues, and I believe that her confidence in me gave me the hope to keep trying. But in spite of all she did, it was not enough to heal me. I needed *spiritual* guidance because my depression—though it affected me physically and emotionally—was rooted in my spirit.

Jim Robinson says, "A gifted counselor will keep one ear on the client, and the other ear on God."[6] Berys Richardson did that. After a few sessions of hearing me recount my life story (for what seemed like the millionth time) and my struggle with depression, Berys was able to offer insight into areas in my life and spirit that were in need of repair and gave me tools to use. She pointed out my need to forgive those who had wounded me. She identified areas of spiritual oppression and led me through deliverance ministry. (I'll share more about that in the next chapter.) She taught me how to hear God's voice through the study of His Word. Berys led me in "listening prayer" for inner healing to address the lies I believed about others and myself. (You'll read more about that in chapter 13.) She taught me how to defend myself by praying prayers for spiritual protection and renouncing Satan's attempts to infiltrate my thoughts. These were all things I desperately needed to learn if I were to gain lasting freedom from depression, but things no doctors or psychologists had addressed.

The returned exiles of Nehemiah's day had grown accustomed to the ruins all around them and made no effort to change their situation until Nehemiah rallied them. Sometimes depression affects us the same way; we live among the wreckage of our lives for so long that we forget what normal feels like, we lose our grip on our dreams, we accept our misery and live in defeat. In times like these, we need someone to stir us to action and guide us to reclaim our lives. As God equipped Nehemiah for that task, He equips others today.

If you feel defeated and overwhelmed, heed Nehemiah's message to the Israelites. You don't have to accept defeat by depression. You don't have to live in the ruins of your past. You can repair. You can rebuild. With a treatment plan that includes wise, godly counsel, you too can be restored.

SELF-REFLECTION

- Have you accepted depression as your lot in life? What would it take to rally you into a rebuilding project?
- Have you explored the potential spiritual roots of your depression with a counselor? If not, what's preventing you from doing so? What steps will you take to find a qualified Christian counselor?

MEDITATION

"Without good direction, people lose their way; the more wise counsel you follow, the better your chances." (Proverbs 11:14, MSG)

"I will ask the Father, and he will give you another Counselor to be with you forever—the Spirit of truth. The world cannot accept him, because it neither sees him nor knows him. But you know him, for he lives with you and will be in you." (John 14:16-17)

CHAPTER 12

DELIVERANCE MINISTRY

Man lives in three dimensions: the somatic, the mental,
and the spiritual. The spiritual dimension cannot be
ignored for it is what makes us human.
Viktor Frankl, Holocaust survivor, psychiatrist

My first attempt had been impulsive. I hadn't really wanted to kill myself. But this time it was different: My family's future depended on my death (or so I believed).

I'd managed to drag my weary soul through another seven years since my first suicide attempt, but the depression had dug in its heels and refused to budge. Now accompanied by anxiety, the torment proved more than I could bear.

I'd been seeing Berys for nearly three months. Though she seemed competent and qualified, we weren't making much progress. I figured it was only a matter of time until she discovered I was incurable.

The recording in my head that had been playing on and off for about a year was now constant. Rewind; repeat. Rewind; repeat.

It's not easy for your family to watch you suffer.
Your illness has robbed them.
Everyone would be better off if you were dead.

I believed the messages but reasoned that suicide would devastate my family; I couldn't kill myself.

They'll get over it in time. Besides, their pain can't compare to the agony you'll have to endure every day if you choose to live.

Rewind; repeat. Rewind; repeat.

If you were gone, Tim would be free to find someone else—someone who could bring joy back into this home and be a mother to your children.

And then it dawned on me. For the first time in nine years of battling for my life, I thought, *I'm being really selfish by staying alive.* No longer did I see my choice to live as a sacrifice I was making for my family (when death would be the easier option for me); now I saw my existence as the one thing keeping them from a happy, normal life. I knew what I had to do.

While sorting out my plans for death, I returned for my scheduled biweekly session with Berys and shared what the last two weeks had been like for me: I had been unable to sleep, terrified of morning, anxious, afraid to be alone. When I was done describing my torment, she asked if I'd been contemplating suicide. I confessed I had, then she said something I'd never heard before: "I think you're under demonic attack." *I'm under what? Maybe* she *was the crazy one.*

How could a Christian be attacked by demons? I wondered. It didn't seem to make sense, but I was open to hearing Berys' rationale. She wondered what might have happened in the previous two weeks to make me vulnerable to this level of attack and asked if there was anything I was doing differently. Besides worrying and listening to the tape in my head, the only other thing occupying my time was the homework she'd assigned.

Better Late Than Never

Two years earlier, during unexpected visits from a couple of friends I hadn't seen since I was a teenager, came dual recommendations of a book by Neil T. Anderson called *The Bondage Breaker.* My friends said this book that taught about spiritual warfare had made a difference in their lives, but as I heard about it, I had a strong, inexplicable urge to avoid the book at all costs. Although I appreciated my friends' compassion and concern, I secretly resented the implication that my depression might have anything to do with the state of my spirit. That's impossible, I thought. I've been a Christian most of my life; have served God faithfully; and am a decent, moral person. I decided then and there to never read *The Bondage Breaker*.

But when Berys gave the book to me as a reading assignment, I had run out of options for healing, so I complied. When I told her that reading *The Bondage Breaker* was the only difference in my life since we'd last met, she seemed to think we'd hit the jackpot.

After praying with me that afternoon, Berys called two prayer chains she was involved with and asked them to pray for my safety. I called my pastor and asked if he would pray for me at prayer meeting that evening—a first for me. I'd always believed that to ask for prayer was to admit you had a problem, and to admit you had a problem was to admit you were weak. Not exactly the image I wanted to project. But that week my eyes were opened to the power of prayer. Within two days, the anxiety disappeared, along with my ideas of suicide. I was able to sleep peacefully without frightening thoughts invading my mind, and I was able to stay at home alone without panicking. The change in me was nothing short of miraculous.

Deliverance Ministry

Two weeks later, after I'd finished reading *The Bondage Breaker*, Berys led me through the "Steps to Freedom in Christ," a form of deliverance ministry and a huge step toward wholeness for me. The Steps to Freedom, outlined in *The Bondage Breaker*, required that I confess, renounce, and request forgiveness for six areas of sin: involvement in false religions and occultic practices, believing lies about myself and others, bitterness and unforgiveness, rebellion against human and godly authority, pride, and habitual sin.[1] My sin not only hurt others and me, it gave my spiritual enemy opportunities to oppress me—"footholds" in my life (see Ephesians 4:26-27).

The final area, and Step to Freedom, involved cutting off any possible curses or demonic footholds passed on to me from other generations. The second of the Old Testament's Ten Commandments warns those who commit the sin of idolatry that the punishment will be passed on to their descendants, even to the third and fourth generations (see Exodus 20:3-6). In order to cut off these kinds of curses, there is a pattern of confession we must follow, declaring our ancestors' sins as well as our own. When we do this, we remove the Enemy's right to oppress us because of these sins.[2]

The session that day would be a long one. Berys had invited two friends—"prayer warriors," she called them—to sit in on the session and pray throughout it while she led me through The Steps to Freedom. Having a trusted friend, counselor, or pastor help you in this process is a wise plan, supported by Scripture. Through the Bible, we're instructed, "Confess your sins to each other and pray for each other so God can heal you. When a believing person prays, great things happen" (James 5:16, NCV).

The first action was to review the events of my life in order to reveal areas that needed to be addressed. This was done using a Non-Christian Spiritual Experience Inventory (identifying occult experiences, cults, and other religions I may have been involved in) and a Personal Inventory (addressing my family, religious, marital, and health history; the moral atmosphere in which I was raised; and my salvation experience and spiritual history).

I prayed, acknowledging God as omniscient (all-knowing), omnipotent (all-powerful), and omnipresent (always present). I declared my belief that all power on heaven and earth has been given to Christ and as a follower of Christ I share that authority. I asked God to fill me with His Holy Spirit, lead me into truth, protect me, and guide me.

Then, with Berys' guidance, I prayed aloud through each Step to Freedom using prayers given in *The Bondage Breaker*. Because God is omniscient, He knows our thoughts and hears our silent prayers. But Satan does not have that kind of power and insight, so it was important that I pray aloud so the Enemy could hear me verbally confessing and renouncing sin.

To help you see what this process entailed, let me give you a glimpse into one of the steps, "Pride Versus Humility." I began by praying a prayer of confession identifying that there were times in my life that I had been prideful—that I'd believed I could live successfully by my own strength and resources. I confessed that I had sinned by placing my will before God's will and centering my life on myself rather than on Him. I renounced this "self-life" and, in so doing, cancelled all grounds given to the enemies of Jesus Christ (Satan and his emissaries). I asked God to guide me so that I would no longer act out of selfish or independent motives. Then I identified specific areas in my life in which I had been prideful, verbally confessing them, asking God's forgiveness, and announcing my decision that I would choose to humble myself and place my confidence in God.[3]

Set Free

One of the people who had been praying for me during this session had spent some of that time quietly writing. At the end of the session, her husband (the other prayer warrior) anointed my head with oil and prayed over me while she presented me with six passages of Scripture that God laid on her heart for me. Two of them were:

> The Lord says, "Do not cling to events of the past or dwell on what happened long ago. For I am about to do a brand-new thing. It is happening already—you can see it now! I will make a pathway through the wilderness for my people to come home. I will create rivers for them in the desert!" (Isaiah 43:18-19)[4]

"For I know the plans I have for you," declares the Lord, "plans to prosper you and not to harm you, plans to give you hope and a future." (Jeremiah 29:11)

Six Steps and three hours after we began this deliverance session, Satan's chokehold on my life was broken. I walked out of my counselor's office knowing I was free. My depression wasn't replaced by a sudden exuberance. I didn't feel weightless, and I heard no angelic choir singing the Hallelujah chorus (though they may have been rejoicing in heaven). I just felt a deep assurance that the battle was over.

In the months and years that followed, it was apparent that my gut feeling was well-founded: I never returned to the psychiatric ward and never had another electroconvulsive treatment. Four months after my depression ended, I was off all antidepressant medication for good and scheduled a final appointment with my psychiatrist.

Though I'm sure I tried her patience over the years, Dr. Colford had combined intellect, common sense, and compassion to offer me the kind of care I've come to realize is extraordinarily rare. Her belief that I was a person of worth and value with much to offer the world challenged my notions to the contrary. Now, after nearly nine years together, the time had come for me to bid farewell to the woman who had enriched my existence, helped me hang on to hope, and saved my life a thousand times over.

I was finally free from depression, but the journey to wholeness was just beginning.

SPIRITUAL BATTLE

I realize that the concept of spiritual warfare and demonic oppression seems unsettling, even far-fetched, to some. It's something many would prefer not to think about. But the old adage "What you don't know won't hurt you" does not apply in battle. An important step in my journey to wholeness was to deal with spiritual oppression.

One of our Enemy's most advantageous accomplishments is to make himself invisible to his targets by convincing us he doesn't even exist. Some Christians believe that Satan and demons were active in biblical times but not in today's modern world. A study conducted by the Barna Group in 2006 revealed that 45 percent of born-again Christians in the United States say that Satan, or the Devil, is not a living being but rather a symbol for evil.[5] There's another camp of Christians who believe that Satan is real but can't influence or harm those who belong to Jesus. I was once of that mind myself; I didn't give Satan a second thought because I believed Jesus had me covered. In *The Bondage Breaker*, Neil Anderson asks,

> If Satan can't touch the church, why are we instructed to put on the armor of God, to resist the devil, to stand firm, and to be alert? If we aren't susceptible to being wounded or trapped by Satan, why does Paul describe our relationship with the powers of darkness as a wrestling match?[6]

Even though we may not acknowledge him, Satan is alive and well on planet Earth and very active. He has legions of other invisible spiritual beings, called demons, working with him and against us. Through attack and oppression, demons carry out their mission to torment those God loves, trying to rob us of peace, security, wholeness, and even life.

Is satanic or demonic attack aimed at only those who are spiritually weak? No. Even God's Son was targeted.

Following Jesus' baptism, Satan met and tempted Him during His forty-day fast in the desert. Jesus was probably at His weakest, physically and emotionally, but He was filled with the Holy Spirit and able to resist the temptations. So did Satan give up on the soon-to-be Savior? No way! The Bible tells us he left to wait for another opportune time (see Luke 4:13). Not even those who are Spirit-filled and following God are safe from Satan's schemes, and the Enemy is always looking for new opportunities to lead us astray.

The Weapons of War

Our Enemy knows better than to make the battle obvious, otherwise we'd be expecting him, ready to defend ourselves. He attacks in subtle ways, so crafty that many don't even notice him. Satan slithers into our minds because he knows that's where the real battle lies. He cannot own anyone who belongs to Christ, and he can't force us to do anything we are opposed to, but he can whisper into our thoughts ideas that aren't our own (like telling me my family would be better off if I were dead). He can try to replace God's truth with his lies. And if he can get us to entertain his thoughts long enough, he knows we will begin to believe them and live as if they were true.

Satan will condemn us, even though God has forgiven us. Our Enemy wants to paralyze us so we won't mature in Christlikeness. He wants to discourage us and make us think we're unforgivable, unchangeable, and of no use to God. His ultimate goal is to have us give up on God, ourselves, and even life. Satan can control our behavior if he can control our thoughts, and that's how he leads us astray and holds us captive.

The Bible warns, "Be alert, be on watch! Your enemy, the Devil, roams around like a roaring lion, looking for someone to devour" (1 Peter 5:8, GNT). This Enemy is also likened to a thief who "comes only to steal and kill and destroy" (John 10:10). But the Bible assures us, "The Son of God came for this purpose: to destroy the devil's work" (1 John 3:8, NCV). "God anointed Jesus of Nazareth with the Holy Spirit and power, and . . . he went around doing good and healing all who were under the power of the devil, because God was with him" (Acts 10:38).

Jesus cast out demons numerous times[7] and healed those under demonic oppression.[8] He had the authority to hurl demons into the Abyss (see Luke 8:31) and forbid them to return (see Mark 9:25). Jesus passed that authority and power on to His followers; Peter healed people tormented by evil spirits (see Acts 5:16) and many others were instrumental in bringing freedom to those held hostage by demons (see Luke 10:17-19; Acts 8:7; 19:12).

Following Jesus' death and resurrection, He was given all power in heaven and earth (see Matthew 28:18). But the spiritual battle didn't end at the cross or the empty tomb. The Enemy continues to wage war against those God loves. Paul warned believers about the seriousness of this war: "This is no afternoon athletic contest that we'll walk away from and forget about in a couple of hours. This is for keeps, a life-or-death fight to the finish against the Devil and all his angels" (Ephesians 6:12, MSG).

The good news is, as Christ's followers, the authority Jesus won is part of our spiritual legacy (see Ephesians 2:5-6). But there's a catch: Spiritual authority is no good to us unless we choose to actively use it. If you don't know how to do that, I recommend you read *The Bondage Breaker.*

Climbing Out

Satan doesn't want you to be free, and he'll probably try to convince you that you're beyond help. That was the tactic he used with me. Just months prior to my deliverance from depression, I believed I'd never been closer to the bottom of despair's pit. But Satan knew what I didn't and stepped up his attack against me.

He saw me finally reaching out to a counselor who had spiritual training. He saw me reading the very book the Lord had introduced me to years earlier, the one my pride had prevented me from picking up. He saw that I was learning the truth about spiritual warfare—the truth that could lead to my freedom from the illness that had imprisoned me for nine years, to freedom from the beliefs and behaviors that had bound me for a lifetime. Satan knew that I wasn't at the bottom of the pit; I'd actually never been nearer to the top.

If you feel that your own life is hopeless, you're wrong. It's possible there's never been more hope for your wholeness than right now. Depression may make you feel as though your soul is trapped in the darkest night, but freedom's light is just about to break on the horizon.

ENCOURAGEMENT FROM GOD'S WORD

When we are first introduced to David in the Bible, it's hard to believe he would ever feel so hopeless and afraid that he'd long for death. When David was a young man, it seemed his life was filled with promise and there was nothing he couldn't do. He killed bears and lions with his bare hands while defending his father's sheep and then killed a giant Philistine, Goliath, while watching the Israelite army hide in their tents, quaking with fear. But later in his life, David was the one trembling in terror. He was transformed from fearless warrior to frightened child, pleading for his Father's help:

> Be kind to me, God—I'm in deep, deep trouble again. I've cried my eyes out; I feel hollow inside.[9] I'm at the end of my rope, my life in ruins.[10] Help me, oh help me, God, my God, save me through your wonderful love;[11] I want to hide in you.[12] You're my only hope![13]

As David's fame increased, he often felt overwhelmed by enemies who relentlessly pursued him.

> My enemies have hunted me down and completely defeated me. They have put me in a dark prison, and I am like those who died long ago. So I am ready to give up; I am in deep despair. (Psalm 143:3-4, GNT)

Perhaps you feel the same as your spiritual enemies pursue you with their weapons of fear, shame, bitterness, or self-hatred. This once-brave hero was forced to hide in caves, crying out for God to come to his rescue. God answered. Psalm 18 is David's praise after the Lord had delivered him from his enemies:

The LORD is my rock, my fortress and my deliverer; my God is my rock, in whom I take refuge. He is my shield and the horn of my salvation, my stronghold. In my distress I called to the LORD; I cried to my God for help. From his temple he heard my voice; my cry came before him, into his ears. He reached down from on high and took hold of me; he drew me out of deep waters. He rescued me from my powerful enemy, from my foes, who were too strong for me. They confronted me in the day of my disaster, but the LORD was my support. He brought me out into a *spacious place.* (verses 2,6,16-19, emphasis added)

Spiritual oppression confines us. Our spiritual enemies back us into corners through addictions we can't break, destructive habits we can't overcome, and painful thoughts and feelings we can't get rid of. Like David, we're forced to cower in caves, unable to experience the fullness of life that is ours as those who follow Jesus Christ. But when God defeats our enemies through the power of Christ, we are free to emerge. We are free to enjoy freedom! We are liberated from the prisons and pits we've been trapped in and are brought out into a spacious place.

Prior to my deliverance from depression, I lived life in a cave, restricting myself to doing only things I was good at, expressing only opinions that were acceptable, associating only with people who seemed safe, and loving only people I deemed worthy. When God released me from the bondage of unforgiveness, people pleasing, perfectionism, pride, shame, low self-worth, fear, worry, and doubt, I was free to do anything God asked, love everyone regardless of their deeds, be comfortable in the company of anyone, accept those who were different, speak up for what I believed in, discover what I was passionate about, and live true to my calling and purpose regardless of what others thought about me. I was free to live without restrictions, stepping out of the cave into the spacious place!

Paul wrote, "It is for freedom that Christ has set us free. Stand firm, then, and do not let yourselves be burdened again by a yoke of slavery" (Galatians 5:1). Satan and his forces will attempt to oppose and overwhelm us and cause us to live in bondage, but they have no right to interfere unless we invite or allow them to. God will deliver us from our spiritual enemies, but first we must recognize the battle we are engaged in, realize we cannot win in our own power, and request rescue. We must take authority in the name of Jesus Christ, the One who has already defeated our foes. As we do so, the chains binding us to our wounded pasts, our addictions, and our dysfunctional behaviors will be broken. Then we will be free to live victoriously.

May the God of heaven give you success as you move forward to reclaim and rebuild your life!

SELF-REFLECTION

▷ The illness of depression causes negative thinking. How has Satan capitalized on that—what kind of thoughts has he infiltrated your mind with?

▷ What has your spiritual enemy used to make you "cower in caves"?

▷ Prayer is a supernatural means of fighting our spiritual enemies. Name at least one mature follower of Christ you can enlist to pray for you in this battle, and commit to calling that person this week. Make sure you pray as well, asking God to reveal what you need to learn to gain freedom and grow in Christlikeness.

▷ Consider reading *The Bondage Breaker* (making sure to have others praying for your protection as you do), and then ask your counselor (or pastor) to lead you through The Steps to Freedom in Christ.

▷ Visit the website of Freedom in Christ Ministries (http://www .ficm.org) and read the encouraging statements in the document "Who Am I in Christ?"[14] You may want to choose a few of the Scriptures listed in the document and meditate on them in the days ahead.

MEDITATION

"I am convinced that neither death nor life, neither angels nor demons, neither the present nor the future, nor any powers, neither height nor depth, nor anything else in all creation, will be able to separate us from the love of God that is in Christ Jesus our Lord." (Romans 8:38-39)

"Now it is God who makes both us and you stand firm in Christ. He anointed us, set his seal of ownership on us, and put his Spirit in our hearts as a deposit, guaranteeing what is to come." (2 Corinthians 1:21-22)

"I have the strength to face all conditions by the power that Christ gives me." (Philippians 4:13, GNT)

CHAPTER 13

LISTENING PRAYER
for INNER HEALING

What you perceive, your observations, feelings, inter-pretations, are all your truth. Your truth is important. Yet it is not The Truth.

Linda Ellinor, author

Following my healing from depression, I continued to see Berys regularly. Though I was no longer captive to the illness, she explained that it was important to discover the things that had led to my descent into a near decade of despair. It was time for the spiritual postmortem to begin. In this process of dissection and discovery, it became clear that much of the pain and dysfunction in my life was the result of lies I believed. The next step in my journey to wholeness would be to receive God's truth.

Our emotions and behaviors are not caused by external things, such as people, situations, and events, but by our *thoughts*[1] —what we believe. Most false beliefs are rooted in a wound from the past. Berys was trained in listening prayer for inner healing, and it proved to be the tool God used to heal my many crippling wounds.

Through prayer, Berys and I invited the Holy Spirit into our sessions. Then we explored whatever situation I was dealing with at the time that was generating unpleasant emotions — stress, for example. I was still dealing with the pressure of trying to do things perfectly and to keep everything in my life under control. Berys thought it would be wise if we delved into the reason for my perfectionism and desire for control, so she led me through one of my first experiences with listening prayer to discover the source of my dysfunction.

Uprooted

If I were going to "pull out" the spiritual roots that had caused my depression, I needed to revisit the wounding events that had planted those roots in my heart. I needed to uncover the lies I'd believed and replace them with God's truth. The first step in this process was to ask Jesus to take me back to a time in my childhood when I first felt the upsetting feelings connected to my present stress. I was transported back to the day my world fell apart.

The sun was shining brightly. I was on my grandfather's farm in the rural countryside of New Brunswick. It was summer, and this corner of the world was green, verdant, and alive. Tall grass swayed in the hay fields. Spruce trees towered over the tidy, gray farmhouse, providing shade for the yard and a sturdy bough from which to dangle a swing. Next to Grampy's ancient tool shed, a well-tended garden was neatly lined with rows of peas, pole beans, and every other vegetable that grew in these parts. The early settlers had named this place Canaan; perhaps to them it seemed a fertile land flowing with milk and honey. For a city girl, it was absolutely enchanting, and I looked forward to spending time with my family here every summer. But not today. On this dark day in my young life the thrill of vacation abruptly ended, and all I could think about was going home.

My parents had been away from their country roots for fifteen years and felt a yearning to return. Unknown to me, they'd been exploring employment options in New Brunswick, where most of their families still lived. I'd never heard them express any dissatisfaction with life in Toronto or a desire to move, so when they sat my sister and me down that morning in mid-August and told us of their plan, I was stunned.

My dad had decided to work with his brother on the dairy farm where they'd been raised, twenty minutes from Canaan. We'd return to Toronto, put the house up for sale, and move as soon as possible. I was about to leave behind the only home I'd ever known, a city I loved, and all my friends.

The worst pain of all was the thought of losing my best friend and her parents, who lived down the street from us. Heather was a year younger than I and like a sister to me. Her mother, Auntie Betty, had cared for me since I was five months old, while my mom worked. Uncle Tom was a hardy Scotsman with a twinkle in his eye and a soothing Scottish brogue. In chapter 9, I wrote about this trauma and the harmful belief I developed as a result: *I won't experience the agony of loss if I keep people at a distance.* But that wasn't the only lie spawned from this event.

On this day in the summer of my eleventh year, I retreated to the solitude behind a shed on my grandfather's farm. Sitting in shock on the stone slab next to the old water pump, I tried to comprehend the drastic turn my life was about to take. I'm not sure if I allowed myself the luxury of tears—I'd grown adept at withholding them—but my bewildered soul cried out in anger and grief.

How can they just uproot my life without my having any say in the matter? I don't want to move. Toronto is my home. I don't want to leave my friends. I don't want to change schools. How can this be happening to me? I felt betrayed and forsaken—by my parents and by God—and many seeds of untruth were sown in my spirit.

The next step in the listening prayer process was to ask Jesus to reveal the lies I'd come to believe as a result of this wounding event. I remembered my feelings of frustration, fear, and despair and heard the lies again in my head: *If my parents would make a life-changing decision like this without even asking how I feel, my opinions don't matter. If God would let something this horrible happen to me, I know I can't trust Him. I am alone. From now on, I'll have to take care of myself.* The ramifications of that day changed more than my address; they scarred my soul. These false beliefs rooted and sprouted and, over time, produced a bumper crop of fear and dysfunction. At the core, I didn't believe that God would take care of me. I didn't believe He had my best interests at heart. Subconsciously, I did not believe that God had proven Himself trustworthy.

God's Good Plans

Jesus had more to reveal about that pivotal day in my life. The next step was to ask Him to tell me the truth to replace the lies I'd just heard again in my mind. His revelation changed me. He assured me that even though I was separated from my friends and others I loved in Toronto, I had never been alone; God had never abandoned me.

Then came this astounding announcement from the Lord: Not only had God been with me but He'd also been in control. The move from Toronto had not been strictly my parents' idea but actually part of God's good plan for my future. He brought to my mind Romans 8:28: "We know that God causes everything to work together for the good of those who love God and are called according to his purpose for them" (NLT).

I'd spent decades of my life trying to maintain control and protect myself for no valid reason; *God* was in control and always had been. Even when it seemed my life was unraveling, the Lord was weaving its threads into the rich tapestry of a promising future. Once committed to worry and what-ifs, I never wasted another moment on those kinds of thoughts after I learned the truth.

I don't know all the reasons God orchestrated my move from the city to the country, but I do know one: to introduce me to the man who would become one of His greatest earthly gifts to me, my husband, Tim. Without Tim's love and unwavering support, I don't believe I would have survived depression. Without the children we had together,

I don't believe I would have tried. Perhaps God's purpose in that move was to prepare me for a greater time of trauma in my future and to position me to gain victory over it.

LISTENING PRAYER FOR INNER HEALING

Emotional pain is not always the result of believing lies. Feelings of hurt and grief, for example, are natural results of being wounded or suffering loss. But lingering or crippling emotional pain is often lie-based. In order to gain lasting freedom from depression, we must unearth those lies and replace them with truth. Listening prayer[2] is a powerful, effective way to do that. Through it, Jesus illuminates the source of our pain and dysfunction and brings healing.

King David asked God to investigate his spirit and thoughts to determine if there was anything within him that needed to be changed:

> God, examine me and know my heart; test me and know my anxious thoughts. See if there is any bad thing in me. Lead me on the road to everlasting life. (Psalm 139:23-24, NCV)

What David requested is essentially the process of listening prayer for inner healing. Through listening prayer we ask Jesus, through His Holy Spirit, to identify the issues He wants us to address — things preventing us from living the abundant life He longs to give us (for instance, anxiety over a certain situation, bitterness toward someone, or conflict in a relationship). Then we follow the Lord back to the time in our lives when this issue originated (often a wounding event in childhood). We listen as Jesus identifies the lie we came to believe as a result of this event, and the truth to replace that lie. This truth brings emotional healing to the memory and removes the trauma.

Next, we follow Jesus to the cross, where we release our offenders. We repent and receive forgiveness for any sins we committed or unholy habits we developed as a result of the wounding event. At the cross, we also cut off any legal right for our spiritual enemy to oppress us. And we leave, free.[3]

Listening prayer for inner healing does not result in complete recovery from all wounds at once. For me, it resulted in complete recovery of at least one wound each time, but I returned to my counselor's office regularly for two years after I was healed from depression. Each time I followed the listening prayer process, the Lord led me to another issue He wanted me to address. Genuine recovery is found in areas of our lives wound by wound, lie by lie, and sin by sin. There are still times in my life when I need to hunker down and address some issue or pain with listening prayer, and I'm now able to do that without the guidance of a counselor.

Experiencing Truth

As I recall all the dark, oppressive untruths I've been set free from, what really strikes me is that many of the lies I believed were not surprising when the Holy Spirit revealed them; Dr. Colford had already identified them. We had discussed many of the false beliefs I held, and she'd tried to help me understand the truth. I often knew in my head she was right— *Of course the fact that I'm not perfect doesn't mean I deserve to die*, I reasoned—but hearing and acknowledging the truth she offered rarely made me feel better about myself. The lies continued to recycle in my head. However, when I confronted these lies on a spiritual level and the Holy Spirit revealed God's truth to me through listening prayer, something finally registered.

The Spirit reveals truth not to our heads but to our hearts. I didn't receive a mental recognition of truth; I actually *experienced* it.

I am good enough.

God cares for me.

I don't have to please others to have worth.

Once these truths took root in my heart, the lies were no longer believable. In *Fear No Evil*, Brad Jersak explains,

If the Living Truth tells you that you are never alone, you *cannot* feel fear of isolation. If he speaks to your heart, "I will never leave you," you *cannot* feel fear of abandonment. If you receive the heart knowledge that God always watches over you as a Good Shepherd, you *will not* feel fear of the unknown. The truth devours the lie as light devours darkness, and the fear it generated simply vanishes.[4]

Jesus promises, "You will know the truth and the truth will set you free" (John 8:32, GNT). The word *know* is from the Hebrew root word *yada*. It has a broader meaning than our English word *know*, including perceiving, learning, understanding, willing, performing, and experiencing.[5] To know isn't to simply be informed of a principle or truth but to grasp hold and experience its reality.[6] The translation of this verse in *The Message* more accurately captures the meaning of *yada*: "You will experience for yourselves the truth, and the truth will free you."

What does the truth free us from? Fear, guilt, sin, misery, and spiritual bondage.[7]

Detecting Lies

Discovering flaws in our belief systems is rarely easy, partly because we've lived these lies so long they've become our reality and also because our Enemy masters in deception and uses it as a weapon against us. Those who have spent countless hours counseling the wounded are familiar with the most pervasive misbeliefs. Do any of those listed here sound familiar to you?

- I am no good, worthless, unimportant, a failure, unworthy.
- I deserve bad treatment; I'm always to blame.
- I must earn others' approval by work, being perfect, doing what pleases them.
- People would reject me if they truly knew me.
- I can't forgive.

- Things are hopeless (self, relationships, depression, spiritual problems).
- Life is not worth living; I'd be better off dead.
- I have to be good enough/work hard enough so God will accept me.
- I am too bad to be forgiven or loved by God.
- I should depend on God only when all else fails.
- God cannot use me.
- God has forsaken me.
- God can't hear me/speak to me.
- God is not a good God; God is punishing me.
- I cannot change.
- I've run out of chances.
- I must look out for myself; God can't be trusted to protect my interests.[8]

Some additional lies I believed were:

- My needs aren't important to other people.
- People won't accept me if I don't share their opinions; my own opinions matter to no one but me.
- It's better not to speak than to suffer humiliation.
- If I don't impress people, I'm not special.
- I will never be enough to hold first place in anyone's heart.
- It's better (and easier) to ignore my fears than to address them.

For the first few decades of my life, false beliefs stunted my emotional growth and prevented me from experiencing healthy relationships with God and others. Lies enslaved me, robbed me of joy, and made me resentful of people. I was chained to the opinions of others, and at the same time I isolated myself from the world, shying away from conversation and relationships. I avoided conflict at all costs, even when the price was my voice and my identity.

But God's truth has, and is, setting me free to be the person He created me to be, experience the relationships He designed me for, and follow the passion He has placed in me—not driven by the opinions of others but directed by my heart and His Spirit. Oh, how I long for this same sweet freedom for you!

ENCOURAGEMENT FROM GOD'S WORD

Truth was foundational to the Messiah's ministry and identity. John wrote that Jesus "came from the Father, full of grace and truth" (John 1:14). To his disciples, Jesus claimed to *be* the truth (see John 14:6). Prior to Christ's return to heaven, He promised, "I will ask the Father, and he will give you another Counselor to be with you forever—the Spirit of truth. . . . When he, the Spirit of truth, comes, he will guide you into all truth" (John 14:16-17; 16:13).

God, through the Holy Spirit, is still speaking truth to His people today. You don't have to hold a degree in theology, be an ordained minister, or write Bible studies to hear your Maker's voice. Your heavenly Father longs for a relationship with you. Doesn't it make sense, then, that He'd also want to engage you in conversation? Jesus told this parable:

> The man who enters by the gate is the shepherd of his sheep. The watchman opens the gate for him, and the sheep listen to his voice. He calls his own sheep by name and leads them out. When he has brought out all his own, he goes on ahead of them, and his sheep follow him because they know his voice.... I am the good shepherd; I know my sheep and my sheep know me—just as the Father knows me and I know the Father—and I lay down my life for the sheep. (John 10:2-4,14-15)

Jesus didn't say that only prophets and priests hear His voice or that the most holy or learned among us would provide interpretation for the rest. He doesn't speak to the hired hand and ask him to pass along His messages. The Shepherd speaks to the sheep.

Notice that Jesus didn't say the sheep would hear His voice if they were dressed in their Sunday best and sitting in straight rows. Neither did He say that they *might, could,* or *should* be able to hear Him. He said, "My sheep hear my voice" (John 10:27, KJV).[9]

The Shepherd speaks directly to His followers: "He calls his own sheep by name" (John 10:3). Do we listen? Do we dismiss His voice in favor of another? Do we drown it out with messages from society, media, and other people?

Sometimes the Shepherd speaks through a nudging of our spirits, the conviction of conscience, or the divinely inspired words of a teacher. We may hear Him through a gentle whisper in the mind, an audible voice, a dream, or a vision. In biblical times, He spoke through angelic visitations,[10] writing on a wall,[11] and the mouth of a donkey.[12] Those who know the Shepherd hear and understand His voice; no interpretation is required. The question is, are you ready to heed the words He's speaking? Hearing God brings a measure of responsibility with it. Once you know His heart, His dreams for you, His truth, you have to decide what to do with that information. Will you act on it or ignore it?

The Lord wants to turn your life around, but first you have to listen. In *Can You Hear Me?* Brad Jersak reasons,

> If Jesus can speak through children and the disabled, to prisoners and prostitutes, then he *will* speak to you. In fact, I am certain that he already has. Have you perceived it? It's time to dial in to God's station. In fact, I believe that God is saying to you today, "Maybe you should check *your* messages."[13]

The danger of ignoring God's voice is not that He will resort to the silent treatment, but that He will begin to speak more clearly and forcefully.[14] In *The Problem of Pain*, C. S. Lewis writes, "God whispers to us in our pleasures, speaks to us in our conscience, but shouts in our pains: It is His megaphone to rouse a deaf world."[15] For me, that shout came in an illness that seemed incurable, grinding my life to a halt and making the world so quiet I couldn't ignore His voice any longer. You have the choice to be in tune to God's whispers or let Him holler, but when you do listen you'll find that His words bring freedom, restoration, and life.

The old adage "The truth hurts" isn't entirely correct. Heavenly truth also heals; receiving it sets us free. While the prophet Jeremiah was in prison, the Lord told him, "Call to me, and *I will answer* you; I will tell you wonderful and marvelous things that you know nothing about" (Jeremiah 33:3, GNT, emphasis added). God has some amazing things to tell you. Are you ready to listen?

SELF-REFLECTION

- Review the list on pages 191–192 of the common lies people believe as well as those I believed. If you've believed any of these yourself, reflect on how they have negatively impacted your life and your spirit.
- What areas of your life could be improved by divine truth therapy? Seek help from a Christian counselor or pastor trained in listening prayer for inner healing so you can be released from the burden of deception and receive the liberating power of truth.

MEDITATION

"Know that the LORD is God. It is he who made us, and we are his; we are his people, the sheep of his pasture." (Psalm 100:3)

"No other nation, no matter how great, has a god who is so near when they need him as the Lord our God is to us. He answers us whenever we call for help." (Deuteronomy 4:7, GNT)

"All truths are easy to understand once they are discovered; the point is to discover them." (Galileo Galilei)

JOHN STEPHEN AKHWARI: THE POWER *of* PERSEVERANCE

The greatest glory in living lies not in never falling, but in rising every time we fall.

Nelson Mandela

It's the stuff legends are made of. John Stephen Akhwari of Tanzania set a marathon record at the Mexico City Summer Olympics of 1968—a record that has remained unbroken, though Abdul Baser Wasiqi from Afghanistan matched it in the 1996 Olympics.

People continue to talk about this inspiring man forty years after the event that propelled him to fame. In January 2008, sixty-nine-year-old Akhwari was invited to Beijing to celebrate the start of the Olympic year. There he met with media and schoolchildren and starred in a music video for the song "Hero," by a Taiwanese singer.

In 1983, Tanzania awarded a National Hero Medal of Honor to Akhwari, the man who failed to bring home a medal from the Olympics. That's right, what launched John Stephen Akhwari to stardom at the

'68 Olympics was not a winning performance but the fact that he had become the greatest last place finisher ever!

As seventy-five marathon competitors arrayed themselves across the starting line in Mexico City, the crowd buzzed with speculation about the ultimate winner. At the sound of the starter's pistol, they were off in a jumble of arms, legs, and lean bodies. Nineteen kilometers into the race, thirty-year-old Akhwari found himself trapped in the middle of a pack of other runners. He stumbled and fell, hitting his head, badly injuring his knee, and dislocating his shoulder as he was trampled. But the race continued without him, and Mamo Wolde of Ethiopia won the gold medal.

As night descended and photographers' cameras were being packed up, the sound of police sirens captured the attention of the crowd that had begun to filter out of the stadium. A voice announced over the speakers that the final runner of the marathon was approaching. Spectators were confused: The winner had crossed the finish line more than an hour earlier, medals had been awarded, and it seemed this marathon was history. But the greatest story to emerge from these Olympic Games was still unfolding. The announcer asked the crowd to take their seats as a police escort reached the stadium. Then the marathon gate swung open and Akhwari hobbled into the light and onto the track, grimacing with every painful step. His thin, brown leg was wrapped in white bandages, beginning to unravel, fluttering in the breeze as he made his way around the track. The astounded crowd was soon screaming and cheering Akhwari on as if he were the winner. Paramedics and cameramen edged closer to reach him as the crowd's shouts swelled to a roar. John Stephen Akhwari shuffled across the finish line and collapsed into the arms of medical personnel, who whisked him off to the hospital. For the first time, the Olympics had witnessed a rally for an athlete who came in last place.

At a press conference the next day, a reporter asked the Tanzanian runner, "Why, after sustaining the kinds of injuries you did, would you ever get up and proceed to the finish line when there was no way you could possibly place in the race?" There was a pause before the answer came. Looking bewildered by the question, John Stephen Akhwari responded, "My country did not send me to Mexico City to start a race. They sent me to Mexico City to finish one."

Eighteen other runners had given up and dropped out of the marathon, but that was not an option for Akhwari. Forty years later, he shared what was going through his mind as he picked himself up and pressed on. "I just thought about my father and my mother. I just thought about my country. Once I am on the road, there is no way I am going to quit."[1]

There is a saying from Akhwari's homeland:

Every morning in Africa, a gazelle wakes up. It knows it must outrun the fastest lion or it will be killed. Every morning in Africa, a lion wakes up. It knows it must run faster than the slowest gazelle or it will starve. It doesn't matter whether you're a lion or a gazelle—when the sun comes up, you'd better be running.[2]

No matter where we are in life, the dangers or trials we're facing, we won't survive or succeed unless we keep running, unless we continue to press on. John Stephen Akhwari realized the importance of this truth. The message he delivered in Beijing was in keeping with the one he lived out in Mexico City: "I want to tell the young people in China that they should never give up, that they should always pursue their dreams and face challenges with courage," he said. "It doesn't matter if you are a doctor or a teacher or whatever, go for your dream and stick to it."[3]

I don't know what dreams you have, but I do know the kinds of challenges you're facing as a result of depression. Will you choose to face them with courage? Perseverance requires a shift in perspective, taking our focus off the momentary struggles we face and placing it on the bigger picture of our lives and futures, knowing that each small battle we overcome builds character and strength. Next to faith, perseverance is the most powerful weapon we have to fight depression. If you press on and continue to believe there is hope for wholeness, I believe you'll find it. Remember, God didn't send you just to start the race but also to finish it.

PART FOUR

PRESERVING AND ADVANCING

CHAPTER 14

CONSISTENT SPIRITUAL SUSTENANCE

"You will seek me and find me when you seek me with all your heart. I will be found by you," declares the LORD, "and will bring you back from captivity."

Jeremiah 29:13-14

Collapsed in a heap on the cold tile floor of the hotel bathroom, I desperately waited for morning and the plane that would take me home. Though I'd been free from depression for two years, at this moment I was filled with despair. Dreading the possibility that depression might have returned to reclaim my soul—and thinking, *I don't want to live through that again*—I considered flinging myself from the window, until I realized it didn't open.

I'd been away from God's Word for a while. A two-week vacation with Tim, followed by another week visiting my sister and her family, had kept me preoccupied. In all my busyness rekindling these relationships, I'd neglected the one I needed most. Now, after nearly a month with barely more than bedtime prayers, I was reaping the disastrous repercussions.

In the past few days, I'd been feeling a little down and knew something wasn't quite right within me, but I was unprepared for this sudden, aggressive attack on my spirit. I knew that God was my only hope, so I grabbed the Gideon's Bible from the nightstand and returned to the bathroom, which was as far away from the window as I could get. As I huddled in the corner and searched for something to help me hang on, these words became my plea:

> Rescue me from the mire, do not let me sink; deliver me . . .
> from the deep waters. Do not let the floodwaters engulf me or
> the depths swallow me up or the pit close its mouth over me.
> (Psalm 69:14-15)

I'd forgotten that part of my success in remaining free from depression was attributed to the fact that I had become a seeker after God. After my healing from depression, my counselor taught me how to hear God through His Word. And hear Him I did. I began to live for those quiet times spent in my bedroom reading the Bible, listening to the Holy Spirit's explanation of how each passage applied to my life, and reflecting on it. Study, meditation, and prayer were the keys to building a relationship with God and to protecting me from my spirit's enemy and depression, yet I'd been depriving myself of them.

The apostle Paul describes God's Word as a "sword" (Ephesians 6:17) and urges Christ's followers to use it to "stand against the devil's schemes" (Ephesians 6:11). But in the month leading up to the hotel incident, I'd neglected God and His Word and left myself wide open for another spiritual attack. I desperately needed help.

Somehow God led me to Psalm 40 and through its words reminded me of all He'd accomplished in my life and assured me that He would get me through this present darkness:

I waited patiently for the Lord; he turned to me and heard my cry. He lifted me out of the slimy pit, out of the mud and mire; he set my feet on a rock and gave me a firm place to stand. . . . Many, O Lord my God, are the wonders you have done. (Psalm 40:1-2,5)

The long, terrifying night finally gave way to morning and I was left with the profound understanding that I needed to stay close to God. My very survival depended on it.

Now I know that my mental, spiritual, and emotional health require time spent in God's presence. If I fail to carve out that time, I begin to feel it. I can sense a spiritual fatigue that makes my soul seem grimy, heavy, and dark. But this feeling always vanishes when I reconnect with God. *He* is the medication I need, the food my spirit requires, to stay healthy and strong.

Many Christians complain that they don't have time to read God's Word, to be disciplined spiritually. Prior to my depression, I would have echoed their lament. But God gives us all twenty-four hours each day and the freedom to choose how we'll spend them. Our choices reflect our priorities and affect our spiritual, mental, and physical health. I know that spending time with my Creator is the only way to develop the life-giving relationship I crave and build a spiritual foundation that will protect me from future relapses. The truth is I don't have time to *not* be serious about drawing closer to God. I can't afford to lose another nine years.

A BALANCED DIET

Just as our body's health is impacted by what we feed it, our spirits thrive—or wither—to the extent that they're nourished. Consistent spiritual sustenance is a crucial step toward wholeness and lasting freedom from depression. People who fail to feed their faith become spiritually sick. They don't have what it takes to live victorious lives. I lingered in this stage for years, and you know what it cost me.

Other people are willing to eat only what's quick and easy. A few minutes from a devotional guide in the morning and they're on their way. They never really get into God's Word and study it for themselves; reading what God has revealed to others is good enough for them. It's like grabbing a donut on the way to work or a burger from a drive-thru window for supper. We may not have eaten well, but at least we've eaten something. (I've spent a lot of time in this stage, too.)

You cannot gain the spiritual fortitude you'll need to become whole and remain free from depression unless you take the time and make the effort to nourish your spirit. Christian classics, pocket devotionals, and Bible study guides are great supplements, and secondary aids, but they cannot replace our own study of God's Word. Our bodies can't thrive on supplements and neither can our spirits. We need solid food, and we need to eat and experience it for ourselves.

In order to provide our physical bodies with proper nutrition, experts have divided the food we eat into four distinct groups and recommend that we eat a variety of foods from each group every day. Our spiritual diet should also be wholesome and varied. In his book *The Celebration of Discipline*, Richard Foster refers to the key spiritual elements as spiritual disciplines, identifying them as: meditation, prayer, fasting, study, simplicity, solitude, submission, service, confession, worship, celebration, and guidance (or community).[1] In the beginning of my journey beyond depression, the elements that I "consumed" in the greatest quantities were study, prayer, and meditation, so I'll focus on those.

Study

In chapter 13, we looked at Jesus' statement that knowing the truth would set us free (see John 8:32). A wealth of liberating truth is found in God's Word. Many of us faithfully attend church, lead Sunday school classes and small groups, pastor congregations, sing our hearts out during praise and worship time, and try to live moral lives, yet we remain unchanged. How can it be that with all we do for the Lord and all the love we feel for Him, we fail to grow? Richard Foster asserts that it's because we neglect "one of the central ways God uses to change us: study."[2] Many of us remain limited in our understanding of God and ill equipped for victorious living because we simply don't know the truth.

In the Bible, we read, "All Scripture is given by God and is useful for teaching, for showing people what is wrong in their lives, for correcting faults, and for teaching how to live right" (2 Timothy 3:16, NCV). If you are reading this book because you're depressed, you need God to show you what's wrong in your life. If you're like me, you have a few faults that need correcting. And if you're on your way out of depression, it would help to have some instruction on how to live rightly, a map to guide you toward a victorious future. God can do all those things through His Word.

When I study the Bible, I reflect on each passage of Scripture using the questions my counselor taught me to hear God through His Word:

- What does it mean?
- What does it reveal about God, the Holy Spirit, and Jesus?
- What truth does it teach?
- How does it apply to my life?
- What might God want to say to me through this passage?

In the years since I began writing down these lessons, I've been amazed to experience the truth that God's Word is *alive* (see Hebrews 4:12). Though He never contradicts Himself, God has used the same passages to teach me completely different lessons over the years. He opens my eyes to different themes based on my needs at the time.

Every year before Christmas, I read the story of Christ's birth from several biblical accounts. One year, as I read about expectant Mary's visit to her cousin Elizabeth (see Luke 1:39-56), God emphasized verse 53 in Mary's Song: "He has filled the hungry with good things but has sent the rich away empty." Through this verse, God spoke to me about how we stuff ourselves with the things of the world and gain a false sense of fulfillment. He taught me that only when we realize that the world cannot satisfy will we hunger after something that does: God.

The next winter when I read the same passage, God pointed out how "unqualified" Mary was, by worldly standards, to be the mother of the Messiah. But Mary had the qualities God was looking for: obedience and faith. It wasn't an easy assignment, and surely there were times when Mary wondered and wept, but even when she couldn't understand what God was doing, she trusted He would do what He promised. God used this passage to speak to me during a difficult time of wondering—and feeling unqualified—as I accepted His assignment to write this book.

God will speak to our spirits through His Word and use it to nourish, teach truth, and transform our lives. For this to happen, all we need, according to author Max Lucado, is a regular time, an open Bible, and a listening heart.[3]

Prayer

Prayer is a challenge for me. I don't have a hard time asking God for things, but prayer is more than just presenting our petitions, more than a one-sided conversation. Through prayer we praise God. We confess our sins and weaknesses. We thank Him for His goodness. We relinquish our will and ask that His will be done, *and we listen.* Our spirits need to be still and quiet to hear God's voice, a great challenge for one who feels she has so much to accomplish. Seventeenth-century French theologian, poet, and writer François Fénelon said it well: "How rare it is to find a soul quiet enough to hear God speak."[4]

We know that prayer is important because it was a priority for Jesus. In spite of all He had to accomplish, in spite of people following Him from town to town, others scrutinizing His every action and word, and having a group of disciples to teach, Jesus made time to be with God. Luke tells us, "Jesus went off to a mountain to pray, and he spent the night praying to God" (Luke 6:12, NCV). Mark reports, "Very early in the morning, while it was still dark, Jesus got up, left the house and went off to a solitary place, where he prayed" (Mark 1:35). "Jesus often withdrew to lonely places and prayed" (Luke 5:16). If prayer was so important that the sinless Son of God would give up a night's rest, climb a mountain, and regularly seek solitude for it, shouldn't we make it a priority in our lives?

I can almost hear your protest: "But I'm so busy. My kids are noisy and needy. My job is demanding. I don't have a minute to myself; how can God expect me to fit *Him* in, too?" Max Lucado writes that God intends for prayer to "lighten — not heighten — our load."[5] When we fail to foster an intimate relationship with God, our spirits feel the effects of malnourishment: unsatisfied hunger, weariness, vulnerability to sickness and disease. Martin Luther declares, "I have so much business I cannot get on without spending three hours daily in prayer."[6] (I'm not there yet!) Luther realized that life is harder when we don't make time for prayer.

Prayer not only draws us closer to God but also provides what we need to cope with major challenges. In determining whether one survives an extraordinary life crisis, Al Siebert, author of *The Survivor Personality*, states, "Praying can make a real contribution. It can give a person calmness, focus, increased hope, and decreased feelings of helplessness."[7] If prayer is so important and empowering, why does it seem so difficult at times? Perhaps there's someone willing to devote a lot of energy to see that we devote very little to this important spiritual practice.

Just as Satan tries to discourage us from reading the Bible by convincing us that it's too difficult, too time-consuming, or too ancient to have any relevancy, he also tries to interfere in the matter of prayer. Author Beth Moore writes,

> [Satan] would rather see us serve ourselves into the ground, because he knows we'll eventually grow resentful without prayer. He'd rather see us study the Bible into the wee hours

of the morning because he knows we'll never have deep understanding and power to live what we've learned without prayer. He knows prayerless lives are powerless lives, while prayerful lives are powerful lives.[8]

Our Enemy would rather we do *anything* but pray.

Depression can make prayer even more difficult. When seriously depressed, we lack the joy to praise God as well as the ability to recognize our blessings and express gratitude. We may feel as though God is far off or can't hear us. If this is your experience, don't feel guilty; it's not unusual for those who suffer depression. During my illness, my pastor once assured me that even though my spirit couldn't pray, the Holy Spirit was petitioning God on my behalf. "The Holy Spirit helps us in our distress. For we don't even know what we should pray for, nor how we should pray. But the Holy Spirit prays for us with groanings that cannot be expressed in words" (Romans 8:26, NLT).

Learning to live a prayerful life is a journey. Instead of being discouraged, remember that God always meets us where we are. Commit to doing as much as you can, and ask God to help you progress.

Meditation

The discipline of meditation is practiced in many religions but in different forms. Objective is what differentiates Christian meditation from the kind practiced in Eastern religions. Eastern meditation is an attempt to empty the mind and detach from the world. Christians meditate to *attach* to the person of God.[9] Rather than emptying our minds, we try to fill them up with God and a better understanding of Him.

Richard Foster states that Christian meditation is simply the ability to hear God's voice and obey His word. "It involves no hidden mysteries, no secret mantras, no mental gymnastics, no esoteric flights into the cosmic consciousness."[10]

Many of the godly people we read about in the Bible understood the value of meditation. God instructed Joshua to meditate on the book of the law "day and night" so that he might do everything written in it.[11] Isaac meditated in the evening while taking a walk through the fields.[12] David meditated on God;[13] His unfailing love[14] and wondrous works; the wonderful deeds of long ago;[15] and His commandments and principles.[16] He stayed awake through the night, thinking about God's promises.[17]

The disciplines of study, prayer, and meditation overlap one another. We can meditate on Scripture by using our imaginations and allowing our senses to place us in the midst of the story, receiving the personalized message God intends for us. We can ponder the truths that we discover in God's Word. When we pray, we can meditate by quietly waiting to hear God's voice.

One of my favorite ways to meditate on God is by observing nature. As I remove myself from activity and conversation to cycle through the country, inhaling the sweet scent of clover, or to simply sit on my lawn and watch bees pollinating blossoms in the tree overhead, I'm filled with wonder and gratitude. Nature reflects God's creativity, intelligence, attention to detail, and power. "The heavens declare the glory of God; the skies proclaim the work of his hands" (Psalm 19:1). We can use all our senses to guide us in meditation and usher us into God's presence. He's all around us, waiting to delight and inspire those who will make an effort to notice.

Eating well isn't always easy, but it's worth the effort. God has provided all that we need; we just have to be willing to receive it. Author David Jeremiah writes,

> The truth is that we all have as much of God as we truly want. . . . Don't even attempt to say, "I want more of God. But this is as far as I've been able to go." The truth is, there is *always* more of God, and that more is always within reach. . . . God leads us onward with the intensity with which we are willing to come. It's a matter of how hungry we are.[18]

ENCOURAGEMENT FROM GOD'S WORD

A story in the Old Testament provides a beautiful illustration of how God provides sustenance for us. After the temple was destroyed and the Israelites were exiled to Babylon, God gave the prophet Ezekiel a vision of a new temple that would one day be built, an assurance that He would once again live among His people. An angel led Ezekiel around the temple and showed him a life-giving river that flowed from beneath God's dwelling place. The farther along the river Ezekiel ventured, the deeper the water became. The angel told him, "Wherever the stream flows, there will be all kinds of animals and fish. The stream will make the water of the Dead Sea fresh, and wherever it flows, it will bring life" (Ezekiel 47:9, GNT).

What promise the river held: In a sea so salty it could not support life, the waters would teem with fish! And fishermen from all the villages along its shore would be seen drying their nets on the beaches. But there was even more:

> On each bank of the stream all kinds of trees will grow to provide food. Their leaves will never wither, and they will never stop bearing fruit. They will have fresh fruit every month, because they are watered by the stream that flows from the Temple. The trees will provide food, and their leaves will be used for healing people. (Ezekiel 47:12, GNT)

Vegetation along the riverbank would flourish. Fish and animals would be plentiful. Everything the water touched would be alive. "But the water in the marshes and ponds along the shore will not be made fresh," the angel pointed out (Ezekiel 47:11, GNT).

For us, life-giving water also flows from God. We drink it in through such spiritual practices as prayer, Bible study, and meditation. Deep within the water there is life, but in the shallows around the shore—the marshes and the ponds—nothing grows or thrives.

So why do so many of us choose the pond? Why are we often content to just gaze at the river? Why do we settle for reports from others who have waded in and found life in the depths instead of venturing in ourselves? Many pack a picnic, park themselves at the pond, and then wonder why their lives seem shallow and their growth stunted. *God doesn't speak to me. My faith isn't working. I want more of God, but I can't find Him,* you may hear them say. Ah, but remember: *We have as much of God as we truly want.*

Are you willing to pursue Him? Are you so thirsty for God that you're ready to abandon your folding chair near the shallows and wade into the river? Richard Foster writes,

> Psalm 42:7 reads "Deep calls to deep." Perhaps somewhere in the subterranean chambers of your life you have heard the call to deeper, fuller living. You have become weary of frothy experiences and shallow teaching. Every now and then you have caught glimpses, hints of something more than you have known. Inwardly you long to launch out into the deep.[19]

Maybe it's time for more than just river-gazing, for more than toe-dipping or ankle-wetting. Maybe it's time to go after what you're truly longing for. Maybe it's time to dive in.

SELF-REFLECTION

▸ Give some thought to how well you nourish your spirit. Is your diet lacking in prayer, study, or meditation? If so, what changes are you willing to make to give your spirit the opportunity to flourish?

▸ Reread Ezekiel 47:12. What would it mean for you to not only flourish but also one day be used to heal other people? By making an investment in your spiritual health today, you may be investing in the healing and freedom of someone else in the future.

MEDITATION

"Instead you thrill to GOD's Word, you chew on Scripture day and night. You're a tree replanted in Eden, bearing fresh fruit every month, never dropping a leaf, always in blossom." (Psalm 1:2-3, MSG)

"Cry out for wisdom, and beg for understanding. Search for it like silver, and hunt for it like hidden treasure. Then you will understand respect for the LORD, and you will find that you know God." (Proverbs 2:3-5, NCV)

CHAPTER 15

THE FINE ART
of BALANCE

In our busyness we become barren.

Bob Meisner, author, television host

I t was dark. The moonlight shimmering on the ocean guided our journey as Tim and I bounced across the waves on our way to a vacation
unlike any we'd experienced before. The regular, more sophisticated,
launch that ferried guests from a larger island — where the airport was
located — to our destination on a more remote shore had made its last
trip hours earlier, so we found ourselves in a small motorboat hired to
shuttle the late arrivals. I tried to focus on my breathing as the engine's
fumes joined forces with my tendency toward motion sickness. But
the slight nausea failed to dampen my excitement; I couldn't help but
laugh out loud at the absurdity of what we were doing and where we
were headed.

In the first few years following my freedom from depression, I lived
with the sense that I had a lot to catch up on and returned to busyness
as usual. But part of me longed for a true departure from our routine,
and I found what I believed would be the answer: a quiet, eco-sensitive

resort inviting us to disconnect in pristine, natural surroundings. Guest rooms without telephones, computer jacks, televisions, radios, or even clocks. Wake-up calls (if truly required) in the form of a quaint knock on the door. Guest activities including watercolor painting, stargazing, and nature walks.

Tim and I were accustomed to bringing whatever electronic devices we required to stay in touch with business and family while vacationing, so the concept of unplugging for a week was challenging. But we were driven by a desire to be reckless for a change. Besides, I reasoned, there'd be so much to do in paradise we'd never miss the gadgets.

After a wild twenty-minute ride, the motorboat delivered us to a dock lined with flaming torches and welcoming staff who led us to our room. It was late, so after a snack we went straight to bed, with the window louvers open, listening to waves caressing the shore.

Morning broke bright and beautiful, the scent of flowers wafting into our room. I eagerly unpacked, ready to begin the first of many planned adventures. Though my family prefers more laid-back vacations, I enjoy them filled with activity and spend weeks — even months — researching a destination. I scope out interesting sights, shops, and restaurants, not wanting to miss a thing. But as I searched through my luggage that first morning on the island, I was dismayed to discover I'd left the itinerary at home — all eighteen pages of it.

Without my treasure trove of information, we'd have to settle for guided tours and activities, so we stopped by the tour desk after breakfast and booked enough to keep us occupied. Then we went to the beach to while away the time until our first tour, the next day.

As we spent the afternoon on that quiet stretch of sand, doing nothing more than watch sailboats glide by, something unexpected happened: I enjoyed myself. Ms. Must Be Active Every Waking Moment *enjoyed* doing nothing. In fact, Tim and I liked it so much we eventually cancelled all the activities we'd booked, except my watercolor painting class and his scuba diving. We spent most of the week in the same chairs on the same beach, languishing in the shade of sea grapes and palms, sitting, reading, napping, observing—and burning a bit. (Who knew you needed sunscreen in the shade?)

Though it seemed I was accomplishing nothing, God was accomplishing much in me. Relaxing on the beach, being still and quiet, I felt close to my Creator. He whispered in the gentle lap of waves, in the twittering of birds, and in the rustle of leaves. I felt Him in the warmth of the sun, in the refreshing breeze, and in the vastness of the ocean. Somehow, as I rested I began to feel complete and content deep down in my soul.

Each day after the sun set, Tim and I talked for hours. With no distractions, our conversation became the evening's entertainment. We discovered that we'd been missing out on the simple, uninterrupted pleasure of one another's company for many years.

The Vacation of the Lost Itinerary ended up giving me so much: I reconnected with my husband, learned how to truly relax, and realized that spending a day in stillness and silence is not a missed opportunity but a chance for discovery.

Though all my vacations since this one haven't been as laid-back, I do travel differently now. I look for moments to sit and soak in my surroundings. I relish pauses to quietly observe and to focus on the feelings each new place stirs in me. In exploring less, I'm free to experience more. This is a valuable lesson I've carried through to daily life as well—do less, feel more—and it's birthed a deep sense of peace and contentment that I now consider one of my greatest treasures.

BREAKING FREE

Western society is moving faster than ever. We race to do more, be more, and acquire more, as if accomplishments, status, and possessions are the keys to happiness. Jesus' teaching reveals how wrong that notion is, yet we still get sucked in to going with the flow and speeding toward burnout. We work our fingers to the bone and our brains into a frenzy, assuring ourselves that we're doing it for our own good.

(We'll retire early, buy a cottage on a lake, and have the life we're too busy to enjoy now.) But in time our relationships rupture, our souls starve, and God's voice becomes a distant memory.

In his book *The Rest of God*, Mark Buchanan notes that the Swahili word for *white man* is *mazungu*, meaning "one who spins around." He writes, "That's how the East Africans see Westerners: turning ourselves dizzy, a great whirl of motion without direction. We're flurries of going nowhere."[1] But even though our frenetic motion doesn't get us far, it can cost us plenty.

Stress is one of the negative consequences of living life in the fast lane. Though it can have a positive, motivating effect on us in smaller doses, high levels are hazardous. Stress affects the mind; the National Institute of Mental Health reports that stress triggers an enzyme in the brain that causes "disturbed thinking, impaired judgment, impulsivity and distractibility."[2] Stress affects the body; working or living in stressful environments for extended periods of time can weaken the immune system, making it more susceptible to disease. High mental stress can increase one's risk of fatal stroke by 50 percent[3] and double the risk for heart-related death.[4] And an estimated 75–90 percent of all visits to primary care physicians are for stress-related problems.[5]

Blessed Are the Busy?

The tyranny of the Western world's fast-paced, overachieving, self-sufficient lifestyle is evident in even our churches. We seem to equate busyness with godliness, believing that the more we serve and the harder we work, the more impressed God and others will be. I believed it, I tried it, and I ended up in a psychiatric ward. Not so impressive.

Mike Yaconelli writes, "While the church earnestly warns Christians to watch for the devil, the devil is sitting in the congregation encouraging everyone to keep busy doing 'good things.'"[6] Why? Because busyness keeps us from nurturing relationships and knowing God.

As we cram more and more into our schedules, we find out that we can't do it all—at least not very well. So we then resort to using busyness as an excuse to justify poor performance, lack of follow-through in our commitments, and stunted spiritual growth. But God never called us to be overworked or overwhelmed. On the contrary, Jesus said,

> Are you tired? Worn out? Burned out on religion? Come to me. Get away with me and you'll recover your life. I'll show you how to take a real rest. Walk with me and work with me—watch how I do it. Learn the unforced rhythms of grace. I won't lay anything heavy or ill-fitting on you. Keep company with me and you'll learn to live freely and lightly. (Matthew 11:28-30, MSG)

Comfortably Numb

Not only does busyness negatively affect our relationships with others, it also prevents us from knowing ourselves. It allows us to ignore the uncomfortably empty feeling in our souls. It's a drug that dulls the piercing pain of past wounds, present failings, anxiety, fear, and shame while those feelings continue to release deadly toxins into our bodies and spirits.[7]

Subconsciously, we believe that if we can fill our days with enough activity and noise, we may not have to deal with the void within us. We clutter up our souls so we don't have to do the hard work of discovering who we are and what we were truly made for. But clutter is the enemy of completeness. If you are on a journey toward healing and restoration, heed Jerome Daley's warning, "A cluttered soul will never even find its wounds, much less pursue the path of healing!"[8] You will never experience wholeness until you address your woundedness. And you can't do that without time and room to reflect, pray, and listen.

Investing in You

Naturally, the business of living requires some effort on our parts. We have to earn money to pay for food, clothing, and shelter. Then we have to prepare the food, wash the clothing, and clean the shelter. And beyond the basics lies the lure of many other "good things" we may choose to devote time and energy to. The challenge is to choose wisely and remember our own needs.

You may feel that family interests, church obligations, and the demands of your job take priority. For women in particular, society sends the message that we're selfish and negligent if we don't put everyone else's needs ahead of our own. But if we neglect our own needs, we can't give our best to others.

Psychologist Dr. Phil McGraw says,

> We're like bank accounts: If we make only withdrawals (carpooling, working late, helping out a friend), we wind up emotionally and physically bankrupt. We all must make regular deposits to our minds, souls, and bodies. You must take time for you.[9]

While striving for balance may be revolutionary, it's not selfish. When you attend to your own needs, you become stronger, calmer, and more pleasant to be around, and everyone whose life you touch benefits. As you cultivate a life of balance, you take an important step on the path to wholeness and to maintaining freedom from depression.

So how can you invest in yourself?

Seek solitude: A deposit to your mind. Solitude is intensely healing and restorative. It allows us to reflect on our lives, rediscover our dreams, and reenergize. Jesus took time to seek solitude. I expect that it strengthened Him and helped Him clarify His mission. And when He returned to the demanding crowds, He was able to give freely of Himself.

Schedule solitude into each week (or even each day, if you can), an uninterrupted time where you are free to do whatever you enjoy, preferably something that allows you to relax and reflect. (Balancing your checkbook alone at the kitchen table won't cut it.) Some days you may just want to curl up with a good book; other times a walk outdoors enjoying creation may be refreshing. Close your eyes and feel the sun's warmth on your skin. Listen to the sound of rustling leaves or beautiful music.

By yourself you can spend time weighing the difference between who you are and who you long to be. Reflect on those moments in your life when you've felt most alive and satisfied and strategize ways you can recapture those feelings. Grapple with some weighty questions, such as, *What passions has God placed in me?* and *How can I position myself to pursue those passions?*

Seek God: A deposit to your soul. Solitude offers time for self-discovery and also time to get to know God. In the previous chapter, I shared the importance of seeking God for spiritual sustenance and ways to do that. But there's another reason to seek Him: Spending time with God will not only nourish you, it will free you. This freedom goes a long way in helping you cultivate a life of balance.

As you draw closer to God, He will reveal more of Himself, His complete love and acceptance of you, and your worth and purpose. Experiencing God's love and acceptance (and acknowledging your worth) liberates you from the need for others' approval and all the unhealthy behaviors that accompany that need: people pleasing, workaholism, and busyness, to name a few. This frees up more time to devote to the important relationships in your life, to draw even closer to God, and to pursue the passions He's placed in your heart.

Seek rest: A deposit to your body. The psalmist writes, "It's useless to rise early and go to bed late, and work your worried fingers to the bone. Don't you know he enjoys giving rest to those he loves?" (Psalm 127:2, MSG). Rest is God's gift to you, part of His perfect plan for a fulfilling and healthy life. Rest is also a requisite for a holy life. How can we worship God if we don't take time to contemplate who He is, or the wondrous beauty and complexity of His creation? How can we serve Him effectively and wholeheartedly when we're weary and exhausted?

That's when ministry becomes misery, drudgery, and obligation — a ritual devoid of meaning.

God set an example for us to follow when, after working on creation for six days, He rested. Later, He commanded His people to do the same. The Israelites were to cease working on the seventh day of every week. Even their livestock and servants were to be granted this day of rest so they, too, might be "refreshed" (Exodus 23:12).

Not even busyness was a good reason to reject God's gift of rest. The Israelites were told, "Even during the plowing season and harvest you must rest" (Exodus 34:21). And every seven years, the land was to be given a one-year Sabbath — it was not to be planted, pruned, or harvested (see Leviticus 25:4-5). Do you know what happens after a field has lain fallow for a year? It becomes more productive. Is it possible that observing a Sabbath rest could, likewise, increase our own productivity during the other six days of the week?

Rest is an exercise in humility, an acknowledgement that we are not so important the world can't get along without us for twenty-four hours. It's also an act of faith, believing that God will honor our rest by providing all we need to survive and accomplish the work He's entrusted to us, even if we take a day off.

God's gift to the Hebrews of Moses' day was more than freedom from their Egyptian taskmasters; He promised that His Presence would go with them into their new life and land and that He would give them rest (see Exodus 33:14). This gift was so precious that God commanded that anyone who squandered it by working was to be put to death (see Exodus 35:2). In our society, no one is stoned for laboring on the Sabbath, but we die a little each and every time we reject this gift intended to renew our souls and bodies. Instead of embracing freedom and rest, we voluntarily enter back into slavery, placing the shackles of drivenness around our ankles and the yoke of labor on our necks. We trudge right back into Egypt, dragging balls and chains.[10]

If you desire balance in your life, choose to observe a weekly day of rest — a time when you cease from your labor and all the activities that deplete you. For me, Sunday works best, but if your job requires that you work on that day, pick another day. Discover what brings you maximum peace and fulfillment, and incorporate those things into your day of rest (and eliminate activities that deplete you). Your Sabbath doesn't have to be a burden, laden with rules and rituals; it's meant to be a reward, so enjoy it.

Investing in solitude will renew your mind. Investing in time spent with God will strengthen your spirit. Investing in rest will restore your body. The choice of how you spend the time you've been given is yours. Will you set aside some of it to take care of yourself?

ENCOURAGEMENT FROM GOD'S WORD

Martha struggled with balance. Her makeup made it difficult for her to relax. She was a doer. She was a giver. If Martha saw a need, she rose to meet it. When Jesus passed through her town, Martha welcomed Him and made Him feel at home (see Luke 10:38). (I would have panicked; I like advance warning before someone comes to call.) With very short notice, Martha was entertaining Jesus and probably a dozen of His closest friends.

Though I don't have the gift of hospitality, I do share one thing with Martha: the tendency to become overwhelmed by the technical aspect of entertaining. I admire those people who can attend to their guests and prepare a meal at the same time. I send people as far away from the kitchen as possible and ask my daughters to keep them occupied while my husband and I try to get the meal on the table. Maybe that was Mary's objective—to engage the guests so her sister could devote her attention to the meal preparations. While Martha worked, Mary sat leisurely at Jesus' feet, hanging on His every word, oblivious to the hubbub in the kitchen. As Martha neared her breaking point, she interrupted the conversation and beseeched Jesus to intervene: "Master, don't you care that my sister has abandoned the kitchen to me? Tell her to lend me a hand" (Luke 10:40, MSG).

I would have done the same thing. Why, it doesn't seem fair that one sister would have to do all the work while another got to loaf around making merry with the guests. I'd have demanded justice and equality as well. But I'd have been sorely disappointed.

Jesus didn't see Martha as the heroine in this situation. Yes, she's the one who opened her home and was doing all the work, but apparently busyness was not the most admirable virtue in Christ's eyes. Rather than praising Martha for all she was doing, Jesus chose instead to point out what she was missing: "'Martha, Martha,' the Lord answered, 'you are worried and upset about many things, but only one thing is needed. Mary has chosen what is better, and it will not be taken away from her'" (Luke 10:41-42).

Luke reports, "Martha was *distracted* by all the preparations that had to be made" (Luke 10:40, emphasis added). Her work in the kitchen drew her away from the guest of honor in her home. In her busy attempt to offer hospitality, she neglected to notice what Jesus had to offer her. As Martha bustled about doing good things and baking bread to feed her guests, Mary chose something *better*—to sit at the feet of the Bread of Life and allow her soul to be fed. She was seeking the Lord and rest at the same time.

Every day we face the same choice between doing what's good and doing what's better, between being busy or cultivating a life of balance. In choosing busyness, Martha neglected her spirit's needs.

I admit that up until a few years ago, I would have been caught in the kitchen rather than resting at the feet of my Lord. Choosing what's best is still a challenge, but I'm making the right choices more often. How about you? You may expend a lot of energy doing good things: taking care of family, spending time with friends, working hard at your job, maybe even filling two or three roles in your church. It's all good, but does it prevent you from doing what's *better*? Do you have time to regularly sit at the feet of Jesus and listen to Him speak? Do you rest in His presence? Do you bask in His love?

Is busyness distracting you from the guest of honor dwelling in your heart, from experiencing an intimate relationship with Jesus Christ? Is it preventing you from living out God's plan for you? If so, it's time you invested in yourself.

God wants to see you restored and at peace. All you need is already available to you. Will you take the step to cultivate a life of balance? Will you cease your spinning, push aside life's clutter, and carve out time amidst the chaos? Will you fight to make room for your soul to breathe? If your answer is yes, I'm confident you will be stronger and richer as a result and one giant step closer to finding lasting freedom from depression.

SELF-REFLECTION

- Give some thought to how you spend your time. Is there a healthy balance between activities that deplete you and those that energize you?
- What choices will you make to incorporate time for solitude, God, and rest into your lifestyle?

MEDITATION

"I am leaving you with a gift — peace of mind and heart! And the peace I give isn't fragile like the peace the world gives. So don't be troubled or afraid." (John 14:27, TLB)

"There is a special rest still waiting for the people of God. For all who enter into God's rest will find rest from their labors, just as God rested after creating the world. Let us do our best to enter that place of rest." (Hebrews 4:9-11, NLT)

CHAPTER 16

LIFE BEYOND *the* WASTELAND

The road to the promised land runs past Sinai.

C. S. Lewis

The smell of sulfur smoke lingered in my nostrils. Steam rose from vents in the scorched earth as I carefully picked my way over cracks, crevices, and chunks of black rock. Basting in a layer of sweat, baked by blistering heat, I raised my head and looked toward the horizon where puffy white clouds of steam billowed skyward. *This sure doesn't look like paradise*, I thought. But it was.

From a safe vantage point at the base of massive Mauna Loa ("Long Mountain"), I watched the surf pound against jet-black cliffs as red rivers of fiery-hot lava poured into the sea, vapor mixing with the ocean spray. A spectacular sight! Cooled by the waters of the Pacific, the lava solidified and earth was created.

I was in Volcanoes National Park on the Big Island of Hawaii, where the Kilauea Volcano has been erupting since 1983. Lava flows have wiped out forests, nature trails, and treasured historical and archaeological sites. Entire communities have vanished. Nearly two hundred structures have been destroyed and more than eight miles of highway buried. But without this devastating natural phenomenon, this paradise would not exist.

Hawaii was formed by volcanic eruptions and continues to grow. Eventually, the black wasteland of the lava flow I crossed will be bursting with life. As I carefully navigated the uneven terrain, I saw the evidence: a tiny fern poking up through the broken crust of ground. Looking around I realized that, though barely noticeable, these ferns were everywhere.

After a volcanic eruption, Hawaiian ecosystems can become re-established very quickly. Sword ferns can be found on lava flows within a year, and other plants and trees soon follow. One day these small green shoots will form the basis of a lush forest, thriving in the rich volcanic soil. That which at first glance appears destructive the Creator uses to nurture new life.

Heading Out

Depression may seem like a disaster bound to destroy you, but it needn't be. I realize a trek through the land of emotional and spiritual illness can be very frightening. The future looks bleak from that rock-hard wasteland. However, even in the hardest, blackest earth, life grows.

Sometimes the journey out of the wasteland is long, but it isn't far; you may be one discovery of truth, one choice to forgive, or one listening prayer away from freedom. The future may look bleak to you, but there's so much you've yet to see. Right now as you stand on the scorched earth, seeds of life are waiting to sprout beneath your feet. Don't lose heart, my friend. What you have been through will not be wasted. God can work all things for your good (see Romans 8:28), and He will most surely use your experience, one day, for someone else's good. Paul tells us how God does this:

> All praise to the God and Father of our Master, Jesus the Messiah! Father of all mercy! God of all healing counsel! He

comes alongside us when we go through hard times, and before you know it, he brings us alongside someone else who is going through hard times so that we can be there for that person just as God was there for us. (2 Corinthians 1:3-4, MSG)

A Better Life

I've had trials since my depression ended, and I'm sure I will continue to while I live on this earth. But I have to believe that the God who delivered me in the past will be there for me each day of my future. I trust Him to give me the strength to keep pressing on. I love the way Paul describes this journey:

I'm not saying that I have this all together, that I have it made. But I am well on my way, reaching out for Christ, who has so wondrously reached out for me.

Friends, don't get me wrong: By no means do I count myself an expert in all of this, but I've got my eye on the goal, where God is beckoning us onward—to Jesus. I'm off and running, and I'm not turning back. (Philippians 3:12-14, MSG)

I still have a long way to go until I'm all that God created me to be, but now I understand that I cannot become that person in my own power. No amount of obsessiveness or self-abuse, performing, or perfectionism will get me one step closer. Every measure of growth I have achieved in life thus far has come through pain. We don't have to look at trials as punishment, signs of failure, or harbingers of doom—they are for good, for growth, and for God's glory. Pain is a launching pad to a better life.

For me, there were many years when depression seemed like a grueling trek through a dark and devastating wilderness. But I can now see new life springing forth from jagged cracks in my crusty soul. Though not yet a lush, beautiful forest, I continue to grow. And I now understand that the lessons I so desperately needed to learn could be taught no other way than through burning fire and flame. Though badly blistered, I was not consumed (see Isaiah 43:1-3, NLT). As I sink my roots deep into the fertile soil of what was once a wasteland, I realize that life can, and does, rise up from the ashes.

The Creator has a good plan for you, too. Your path to freedom from depression may resemble the one He led me along or it may be different, but God can give you back your life. You are not defeated. You are not defenseless.

With God's help, you can:

- Accept your limitations
- Be prepared for your spiritual enemy's attacks
- Believe in your God-given worth
- Trust your heavenly Father to take care of you
- Choose to forgive those who have caused you pain
- Accept godly counsel
- Invite Christ to break the bonds of spiritual oppression
- Receive truth
- Nourish your spirit
- Cultivate a life of balance

Each of these steps will bring you closer to the life of peace and wholeness that God offers.

Are you ready to receive it? Are you ready to move forward? Someone is waiting to lead you to freedom.

Arise, my darling, my beautiful one, and come with me.
See! The winter is past; the rains are over and gone.
Flowers appear on the earth; the season of singing has come. . . .
Arise, come, my darling; my beautiful one, come with me. (Song of Songs 2:10-13)

RECOMMENDED RESOURCES

FOR DEPRESSION

Neil T. Anderson, *The Bondage Breaker* (Eugene, OR: Harvest House, 1993).

Neil T. Anderson, *Victory Over the Darkness: Realizing the Power of Your Identity in Christ* (Ventura, CA: Regal, 2000).

David Cox and Candy Arrington, *Aftershock: Help, Hope, and Healing in the Wake of Suicide* (Nashville: B&H Publishing, 2003).

Grant Mullen, MD, *Emotionally Free* (Grand Rapids, MI: Chosen Books, 2003).

Brad Jersak, *Fear No Evil* (Abbotsford, BC: Fresh Wind Press, 2005).

Brad Jersak, *Can You Hear Me? Tuning In to the God Who Speaks* (Abbotsford, BC: Fresh Wind Press, 2003).

Harold S. Koplewicz, MD, *More Than Moody: Recognizing and Treating Adolescent Depression* (New York: Perigee, 2002).

James B. Richards, *How to Stop the Pain* (New Kensington, PA: Whitaker House, 2001).

Anne Sheffield, *How You Can Survive When They're Depressed* (New York: Three Rivers Press, 1998).

Anne Sheffield, *Sorrow's Web: Hope, Help, and Understanding for Depressed Mothers and Their Children* (New York: Fireside, 2000).

WEBSITES

Freedom in Christ Ministries, http://www.ficm.org

Freedom in Christ Canada, http://www.ficm.ca

FOR SPIRITUAL GROWTH

Mark Buchanan, *The Rest of God* (Nashville: W Publishing, 2006).

Jerome Daley, *Soul Space* (Brentwood, TN: Integrity, 2003).

Richard J. Foster, *Celebration of Discipline* (New York: HarperSanFransisco, 1998).

FOR MOOD DISORDERS, ADDICTIONS, AND SPIRITUAL GROWTH

James E. Robinson, *Coming Home to a Place Called Hope: A Journey for the Wounded Soul* (Franklin, TN: Good Apple Press, 2008).

James E. Robinson and Sherry G. Thomas, *Coming Home to a Place Called Hope: A Companion Guide for Your Personal Journey to Hope* (Franklin, TN: Good Apple Press, 2008).

James Eugene Robinson, *Prodigal Song* (Franklin, TN: Good Apple Press, 2003).

WEBSITE

ProdigalSong: Healing the Broken Spirit, http://www.prodigalsong
.com

FOR ENCOURAGEMENT

Jerome Daley, *When God Waits* (Colorado Springs, CO: WaterBrook, 2005).

Max Lucado, *A Gentle Thunder: Hearing God Through the Storm* (Dallas: Word, 1995).

Max Lucado, *You Are Special* (Wheaton, IL: Crossway, 1997).

Joni Eareckson Tada and Steven Estes, *When God Weeps: Why Our Sufferings Matter to the Almighty* (Grand Rapids, MI: Zondervan, 1997).

WEBSITE

Father's Love Letter: An Intimate Message from God to You, http://
www.fathersloveletter.com

HOW TO HELP A LOVED ONE WHO *Is* DEPRESSED

I f you have a loved one who is depressed, you probably feel confused about what you can do to make life easier for her (or him). Here are some suggestions for how you can help:

EDUCATE YOURSELF

Learn as much as you can about depression, and stay informed about advances in treatment.

ADVOCATE TREATMENT

Encourage your loved one to seek professional help or, if already undergoing treatment, to stick with it. If she has been prescribed medication and has difficulty remembering to take it, gently remind her.

Encourage your loved one to incorporate godly spiritual counseling into her treatment plan. (You can read about its importance in chapter 11 of this book.) Help set realistic expectations about treatment. It may take weeks before medication takes effect; progress with counseling is also gradual.

If your loved one refuses to seek treatment, don't harass and nag or you will soon be perceived as part of the problem. Instead, tell her how much you miss the "real person" she is and that you long for the good times the illness has stolen from both of you.[1]

ASSESS TREATMENT

Together, evaluate the treatment your loved one is receiving. Skillful doctors have a variety of ways to help people and are willing to work with patients to create individual treatment programs that meet their needs. A good doctor will be willing to explain the treatment being offered and answer the patient's (and loved one's) questions. She will also seek input from the patient in order to aid in the evaluation of treatment.

A trustworthy doctor will be comfortable directing your loved one to other specialists for additional treatment. No doctor is extensively trained in every aspect of mental health care. Reputable physicians and therapists are aware of their own limitations in education and experience and are willing to seek a second opinion if a patient does not seem to be responding to treatment.

If your loved one is seeing a counselor, it's important to evaluate progress. You can read about how to help her do that in the "Measuring Success" section in chapter 11 (see pages 165–166).

BE PREPARED TO SACRIFICE (IT'S NO LONGER FIFTY-FIFTY)

Don't be surprised if your loved one doesn't take your feelings into consideration or if you no longer can count on her to contribute to the relationship. Among many things, depression causes negativity, exhaustion, and a desire to withdraw. If this is the kind of behavior your loved one is exhibiting, the illness is to blame. When she recovers, she will be appreciative of all you did to support her during this difficult time.

BE A LOVING, ATTENTIVE PARENT TO THE CHILDREN YOU SHARE

Though love is not diminished, depression limits a parent's ability to be nurturing, affectionate, and patient. This can have a serious impact on children. (In chapter 5, you can read about how parental depression affects children and how to help them cope.) Until your loved one can resume her role as a warm, involved parent, your children need you to be willing to play the role of two parents, to do what you can to assure them of their worth, and show them they are loved.

My daughter Lauren offers this advice:

Pay lots of attention to your children. Talk a lot just about stuff: how their day was, friends, and so on. Be as "normal" as possible, but don't ignore the fact that there is a depressed parent. It's a big deal. You can't pretend the depression doesn't exist.

Discipline and structure are also important for children. Though they complain about it, they are lost without it. Knowing what parents expect from them is reassuring to children and shows that you care about what they do. Parents with depression find it difficult to deal with the drama that often accompanies disciplining. If that's the case in your household, it's important for you to step in and pick up the slack,[2] holding children to the behavior that was expected of them prior to their parent's depression.

Make sure children complete homework assignments and get help with their studies when needed. Stick to rules about television viewing, time spent chatting on computer and telephone, chores, and bedtime.

ACCEPT AND LOVE

Assure your spouse of your love and acceptance, no matter how she feels about herself. Commit to seeing her through this experience with depression.

PRAY

Praying for your loved one is the most powerful thing you can do. Bring your concerns before God and ask for His help.

BE PRACTICAL

People who are depressed are easily overwhelmed, by even the simplest tasks. Pitch in with things such as dressing the children for school, making meals, and doing the laundry.

ENCOURAGE INVOLVEMENT

Invite your loved one to participate in activities she used to enjoy, but don't force it. You may find that your "gentle insistence" is met with fierce resistance. Don't take it personally; your loved one may be overwhelmed and frightened by the prospect of being expected to do something she feels incapable of accomplishing.

LISTEN

Be available to listen, but don't try to be a therapist. Your role is to provide support and unconditional love; therapy needs to be conducted by a professional.

DON'T ARGUE

A person with depression is brimming with pessimism and sees nothing but obstacles. If you tell your loved one that everything is going fine in her life, she will believe that you're illogical and that you don't understand; she may feel like a failure for being depressed with the life everyone else thinks is wonderful. Telling depressed people that they should count their blessings and feel grateful for all God's given them is one of the worst things you can do. "Singing cheerful songs to a person whose heart is heavy is as bad as stealing someone's jacket in cold weather or rubbing salt in a wound" (Proverbs 25:20, NLT).

The best approach is to tell your loved one that you're sorry everything looks so bleak to her but that this feeling stems from the depression and that things will get better. This offers affirmation that you have heard her and hope that relief will eventually come.

BE VIGILANT

Depression is a serious, life-threatening illness. Sufferers can slip into hopelessness very quickly, sometimes without others noticing. Look for signs that your loved one's mood may be further deteriorating. If she is in treatment and begins skipping appointments, refuses help, or becomes nonfunctional, hospitalization may be necessary.

If your loved one seems preoccupied with death or talks about suicide, seek immediate help and don't leave her alone. Remove any weapons or large amounts of medication. Call a suicide hotline or your loved one's doctor or counselor. In a crisis situation, call 911 or go to the nearest hospital emergency room. See resources offering help and support for those who suspect someone is suicidal, listed at the end of chapter 4.

HOW TO HELP YOURSELF WHEN CARING *for* A DEPRESSED LOVED ONE

Living with a spouse, parent, or child who views the world through the dark lens of depression is extremely discouraging and even damaging. Eventually, you begin to experience similar feelings to those the illness provokes in the depressed individual: worthlessness and the inability to enjoy or cope with life.

Though it's been known for some time that stress can contribute to depression, researchers now know that the stress of caring for someone who has a mental illness can trigger depression in the caregiver. A study sponsored by the National Institute of Mental Health looked at family members and close friends of people with depression, bipolar disorder, and schizophrenia and found that 40 percent of caregivers exhibited symptoms strong enough to qualify them as being seriously depressed. Many other caregivers were somewhat depressed or at serious risk of becoming so.[1]

To avoid becoming another victim of depression fallout, it's imperative you make every effort to take care of yourself while caring for your loved one. Here's how:

TAKE CARE OF YOUR BODY

Eat nutritious food, exercise, and get adequate rest. Being in good physical shape will give you the stamina you need to deal with your challenging life circumstances.

ENLIST SUPPORT

You may need assistance with your children, help with household chores, or even a reprieve from some of the work you do for your church. Don't be afraid to ask for help if it will relieve some of the added pressure you're under.

DON'T KEEP IT A SECRET

You don't have to tell the world the details of your loved one's limitations and behavior, but don't try to cover up the fact that your family is facing the challenge of dealing with depression. How will you get support, encouragement, and prayer if you keep this a secret? In being open, you may discover other families in the same situation.

INTERACT WITH OTHERS FACING SIMILAR CHALLENGES

Becoming a member of a support group and listening to others' stories may give you new strategies for coping and help you realize you're not alone.

FIND AN OUTLET

One of the hazards of pouring your energy into someone who's depressed is there seems to be no return on the investment. People with depression characteristically do not offer positive feedback or gratitude, and this can cause you to feel worthless and ineffective. Reward yourself by finding something you do well and doing it for people who are in a position to appreciate your efforts. Volunteering is one way to accomplish this. The objective is not to abandon your loved one but to do something that will make you feel like a good, intelligent, generous individual.[2]

RELY ON GOD

Ask God to give you the strength to deal with the turmoil a loved one's depression presents and to keep your commitment to your loved one strong. Release the situation to Him and ask for His guidance and help.

TAKE CARE OF YOUR MIND AND SPIRIT

Be aware of the symptoms of burnout and depression; if you are exhibiting any, seek help. It may be a good idea for you to see a counselor or family therapist to learn ways to cope with your depressed loved one and the added stress you are under.

Though you can do much to support someone with depression, the only person you can take responsibility for is you. When you attend to your own needs—physical, emotional, and spiritual—you'll be in a far better position to cope with and care for the people you love.

NOTES

CHAPTER 1: CAUGHT IN THE DELUGE OF DEPRESSION

1. Postpartum depression "can begin at any time between delivery and 6 months post-birth, and may last up to several months or even a year." Canadian Mental Health Association, "Post Partum Depression," 2008, http://www.cmha.ca/bins/content_page .asp?cid=3-86-87-88 (accessed May 17, 2008).

CHAPTER 2: SEEKING UNDERSTANDING

1. The term "burden of disease" refers to the "overall impact of diseases and injuries at the individual level, at the societal level, or to the economic costs of diseases." World Health Organization, "Glossary of Globalization, Trade and Health Terms: Global Burden of Disease," http://www.who.int/trade/glossary/story036/ en/ (accessed July 31, 2006).
2. M. Peden, K. McGee, and E. Krug, eds., "Injury: A Leading Cause of the Global Burden of Disease, 2000," (Geneva: World Health Organization, 2002), http://whqlibdoc.who.int/ publications/2002/9241562323.pdf (accessed July 31, 2006).
3. Peden, McGee, and Krug.
4. National Mental Health Association, "American Attitudes About Clinical Depression and Its Treatment," March 27, 1996, cited in NMHA Fact Sheet, "Depression: Depression in Women," March 2000, http://www.nmha.org/infoctr/factsheets/23.cfm (accessed July 31, 2006).
5. "National Healthcare Quality Report," 2003, cited by Bob Murray, PhD, and Alicia Fortinberry, MS, in *Uplift Program*, http://www.upliftprogram.com/depression_stats.html (accessed July 31, 2006).
6. National Mental Health Association study reported in *MSNBC*

Health Today, March 10, 2004, cited by Bob Murray, PhD, and Alicia Fortinberry, MS, in *Uplift Program*, http://www .upliftprogram.com/depression_stats.html (accessed July 31, 2006).

7. "Army Corps Takes Blame for New Orleans Katrina Flooding," June 1, 2006, www.foxnews.com/story/0,2933,197783,00.html (accessed August 17, 2007).

8. Anderson Cooper, *Dispatches from the Edge* (New York: HarperCollins, 2006), 175.

9. Frank Minirth, MD, and Paul Meier, MD, *Happiness Is a Choice* (Grand Rapids, MI: Revell, 1994), 122.

10. Melinda Smith and Jaelline Jaffe, PhD, "Causes of Depression: Biological, Psychological, and Social Factors," 2007, http://www .helpguide.org/mental/causes_depression.htm (accessed February 9, 2008).

11. Smith and Jaffe.

12. Smith and Jaffe.

13. Michael Card, *A Sacred Sorrow* (Colorado Springs, CO: NavPress, 2005), 120.

14. Kenneth Barker, ed., *The NIV Study Bible* (Grand Rapids, MI: Zondervan, 1985), 1215.

15. Compiled from NIV, NLT, GNT, MSG, and NCV.

16. Card, 109.

CHAPTER 3: GOOD NEWS ABOUT DEPRESSION

1. C. S. Lewis, as quoted by ThinkExist.com, http://www .thinkexist.com/quotes/with/keyword/turn_out/ (accessed April 8, 2008).

2. Charles R. Swindoll, *God's Provision in Time of Need* (Nashville: Word, 1997), 85.

CHAPTER 4: THE BATTLE BETWEEN LIFE AND DEATH

1. World Health Organization, "Suicide Prevention," http://www .who.int/mental_health/prevention/suicide/suicideprevent/en/ (accessed May 31, 2007).

2. World Health Organization.

3. World Health Organization.

4. National Institute of Mental Health, "Suicide in the U.S.:

Statistics and Prevention," 2004 statistics, http://www.nimh.nih
.gov/health/publications/suicide-in-the-us-statistics-and-preven-
tion.shtml (accessed December 3, 2007).

5. Centers for Disease Control and Prevention, "Eliminate
Disparities in Mental Health," http://www.cdc.gov/omhd/AMH/
factsheets/mental.htm (accessed December 12, 2007).

6. National Institute of Mental Health.

7. Centers for Disease Control and Prevention, "Suicide Facts at a
Glance," Summer 2007, http://www.cdc.gov/ncipc/dvp/suicide/
SuicideDataSheet.pdf (accessed December 3, 2007).

8. National Institute of Mental Health.

9. Compiled from: National Institute of Mental Health, "Suicide in
the U.S.: Statistics and Prevention"; Suicide and Mental Health
Association International, "Suicide Prevention for Physicians,"
http://suicideandmentalhealthassociationinternational.org/
preventionphy.html (accessed June 4, 2007); and David Cox
and Candy Arrington, *Aftershock* (Nashville: B&H Publishing,
2003), 103.

10. Stop a Suicide.org, "Signs of Suicide," 2006, http://www
.stopasuicide.org/signs.aspx (accessed February 26, 2008).

11. Greg Garrett, *Crossing Myself* (Colorado Springs, CO: NavPress,
2006), 51.

12. Cox and Arrington, 1.

13. Cox and Arrington, 5.

14. Job 3:26.

15. Job 30:16, NLT.

16. Job 9:21.

17. Job 10:1.

18. Dale Carnegie, as quoted in Simran Khurana, "Quotes About
Commitment," http://quotations.about.com/cs/inspiration-
quotes/a/bls_Inspiration.htm (accessed December 3, 2007).

CHAPTER 5: WIFE AND MOTHER GONE AWOL

1. Myrna M. Weissman, et al., "Remissions in Maternal Depression
and Child Psychopathology," *JAMA* 295 (March 22/29, 2006):
1389–1398.

2. Mental Health: A Report of the Surgeon General, "Depression
and Suicide in Children and Adolescents," http://mentalhealth

.samhsa.gov/features/surgeongeneralreport/chapter3/sec5.asp
(accessed May 21, 2008). If the parent's depression began before
twenty years of age, the children's risk may be up to nine times
higher. [Findings from study conducted by Myrna Weissman,
Professor of Epidemiology and Psychiatry at Columbia
University, cited by Anne Sheffield, *Sorrow's Web* (New York:
Fireside, 2000), 118-119].

3. Anne Sheffield, *Sorrow's Web* (New York: Fireside, 2000), 31.
4. Sheffield, *Sorrow's Web*, 116.
5. Sheffield, *Sorrow's Web*, 129.
6. Anne Sheffield, *How You Can Survive When They're Depressed* (New York: Three Rivers Press, 1998), 13.
7. Sheffield, *How You Can Survive*, 6.
8. Sheffield, *Sorrow's Web*, 133–134.
9. Dictionary.com Unabridged, s.v. "demoralize," (accessed August 6, 2007).
10. Jerome Daley, *Soul Space* (Brentwood, TN: Integrity, 2003), 129.
11. Albert Ellis, as quoted by Quoteland.com, http://www .quoteland.com (accessed March 13, 2008).

STORY OF HOPE JOHN BUL DAU: THE POWER OF HOPE

1. John Bul Dau, *God Grew Tired of Us* (Washington, DC: National Geographic, 2007), 4.
2. More than two million of southern Sudan's six million people were killed in the civil war that began in 1983, and four million were forced to flee their homes, 600,000 ending up as refugees in neighboring countries. United Nations, "United Nations Mission in the Sudan," 2007, http://www.un.org/Depts/dpko/missions/ unmis/background.html (accessed March 24, 2008).
3. Michael Ordoña, "Finding Their Way," *LA Times*, January 5, 2007, http://www.johndaufoundation.org/LATimes.htm (accessed March 22, 2008).
4. Dau, 135.
5. Dau, 7.
6. Dau, 138.
7. John Dau's journey from the refugee camp to life in the United States and his encounter with American culture are captured in

the award-winning documentary *God Grew Tired of Us*.

8. Dau, 7.
9. John Dau, as quoted in "John Bul Dau—Humanitarian/ Survivor," *National Geographic in the Field*, January 2007, http:// www.nationalgeographic.com/field/explorers/john-bul-dau.html (accessed March 22, 2008).

CHAPTER 6: SPIRITUAL MALNOURISHMENT

1. National Eating Disorders Association, "Anorexia Nervosa," 2006, http://www.nationaleatingdisorders.org/p.asp?WebPage _ID=320&Profile_ID=41142 (accessed March 1, 2008).
2. National Eating Disorders Association, "Causes of Eating Disorders," 2006, http://www.nationaleatingdisorders.org/ p.asp?WebPage_ID=320&Profile_ID=41144 (accessed March 1, 2008).
3. Richard J. Foster, *Celebration of Discipline* (New York: HarperSanFransisco, 1998), 102.
4. Compilation of verses from NCV, MSG, NLT, NIV, GNT.

CHAPTER 7: LOW SELF-WORTH

1. This practice is recommended by Tom G. Stevens, PhD, in his book *You Can Choose to Be Happy*, http://www.csulb .edu/~tstevens/h51worth.htm (accessed February 1, 2008).
2. Stevens.
3. "Self-esteem check: Too low, too high or just right?" July 24, 2007, http://www.mayoclinic.com/health/self-esteem/MH00128 (accessed February 1, 2008); and James J. Messina, PhD, and Constance M. Messina, PhD, "The SEA's Program Model of Self-Esteem," www.coping.org/selfesteem/tools/model.htm (accessed February 1, 2008).
4. Stevens.
5. Messina and Messina.
6. James J. Messina, PhD, and Constance M. Messina, PhD, "Laying the Foundation: Non-Feeling Personality," http://www .coping.org/lowesteem/nonfeel.htm (accessed February 1, 2008).
7. James J. Messina, PhD, and Constance M. Messina, PhD, "Laying the Foundation: People-Pleasing Personality," http:// www.coping.org/lowesteem/please.htm (accessed February 1,

2008).

8. James J. Messina, PhD, and Constance M. Messina, PhD, "Laying the Foundation: Looking Good Personality," http://www.coping.org/lowesteem/look.htm (accessed February 1, 2008).

9. Messina and Messina, "Looking Good Personality."

10. Jennifer Drapkin, "The Pitfalls of Perfectionism," *Psyched for Success*, September 1, 2005, http://www.psychologytoday.com/articles/pto-20050919-000005.html (accessed February 22, 2007).

11. Jerome Daley, *Soul Space* (Brentwood, TN: Integrity, 2003), 120.

12. Brennan Manning, *The Rabbi's Heartbeat* (Colorado Springs, CO: NavPress, 2003), 13.

13. Messina and Messina, "Model of Self-Esteem."

14. See Ephesians 1:4-5, MSG.

15. Paraphrase and compilation of Psalm 149:4, NLT; 1 John 3:1, NLT; Isaiah 40:11, NLT; Isaiah 49:13, NCV; Isaiah 49:16, GNT; 1 John 4:9; Romans 5:8, GNT; Romans 5:5, GNT; 2 Corinthians 6:16, NLT; Romans 8:31, MSG; Ephesians 3:18, NLT; Isaiah 54:10, GNT; Psalm 100:5.

CHAPTER 8: SHAME

1. The American Heritage® Dictionary of the English Language, Fourth Edition, s.v. "shame," (Houghton Mifflin Company, 2004).

2. Jan Luckingham Fable, "Shame," 1999, http://www.forhealing.org/shame.html (accessed March 17, 2008).

3. Ronald and Patricia Potter-Efron, *Letting Go of Shame* (San Francisco: Harper and Row, 1989), as quoted by Jan Luckingham Fable.

4. Fable.

5. William Backus, *Telling the Truth to Troubled People* (Minneapolis: Bethany, 1985), 75.

6. Robert Karen, "Shame," *The Atlantic Monthly*, February 1992: 40.

7. Karen, 42.

8. Fable.

9. Grant Mullen, MD, *Emotionally Free* (Grand Rapids, MI: Chosen Books, 2003), 17.

CHAPTER 9: FEAR

1. Brad Jersak, *Fear No Evil* (Abbotsford, BC: Fresh Wind Press, 2005), 71–73.
2. Michael Yaconelli, *Messy Spirituality* (Grand Rapids, MI: Zondervan, 2002), 123–124.
3. Charles F. Stuckey, *Claude Monet: 1840–1926* (The Art Institute of Chicago, 1995), 186.
4. Stuckey, 189.
5. Charles R. Swindoll, *God's Provision in Time of Need* (Nashville: Word, 1997), 7.
6. Charles Stanley, "The Secret of Being an Overcomer," April 23, 2005, http://www.intouch.org/intouch/site.show_page?p_id=76096&p_devotional_date=04%2F23%2F2005 (accessed May 11, 2007).
7. Charles Haddon Spurgeon, as quoted by QuotationsBook, http://quotationsbook.com/quote/add_to_site/42520/

CHAPTER 10: UNFORGIVENESS

1. A Campaign for Forgiveness Research, 2005, http://www.forgiving.org/Campaign/power.asp (accessed May 15, 2007).
2. A Campaign for Forgiveness Research.
3. A Campaign for Forgiveness Research.
4. Vicki Robb, "Study links forgiveness to less back pain, depression," *Medical News Today*, October 8, 2003, www.medicalnewstoday.com/medicalnews.php?newsid=4446 (accessed May 15, 2007).
5. Robb.
6. Prevention Magazine Health Books, *Age Erasers for Women*, as quoted by MotherNature.com, 2007, http://www.mothernature.com/Library/Bookshelf/Books/44/86.cfm (accessed May 15, 2007).
7. A Campaign for Forgiveness Research.
8. Neil Anderson, *Discipleship Counseling* (Ventura, CA: Regal, 2003), 263.
9. Reverend Majed El-Shafie, "Testimony of Persecution,"

interview with Willard Thiessen, *It's a New Day*, September 1, 2006, Program #31253.

10. Spiros Zodhiales et. al., eds., *The Complete Word Study Dictionary: New Testament* (Chattanooga, TN: AMG Publishers, 1992), 299, as quoted by Beth Moore, *Living Beyond Yourself* (Nashville: LifeWay, 1998), 120.

11. Anderson, 262.

12. Anderson, 259–261.

STORY OF HOPE IMMACULÉE ILIBAGIZA: THE POWER OF FORGIVENESS

1. Immaculée Ilibagiza, *Left to Tell* (Carlsbad, CA: Hay House, 2006), 39–40.

2. Ilibagiza, 92.

3. Ilibagiza, 94.

4. "Rwanda: The Wake of a Genocide," 2008, http://www .rwanda-genocide.org/index.html (accessed March 6, 2008).

5. Ilibagiza, 204.

6. Ilibagiza, 204.

7. Ilibagiza, 204.

8. Ilibagiza, 204.

9. Dr. Wayne W. Dyer, as quoted by Grace Matters, "Guest Interviews," 2008, http://www.gracematters.org/interviews/i .ilibagiza.html (accessed March 10, 2008).

10. Dr. Christiane Northrup as quoted by *Grace Matters*, "Guest Interviews," 2008, http://www.gracematters.org/interviews/i .ilibagiza.html (accessed March 10, 2008).

11. Ilibagiza, 197.

CHAPTER 11: SPIRITUAL COUNSELING

1. Rob Jackson, "Who Needs It? The Importance of Counseling," 2004, http://www.pureintimacy.org/gr/intimacy/redemption/ a0000153.cfm (accessed August 13, 2007).

2. Jim Robinson, "Looking for a Christian Counselor?" 2005, http://prodigalsong.com/articles/article-Looking%20for%20a %20Counselor.htm (accessed August 13, 2007).

3. Rob Jackson, "Guidelines for Selecting a Counselor," 2004, http://www.pureintimacy.org/gr/intimacy/redemption/a0000152 .cfm (accessed August 13, 2007).

4. Jackson, "Who Needs It?"

5. Jackson, "Who Needs It?"

6. Robinson, "Looking for a Christian Counselor?"

CHAPTER 12: DELIVERANCE MINISTRY

1. Neil T. Anderson, *The Bondage Breaker* (Eugene, OR: Harvest House, 1990), 188–209.

2. Chester and Betsy Kylstra, *Biblical Healing and Deliverance* (Grand Rapids, MI: Chosen Books, 2003), 15–16.

3. Anderson, 199–201.

4. Compilation of verses from GNT and NLT.

5. The Barna Group, "Beliefs: Trinity, Satan," http://www.barna .org/FlexPage.aspx?Page=Topic&TopicID=6 (accessed September 11, 2007).

6. Anderson, 21.

7. See Matthew 9:32; 12:22,28; 15:22,28; Mark 1:39; 5:2-13; 7:26-30; 16:19; Luke 4:33-35; 9:42; 11:20; 13:12-16.

8. See Matthew 4:24, 8:16.

9. Psalm 31:9, MSG.

10. Psalm 109:22, MSG.

11. Psalm 109:22, MSG.

12. Psalm 31:4, MSG.

13. Psalm 143:9, MSG.

14. http://www.ficm.org/newsite/index.php?command= textwhoamiinchrist. At time of writing, this site was being updated; the address for the "Who Am I in Christ?" page may have changed by the time you read this book. It may be accessible through the Freedom in Christ Ministries homepage at http:// www.ficm.org.

CHAPTER 13: LISTENING PRAYER FOR INNER HEALING

1. National Association of Cognitive Behavioral Therapists, "What Is Cognitive-Behavioral Therapy?" http://www.nacbt.org/ whatiscbt.htm (accessed October 3, 2007).

2. Some call it "prayer ministry," "prayer counseling," "mind renewal," or "healing of memories." Others have copyrighted a name for their particular approach (for example, Ed Smith's "Theophostic Prayer Ministry").

3. Brad Jersak explains the process of listening prayer for inner healing in detail in chapter 13 of his book *Can You Hear Me?* (Abbotsford, BC: Fresh Wind Press, 2003).

4. Brad Jersak, *Fear No Evil* (Abbotsford, BC: Fresh Wind Press, 2005), 77.

5. Walter A. Elwell, "Entry for 'Know, Knowledge,'" *Evangelical Dictionary of Theology*, 1997, http://bible.crosswalk.com/ Dictionaries/BakersEvangelicalDictionary/bed.cgi?number=T414 (accessed April 8, 2008).

6. Elwell.

7. John Wesley. "Commentary on John 8," *John Wesley's Explanatory Notes on the Whole Bible*, 1765, http://bible .crosswalk.com/Commentaries/WesleysExplanatoryNotes/wes .cgi?book=joh&chapter=008 (accessed March 8, 2008); and Barton W. Johnson, "Commentary on John 8," *People's New Testament*, 1891, http://bible.crosswalk.com/Commentaries/ PeoplesNewTestament/pnt.cgi?book=joh&chapter=008 (accessed March 8, 2008).

8. Compiled from Ken and Carolee Neufeld, Helping Others Find Freedom in Christ Facilitator Training Workshop, guidelines and supplementary materials for those who are spiritual encouragers using the *Steps to Freedom in Christ* as a guide, 17; and Grant Mullen, *Emotionally Free* (Grand Rapids, MI: Chosen Books, 2003), 97.

9. Jersak, *Can You Hear Me?* 17–18.

10. For example, see Genesis 16 and 22; Judges 6 and 13; 2 Samuel 24; 1 Kings 19; Matthew 1–2; Luke 1.

11. See Daniel 5.

12. See Numbers 22:22-35.

13. Jersak, *Can You Hear Me?* 25–26.

14. Jersak, *Can You Hear Me?* 25.

15. C. S. Lewis, *The Problem of Pain* (New York: Macmillan, 1962), 93.

STORY OF HOPE JOHN STEPHEN AKHWARI: THE POWER OF PERSEVERANCE

1. John Stephen Akhwari, as quoted by Cui Xiaohuo, "A lasting memory: Tanzanian runner," *China Daily/The Olympian*,

January 11, 2008, http://www.chinadaily.com.cn/ olympics/2008-01/11/content_6388098.htm (accessed March 25, 2008).

2. Author unknown.

3. Akhwari.

CHAPTER 14: CONSISTENT SPIRITUAL SUSTENANCE

1. Richard Foster, *Celebration of Discipline* (New York: HarperSanFrancisco, 1998), v.

2. Foster, 63.

3. Max Lucado, *Just Like Jesus* (Nashville: Word, 1998), 49.

4. François Fénelon, as quoted by QuotationsBook, http://www .quotationsbook.com/quote/10865/ (accessed October 18, 2007).

5. Lucado, 70.

6. Martin Luther, as quoted by Foster, 34.

7. Al Siebert, PhD, *The Survivor Personality* (New York: Berkley Publishing, 1996), 213.

8. Beth Moore, *Living Free* (Nashville: LifeWay, 2001), 84.

9. Foster, 20–21.

10. Foster, 17.

11. See Joshua 1:8.

12. See Genesis 24:63.

13. See Psalm 63:6.

14. See Psalm 48:9.

15. See Psalm 77:11-12; 143:5.

16. See Psalm119:15,23,48,78.

17. See Psalm 119:148.

18. David Jeremiah, *Life Wide Open* (Nashville: Integrity, 2003), 153–154.

19. Foster, 2.

CHAPTER 15: THE FINE ART OF BALANCE

1. Mark Buchanan, *The Rest of God* (Nashville: W Publishing, 2006), 196.

2. National Institute of Mental Health, "Stress Impairs Thinking Via Mania-Linked Enzyme," October 29, 2004, http://www .nimh.nih.gov/science-news/2004/stress-impairs-thinking-via-mania-linked-enzyme.shtml (accessed October 30, 2007).

3. American Heart Association, "Self-reported stress linked with fatal stroke; unhealthy habits may be factor," Stroke Journal Report, March 14, 2003, http://www.americanheart.org/presenter.jhtml?identifier=3009979 (accessed October 30, 2007).

4. American Heart Association, "High mental stress linked with increased risk of cardiovascular death," Journal Report, August 7, 2002, http://www.americanheart.org/presenter.jhtml?identifier=3004252 (accessed October 30, 2007).

5. The American Institute of Stress, "America's No. 1 Health Problem," http://www.stress.org/americas.htm?AIS=572d66d4337d2250fdc0921b7601343c (accessed October 30, 2007).

6. Michael Yaconelli, *Messy Spirituality* (Grand Rapids, MI: Zondervan, 2002), 97.

7. Fil Anderson, "Resisting a Rest," *InTouch*, August 2006, 14.

8. Jerome Daley, *Soul Space* (Brentwood, TN: Integrity, 2003), 102.

9. Dr. Phil McGraw, "Why You Deserve a Break Today—If Not Sooner," *O*, July 2005, 30.

10. Mark Buchanan's *The Rest of God*, 88–92, inspired these observations.

APPENDIX B: HOW TO HELP A LOVED ONE WHO IS DEPRESSED

1. Anne Sheffield, *How You Can Survive When They're Depressed* (New York: Three Rivers Press, 1998), 83.

2. Anne Sheffield, *Sorrow's Web* (New York: Fireside, 2000), 209.

APPENDIX C: HOW TO HELP YOURSELF WHEN CARING FOR A DEPRESSED LOVED ONE

1. Anne Sheffield, *How You Can Survive When They're Depressed* (New York: Three Rivers Press, 1998), 33.

2. Sheffield, *How You Can Survive*, 151–152.

AUTHOR

SHARON L. FAWCETT is a compelling communicator who offers words of hope through powerful messages on national television and radio as well as in print. She has published stories in *Silver Linings: Breaking Through the Clouds of Depression*, *God Answers Prayers*, and *God Allows U-Turns for Women* and articles in magazines, including *Today's Christian Woman* and *Beyond Ordinary Living*.

Sharon's expertise in depression is hard earned. She battled the illness for nine years, enduring more than one hundred shock treatments, nearly twenty antidepressant medications, and twenty months as a patient in hospital psychiatric wards before finding lasting freedom through the discovery and treatment of her depression's spiritual roots. Sharon also understands the illness from the perspective of a loved one, spending the last six years caring for two daughters with depression. Passionate about humanitarian and environmental issues, Sharon renews her spirit through time spent observing nature and bicycle rides through the country near her home in New Brunswick, Canada, where she lives with her family between the forest and the sea. Visit her website at SharonFawcett.com.

More on spiritual growth for women!

Thirsty

Amy Nappa
ISBN-13: 978-1-60006-093-9
ISBN-10: 1-60006-093-5

There must be something more to life than desert sands and dry heat. Jesus explained to the woman at the well that she needed living water. Amy Nappa writes to women with this thirst, helping them renew their sense of personal worth in light of Scripture.

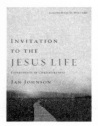

Invitation to the Jesus Life

Jan Johnson
ISBN-13: 978-1-60006-146-2
ISBN-10: 1-60006-146-X

It's easy to learn a little something about Jesus, but to encounter him on a daily basis changes everything. No longer can we live with the same earthly behavior or attitude. Our focus becomes eternal. Jan Johnson helps you experience Jesus in such a way that his love-drenched, others-focused nature shapes your character.

More Than Me

Jim Petersen, Glenn McMahan, David Russ
ISBN-13: 978-1-60006-265-0
ISBN-10: 1-60006-265-2

Life is about relationships, but we increasingly see them broken and suffering. *More Than Me* explains how relationships can become whole with four divinely appointed principles: love, integrity, humility, and forgiveness.

Job

THE SOURCE OF WISDOM

CWR

Elizabeth Rundle

Contents

Introduction

The book of Job has been called one of the greatest works in world literature. Most scholars consider it to be the oldest book in the Bible, and without doubt, Job is one of the most tragic and memorable biblical characters. As a young Christian I saw Job as a miserable and depressing book; all that doom and gloom seemed to have no place within the message of salvation. Where was the joy of the Lord? Now, from the standpoint of experience, I am aware of the power of this story to confront the perennial challenge of indiscriminate suffering.

From the atrocities of warfare to the terrifying results of hurricanes, floods and fires – why do catastrophic things happen to good people? Life can be so unfair. It seems to be in our human DNA to look for someone to blame, and Job blames God. Job's life plummets spectacularly from family happiness, wealth and respectability to devastating personal loss and debilitating disease. Yet from the depths of his suffering in body, mind and soul, Job utters a sublime statement of faith: 'I know that my redeemer lives' (19:25).

The wealth portrayed by cattle, camels and flocks could date Job around the time of the patriarchs, well before the time of Moses – or possibly earlier. Some of the Hebrew words in this book appear nowhere else in the Bible, making it difficult for scholars to determine their exact meaning. The hazy location of Uz was probably somewhere far to the south of Canaan, but the author of this compelling and unforgettable story was far from hazy in his purpose. His overriding mission was to portray the God of creation, not as some distant deity, but as the God who knows, sees and cares.

Nevertheless, Job is not an easy read. So shocking were the catastrophes Job suffered, and so remarkable his endurance,

we can understand how his life became immortalised in poetry. An odyssey passed from generation to generation, centuries before scribes committed the drama to written scrolls.

In Jewish Scripture, the book of Job is the first of the wisdom literature: poetry books we know as Psalms, Proverbs, Ecclesiastes and Song of Songs. All five books confront fundamental issues that face all of humanity, such as suffering, doubt, injustice and love, as well as other everyday issues. Job was mentioned by the prophet Ezekiel (14:14), by James in his epistle (5:11), and we can be sure that Jesus knew about him. He has become a role model for people clinging to faith by their fingertips. This great and godly man's story offers hope to the hopeless.

A dramatic prologue plunges us into a form of courtroom scene between heaven and earth. We need to think ourselves back not just hundreds of years but perhaps almost four thousand years into a world of nomads, farmers and artisans, straggling family clans and scattered urban dwellers. A world rife with superstition and multiple gods, yet a world where people, just like us today, sought meaning and purpose for their lives.

As we read speeches from Job's friends, Eliphaz, Bildad and Zophar, we see how deeply ingrained were the ideas of righteousness and reward, sin and retribution. Mixing sympathy with criticism, they tried to justify the disasters which had brought Job so low. Their arguments merged into grey areas of intellectual concepts, which in themselves sounded plausible enough, but ultimately Job's misery left them speechless. The fourth 'voice', Elihu, rings with a more refined spiritual insight. However, it is the 'blameless and upright' Job who draws us into his search for an answer to random suffering. Job rants and rages against the unfairness of life and the seeming inaccessibility of God; heart-wrenching cries which you may find resonate with your own experience.

There are no neat answers in Job, but glimpses can be caught of how God is beyond the gaps in our knowledge and our own, at times, struggling faith. In Isaiah, God says, 'For my thoughts are not your thoughts, neither are your ways my ways' (Isa. 55:8). In the face of suffering, a second-hand God is not enough. We need to find Him for ourselves.

I pray that Job's refusal to curse God for the unfairness of his situation may continue to be a source of inspiration for those struggling against unfairness in their own lives, or in the lives of others. Like Job's friends, we are often either speechless or talk too much with assumed authority about situations we don't understand. In these times we need to be honest about our doubts, and yes – dare to argue with God. This is our way to inner healing and deeper faith.

Trust, integrity, endurance, perseverance and faith are inadequate words to describe Job's journey, but they are nevertheless the aspiration for every believer. The timeless message within this book is relevant for every generation. So how can this book add to our faith journey? Job finally discovered his utter dependence on God, the creator and sustainer of all things. We are today's witnesses, privileged to keep alive this enigmatic, relevant story for those whose lives have fallen apart – and to claim its hope for ourselves.

WEEK ONE

The prologue

Opening Icebreaker

Which of health, wealth and happiness do you value the most and why? To what extent are they interdependent?

Bible Readings

- Job 1:1–22
- Job 2:1–13
- Romans 8:35–39

Opening Our Eyes

In terms of today's values, Job had everything. Life couldn't be better. The first five verses of this book paint a vivid picture of a wealthy, prosperous and godly man. Then suddenly we find ourselves plunged into a surreal scene between God, His angels and Satan. Instead of dismissing this account, let's consider the background and the purpose of this very odd, even alarming, vision.

Ancient thought placed God 'up' in heaven and humankind 'down' on earth. In the same way earthly kings summoned representatives to their courts and sent them out on missions, it was perfectly normal to accept that God would have heavenly beings to aid His divine business. Any and every natural event on earth was seen as God's direct decree, with a firmly entrenched belief that God rewarded goodness and punished sin; and your life reflected the category into which you fell.

The Lord God praises Job (1:8), to which Satan literally plays devil's advocate. By his remark in verse 9, Satan implies Job is a good man because life has worked to his advantage. Think of it this way: emerging from a supermarket, satisfied with the weekly shop, it's easy to praise God. But would your heart praise Him in the ruins of your home after a hurricane has claimed the lives of your loved ones and left you without food or shelter? This is the core of what Satan is getting at – it is far easier to trust God when things are going well than when skies are leaden and the rains of misery have chilled us into despair. He is convinced Job will turn from God when his life implodes.

Something easily overlooked in this prologue is the fact that not only did Job put his faith in God, but God had total faith in Job. More than this, Job is credited as being God's servant, which aligns him with the great men such as Moses (Exod. 14:31), David (2 Sam. 7:8) and Isaiah (Isa. 20:3).

The stage is set – Satan slinks off to prove he is right and God is wrong.

Then, as now, it is impossible to grasp heavenly motivations with our earth-bound minds. But, however unusual the conversation appears to be, as a dramatic prologue, it remains a vivid, memorable dialogue. Notice that Satan acts on his own accord, despite the interaction with God. However, this conversation between God and Satan offers us the assurance that when we face difficulties, God is present, aware, and isn't categorically dishing out punishment.

Faced with immense suffering, Job was reduced to an outcast. This man of integrity who had taken his seat at the city gate (29:7) and received respect from young and old now heard his wife urging him to curse God (2:9). But let's not be hard on Job's wife – remember she had lost everything too.

The sarcastic term 'Job's comforters' has entered our Christian vocabulary to mean friends who are actually of no comfort at all. We will discover more of the origin of this in future sessions. For now, what we see is that these friends cared enough to leave their homes to sit and weep with Job for seven days. Their shock was palpable, but they sat alongside their friend, willing to share in the ash heap.

Discussion Starters

1. What does the mention of sheep, camels, oxen, donkeys and servants tell you about Job's life?

2. In Psalm 26:11 David declares he has lead a blameless life. Compare Job's life with this.

3. What do you think the scene between God and Satan tells us about suffering?

4. Put yourself in the place of Job's wife. How would you feel?

5. How important is it to have friends that you can trust and talk to about absolutely anything? Are you that kind of friend to someone else?

_____

_____

_____

_____

_____

6. Satan was sure Job would turn away from God in the face of disaster. People today view disasters and tragedies as a reason to not believe in God. How can Christians respond to this view?

_____

_____

_____

_____

_____

7. Which verses in the Bible come into your mind in times of distress?

_____

_____

_____

_____

_____

Personal Application

Job's life challenges us to accept that our faith does not exclude us from the trauma of suffering – emotionally or physically. So when we do face this, do we crumble like Job's wife, blame God and despair, or do we seek to hold on to our faith no matter what? We cannot truly know the answer unless or until we have that experience, but our day-by-day walk with our Lord strengthens us to face such times. Throughout these studies we'll see how Job turned to God with his misery, and it is good for us to do the same. Draw courage from God's Word and pray for the Holy Spirit to support you and similarly lead you to deeper empathy with other people's suffering.

Seeing Jesus in the Scriptures

In God's description of Job, Job is 'blameless' and His 'servant' – words that speak to us of Jesus. The early Christians professed Jesus as the sinless Son of God. Paul wrote to the Corinthian believers: 'God made him who had no sin to be sin for us' (2 Cor. 5:21). Jesus became the sin offering for the world – for all of us. The reference to Job being God's servant underlines his complete obedience. Our Lord Jesus lived in perfect obedience and faithfulness, enduring our suffering and carrying the grief and sins of the world in the agonising pain of the cross.

For Reflection

'We are hard pressed on every side, but not crushed; perplexed, but not in despair; persecuted, but not abandoned; struck down, but not destroyed.' (2 Cor. 4:8–9)

WEEK TWO

'If I were you...'

Opening Icebreaker

What characteristics do you most value in a friend? What can a Christian uniquely offer their friends?

Bible Readings

- Job 3:11–19
- Job 4:1– 9,15–17
- Job 15:7–13
- Job 22:1–11,21–30
- Job 23:3,8–10
- Psalm 139:7–12

Opening Our Eyes

After the week of shocked silence, Job turned to his friends with a verbal torrent of pain, rage and despair. He was wrecked – emotionally, physically and spiritually. Out of the depths of his suffering, he railed against the day of his birth (3:3,11): why had he been born? He now wrestled at a crossroad – he could either curse God, as his wife suggested, or maintain his integrity and trust God. His faith hung by the slenderest of threads. As with so many of life's seemingly impossible situations, Job found the ideas of neither course of action to provide him with relief.

From what we know about the conventions of that culture, we can assume Eliphaz was the senior man and therefore was first to offer his take on things. The author leaves us in no doubt that Eliphaz had difficulty getting a word in edgeways. In his attempt to do what he sees as reconciling Job back to God, Eliphaz reminds Job of the encouragement he had previously given to others. Eliphaz began gently but went on to imply quite emphatically that Job's suffering had to be Job's own fault. He referred to his own spiritual experience to add weight to his argument (4:15).

Eliphaz, albeit in a caring way, offered a 'what I would do if I were you' suggestion (5:8); a temptation with which we are all familiar. This senior 'wise man' then went on to reiterate the commonly held belief of the day: God blesses the righteous and punishes the wicked. How often we find this a belief held even today.

Eliphaz believed that God was so far removed from human nature that nobody could equal His righteousness. All creation was subservient to His wisdom and majesty. Therefore, in Eliphaz's honest opinion, there was no way of avoiding the fact – Job had sinned. With increasing irritation, he dismissed Job's protestations of innocence as empty notions, and condemned his crafty tongue and perceived pride (15:2–7). In Eliphaz's mind, Job's attitude towards God was scandalous. This devout and God-fearing man was disturbed by what he regarded as Job's defiance and outright aggression towards God. However, Job could not be swayed from blaming God for causing his tragedy. Eliphaz could see no other explanation than that Job was speaking shamefully to the point of blasphemy. But, despite everything, Job retained a direct faith in God.

In his final speech, Eliphaz reversed all the good he had said of Job in the beginning verses of chapter 4. His exasperation at Job's refusal to admit any fault leaps out of the poetry. Job needed comfort, but Eliphaz was more concerned with confrontation. And then a flash of divine inspiration: Eliphaz offered a solution of grace (22:21,27). If Job would submit himself to God, he would find the peace that he so desperately sought. According to Eliphaz, in a restored relationship with God, all Job's cries of anguish and bitterness would be channelled into prayer and praise. God would deliver him (22:30). All would be well.

Job, confident in his innocence, was angered by Eliphaz's perception of the situation and unwelcome lectures. He longed for comfort but felt all he had received was criticism. The tragedy of his situation is summed up in the poignant phrase, 'My spirit is broken' (17:1). There are similar examples of despair in other wisdom writings, for example: Psalm 69:20, 'Scorn has broken my heart and has left me helpless. I looked for sympathy, but there was none, for comforters, but I found none' (Psa. 69:20).

Discussion Starters

1. In what ways have you ever felt God to be far away from you?

_____

_____

_____

_____

_____

2. Job felt as if God had turned against him. In times of deep distress, have you ever experienced a similar feeling and found it impossible to pray or praise as a result?

_____

_____

_____

_____

_____

3. How much do you listen to and act on the advice given by your friends?

_____

_____

_____

_____

_____

4. How do you react when you disagree with the advice you are given?

_____

_____

_____

_____

_____

5. Eliphaz declares Job will prosper if only he will submit to God. Compare this with what Jesus said about being His follower in Matthew 16:24.

_____

_____

_____

_____

_____

6. What words would you use to describe Eliphaz?

_____

_____

_____

_____

_____

7. What hope can Job take from Eliphaz's advice?

_____

_____

_____

_____

_____

Personal Application

We live in an amazing world with ever more astonishing advances in technology. Humans have been gifted with incredible intelligence. However, any physical disadvantage, debilitating illness, mental health issue or other difficulty brings us face to face with our vulnerability. When tragedy strikes for no apparent reason, all too often we hear the phrase, 'What have I done to deserve this?' We need to recognise that random suffering does not come from God. We need grace to accept, in some circumstances, that we have no answers. However, we can cling to the promise: '[God] will wipe every tear from their eyes. There will be no more death or mourning or crying or pain, for the old order of things has passed away' (Rev. 21:4).

Seeing Jesus in the Scriptures

The suffering of Job is mirrored in the suffering of Jesus. Against the hostility of the Scribes and Pharisees, Jesus persevered. He was betrayed, arrested, abandoned by His friends, beaten, humiliated and crucified like a criminal. The Son of God knows human suffering first-hand. He is not remote but compassionate. This suffering Jesus, now risen in glory, prays for us (Heb. 7:25). What a glorious hope to lift us to worship and adore Him.

For Reflection

Ask the group to share the names of people, places or situations that are facing suffering, for prayer.

God of grace, healing and wholeness, we lift these to You now. We don't understand, but please strengthen our faith to know we are all held by You. In the name of Jesus Christ, we pray. Amen.

WEEK THREE

'In my opinion...'

Opening Icebreaker

How do people introduce you? Are you Joe Bloggs' daughter? Jane Smith's neighbour or friend? A teacher at the local school or college? Are you introduced to different people in different ways?

Bible Readings

- Job 8:1–7,20–22
- Job 9:2–11,32–35
- Job 18:2–4
- Job 19:1–6,13–27
- Job 25:1–6

Opening Our Eyes

It is possible Job's friend Bildad was a direct descendent of Abraham but removed from the line of Isaac and Jacob. Whatever his background, Bildad was definitely a man of learning and faith in the God of Abraham. Like Eliphaz, he was disturbed to hear Job's accusations against God for causing his distress (6:4–7:20). He began with reasoning from his own deep-held beliefs. It made no sense to Bildad that God would punish a blameless person (8:20). And in Bildad's heart, and from his experience, it was impossible for God to be wrong. Job had to have sinned. He was not the upright man he claimed to be. Bildad reminded Job that against the wisdom of his ancestors, Job was 'born only yesterday' (8:9). However, not wishing to be overly negative, he offered a grain of hope: the God he believed in would restore Job, if Job was prepared to seek Him earnestly and repent (8:5–6).

Job acknowledged God as the creator of all, but in despair he berated God for being distant and unreachable – perhaps a familiar thought for those facing suffering. It is clear that Job was on the edge of a breakdown. Yet even at this low point, an intriguing and new thought spilled into his mind. If only there was someone to act as a mediator between himself and God (9:33).

Bildad tried to apply a positive thinking approach; however, Job was in such a state that positive thinking, rational argument and theological discourse were no help at all: 'Will your long-winded speeches never end?' Job asked in 16:3. To the desperate and suffering Job, his friend's long drawn out explanations missed the point. He needed to know God cared. Bildad, exasperated that his words had no effect, seemed to snap: 'Be sensible, and then we can talk' (18:2). He considered Job to be self-obsessed, in denial over his guilt and resentful towards good advice.

Chapter 19 is one of the shining stars of the book. The agony of Job's isolation is palpable, despite the constant advice from his friends. He lashed out to blame God's anger for his predicament, he pleaded for pity and then verse 25 electrifies the page. Job made an outstanding statement of faith: 'I know that my redeemer lives, and that in the end he will stand on the earth.' The faith and hope within this reminds me of words written by a Jew on the wall of a Cologne concentration camp in the Second World War: 'I believe in the sun, even when it is not shining. I believe in love, even though I do not feel it. I believe in God, even when he is silent.'

It's humbling to think about the millions of people through time who have clung to Job's declaration of faith. These are words inspired by the personal relationship Job had known with God and which enabled him to remain steadfast when all seemed stacked against him. May the Holy Spirit enable us to say those same words from our hearts.

Job is not in any way responsible for his ordeal. Confident that he is blameless and pure in heart, and that this matters to God, he says: 'yet in my flesh I will see God; I myself will see him with my own eyes' (19:26–27). This bears a striking resemblance to the Sermon on the Mount, when Jesus declared: 'Blessed are the pure in heart, for they will see God' (Matt. 5:8).

Discussion Starters

1. Bildad called God 'almighty'. What words would you use to describe God?

2. How do you react when you see someone you know genuinely suffering?

3. What are your thoughts and feelings when you see suffering on the on news and on documentaries?

4. What injustice do you see that tempts you to argue with God?

5. If God is almighty, why does He not eliminate suffering?

_____

_____

_____

_____

_____

6. Refer to Job 9:33. Have you ever had a mediator; someone who has helped to bring you back to God?

_____

_____

_____

_____

_____

7. What words from the New Testament have been helpful to you in times of trouble?

_____

_____

_____

_____

_____

8. What is your reaction to Job's words, 'I know that my redeemer lives, and that in the end he will stand on the earth' (19:25)?

_____

_____

_____

_____

_____

Personal Application

Job responded to his suffering by comparing himself to others. It made him angry with everyone and angry with God. When faced with difficulty, tensions quickly surface in our own lives and Satan, the disturber and adversary, prowls around provoking our anger to flare. That's why it's so important for us to pray for the armour of God so that we can 'stand against the devil's schemes' (Eph. 6:10–17). We must never underestimate the power and subtle attractiveness of evil, nor should we underestimate the power of Jesus Christ to save us and the power of the Holy Spirit to strengthen us.

Seeing Jesus in the Scriptures

In Job's search for redemption and a mediator, we are reminded of our Lord Jesus Christ. Isaiah 59:20 declares, 'The Redeemer will come to Zion', and Hebrews 9:15 says, 'Christ is the mediator of a new covenant'. Jesus is our redeemer, deliverer and mediator. Paul wrote to Timothy, 'there is one God and one mediator between God and mankind, the man Christ Jesus' (1 Tim. 2:5). We don't need to feel isolated from God, because through His death on the cross, Jesus stands to deliver us from our sins and restore us to a right relationship with the Father. Only through Him will we find for ourselves the peace Job sought, the peace that passes all human understanding.

For Reflection

'Love must be sincere. Hate what is evil; cling to what is good... Be joyful in hope, patient in affliction, faithful in prayer... as far as it depends on you, live at peace with everyone' (Rom. 12:9,12,18).

WEEK FOUR

'It's because of...'

Opening Icebreaker

Ask the members of the group if they can think of a saying from the Bible that they find particularly meaningful and would like to pass on to the next generation.

Bible Readings

- Job 11:1–9,13–20
- Job 12:1–6
- Job 13:13–24
- Job 16:7–17
- Job 20:1–8
- Job 21:4–15,34

Opening Our Eyes

Though his speeches were relatively short, Zophar didn't mince his words. He had listened as his two friends reasoned, cajoled and advised – all to no effect. With complete sincerity Job remained adamant that he had not sinned. He was tormented by the thought that God looked on him as an enemy (13:24). At that moment Job could only see God as acting cruelly and unjustly. We catch irritation in Zophar's tone both with Job and the previous speakers. He accused Job of 'idle talk' (11:3), which was somewhat insensitive given Job's situation. Job's spirit may have been broken and his body shrivelled in pain but his mind was working overtime. Zophar, convinced of his superior knowledge and insight, was 'greatly disturbed' (20:2), still trying to have the last word over Job.

The poetry reveals an opinionated and dogmatic friend. Imagine you are sitting listening to this story for the first time. Picture poor old Job slumped in the ashes of his life, torn by grief, head shaven, his physical appearance unrecognisable. Imagine listening to this third friend lecturing him about what he needs to do. Your sympathies would most likely lie with Job as he wails about the injustice of life (21:4–15).

Another towering theme of Scripture – that of light and darkness being synonymous with good and evil – comes across in Job's despair (10:21–22) and Zophar's suggested solution (11:13–17). This theme takes us back to the roots of Genesis where God's first recorded action was to create light to pierce the darkness. Scientists tell us that without light, heat and energy from the sun, our planet would be an ice-covered, lifeless globe. Without the modern wonders of scientific discovery, Job already knew that the almighty creator God was the source of life itself. To God belonged all wisdom, power and majesty; without God, existence would be dark, cold and sterile. Job felt God had abandoned him and become his enemy (13:24). His life seemed truly dark.

In chapter 21 we find another valuable and contemporary theme: why do the wicked prosper? Job is impatient to have answers to this perennial cry (v7). Zophar had failed to explain this conundrum either to Job or the millions down the centuries who have suffered through no fault of their own. Yet the vexed problem of suffering threatened then, and now, to give the impression that God is unfair, uncaring and vindictive. Job berated Zophar with the prosperity he saw accumulated by the 'wicked' (21:7–15). The same kind of questions are heard today.

Way back in the third century, the highly respected Rabbi Yannai wrote: 'It is not in our power to understand either the suffering of the righteous or the prosperity of the wicked.' There are no answers this side of heaven.

Zophar embellished the fate he expected would befall the wicked, by which we realise he had already condemned Job in his heart. The tone of his speech showed his self-appointed monopoly of truth and wisdom. Bitterly, Job replied, 'Nothing is left of your answers but falsehood!' (21:34). *The Message* is more matter-of-fact: 'So how do you expect me to get any comfort from your nonsense? Your so-called comfort is a tissue of lies.' And with that, Zophar left the stage.

Discussion Starters

1. Compare Job's assertion that God will reveal evil deeds (12:22) with the words of Jesus in John 3:19–20. Discuss how our vocabulary today associates good and bad with darkness and light.

2. Like Job's friends, have you found yourself judging someone when they have told you about a painful experience?

3. Zophar says, 'true wisdom has two sides' (11:6). What do you think about this statement?

4. Describe the kind of man you think Zophar would have been. What was his best piece of advice to Job? And does that advice apply to us?

5. What do you believe is righteous anger? Look at
John 2:13–16.

_____

_____

_____

_____

_____

6. Do you become impatient when people disregard your
well-meaning advice?

_____

_____

_____

_____

_____

7. Zophar is convinced that Job is mocking God (11:3). What
is your reaction when you see or hear God mocked today?

_____

_____

_____

_____

_____

Personal Application

It is a common temptation to think we know best, just as Zophar believed. Another common fault is the way we so often quickly jump to conclusions and form judgments. Instead, we need to pay specific attention to God's Word, looking at the context and what the words really mean – not what we think or want them to mean.

Through Job's heart-wrenching story we realise the importance of courage, perseverance and integrity in dealing with difficult life changes. Although we may not know what is around the corner, we can put our trust in the God who is closer than our breath. At the same time, we all have a need to pray for grace to endure what we cannot change and for steadfast faith in the life to come in the presence of God's glory.

Seeing Jesus in the Scriptures

The great sixteenth-century reformer Martin Luther wrote: 'He who does not know Christ does not know God hidden in suffering'. In the vulnerable humanity of Jesus, God endured suffering beyond our imagination. The cross at Calvary was a supreme miscarriage of justice for the blameless Son of God. Millions of words have been written on the subject of why Jesus had to suffer. On the road to Emmaus, Jesus Himself said: 'Did not the Messiah have to suffer these things and then enter his glory?' (Luke 24:26).

For Reflection

'Oh, the depth of the riches of the wisdom and knowledge of God! How unsearchable his judgements, and his paths beyond tracing out!' (Rom. 11:33)

WEEK FIVE

'Listen to me...'

Opening Icebreaker

Ask the group to share light-hearted stories of times when they have been so sure of something, arguing their point of view, only to be proven wrong.

Bible Readings

- Job 32:1–22
- Job 33:1–5,19–33
- Job 34:1–15,34–37
- Job 36:1–5,11–12,26
- Job 37:1–5,14,23–24

Opening Our Eyes

Job's three friends exhausted their arguments. They couldn't break Job's insistence that he had done nothing to deserve such calamity. Listening to all this had been the youngest man, Elihu, who stands as a different 'voice' in the story. Let's look at his unusual credentials.

Elihu is not only known as Barakel's son but also, perhaps significantly, a member of Ram's family. Ram is placed in the illustrious lineage of Jacob, in 1 Chronicles 2. But that is not all – further down Ram's family tree comes the future King David, which could ultimately place Elihu within the extended family of God's Messiah, Jesus. Whatever his background, Ram was an influential name and therefore bestowed authority to Elihu's words.

The previous friends, Eliphaz, Bildad and Zophar had all tried to get Job to admit to sin. They were unable to see beyond the ingrained cause-and-effect mindset of their tradition. Whatever happened to a person, they accepted it as God's direct command because God, El Shaddai, was the mighty creator of heaven, earth, humans and animals. Through his tragic circumstances, Job's thinking on this had shifted, causing him to vehemently challenge God's justice. Job could not *truly* believe his God was a cruel, unjust, capricious deity – yet where was He? Job's world was turned upside down. The faith he had held before no longer seemed fit for purpose.

So what was different about Elihu's speech? Listening to the previous speakers, Elihu had been bursting to put Job right (32:19). He claimed 'the spirit... the breath of the Almighty' had given him special understanding (32:8). This is an important reference to the mysterious, unseen power of Yahweh, the covenant God. It is this Spirit, *Ruach* in Hebrew, who is the life-force of all creation. Our Lord Jesus used the same phrase when in the Nazareth synagogue He read from the scroll of Isaiah: 'The Spirit of the Lord is on me' (Luke 4:18). Elihu considered himself a direct channel of God's wisdom.

As Job's story was told and retold over the centuries, the tiny almost throw-away sentences added pace and tension: 'listen to me' (32:10), 'pay attention' (33:31), 'be silent, and I will teach you wisdom' (33:33). It is as if we can see the stricken Job desperately trying to interrupt to reiterate his argument and yell his innocence.

The thrust of Elihu's speech was that Job's pride had prompted him to imagine he knew better than God. Elihu reminded Job that he had protested he was innocent, right and guiltless but God had inflicted him with an incurable wound (34:5–6). He had declared that God had denied him justice. This attitude was seen by Elihu to be blasphemous, so of course God had correctly punished Job in order to humble him. Like a firebrand preacher, Elihu did his best to correct Job while reminding him what an upright man he himself was (33:1–4). He elevated God's justice, power and righteousness by pointing Job to the order and wonders of nature. In Elihu's estimation, Job deserved his suffering, and his moans and complaints fell as 'empty talk' (35:16) because God is great and beyond human understanding (36:26).

The question may be asked whether the man who charged Job with the sin of pride had himself fallen into that enticing trap, glowing in the assurance he had been able to answer Job's questions in a way the other men had not.

Discussion Starters

1. What is your impression of the young man, Elihu?

2. How often do you say what you think people want to hear and hold back with your honest thoughts in case of offending them?

3. How would you feel if you were suspected of doing wrong when you were innocent? How would you feel if you were punished for this?

4. In what ways may it have looked to Elihu as if Job was showing pride? Do you feel empathy for Job or would you have been frustrated by him like his friends?

5. In 35:1–2, Elihu said: 'Do you think this is just? You say, "I am in the right, not God."' What do you think is justice?

_____

_____

_____

_____

6. The composer Frederic Chopin once wrote: 'Sometimes I can only groan and suffer and pour out my despair at the piano.' How do you deal with times of personal despair?

_____

_____

_____

_____

7. Elihu said, 'Tell us what we should say to [God]' (37:19). What would you like to say to God? Would you describe saying this as prayer?

_____

_____

_____

_____

Personal Application

We often tie ourselves in knots in our efforts to understand the mystery of suffering. At the root of our spiritual wrestling is the desire to make things better, however we can. Let us learn from Elihu's attitude. In his mind Job was to blame, but blame gets us nowhere. It's better to focus on the comfort in friendship, support and compassion we can offer in tragic circumstances, and to thank God for these people in *our* times of need. We also need to take great care to not begin to feel superior to those who don't share our faith, remembering that our horizons are, like Job's, focused on our limited experience.

Seeing Jesus in the Scriptures

Elihu encouraged Job to 'stop and consider God's wonders' (37:14) – the might and majesty of God in creation. Jesus frequently used the mysteries of nature in His miracles. We see this specifically in the raising of Lazarus when Jesus said: 'This illness will not end in death. No, it is for God's glory so that God's Son may be glorified through it' (John 11:4). Thus the Gospel writer aligns Jesus with God the creating Father, having power over nature, life and death. There are many other demonstrations of this power throughout the Gospels (eg Mark 4:39; 8:25).

For Reflection

Blaise Pascal, though fragile in health, became a pioneering inventor of the calculator. After his death in 1662, these words were found on a piece of parchment, sewn into his clothing: 'Certainty, certainty, heartfelt joy, peace. God of Jesus Christ. My God and your God.'

WEEK SIX

Words of wisdom

Opening Icebreaker

Ask members of the group to share which precious stone or precious metal is their favourite. They may have a personal reason behind their choice.

Bible Readings

- Job 28:1–28
- 1 Corinthians 1:18–25
- Colossians 2:2–3,6–7
- Job 1:8
- Proverbs 1:1–7

Opening Our Eyes

Into the thick of this book of agony and argument, before the input from Elihu, drops chapter 28: something completely different. It is not only a calm interlude for reflection, but stands as a superb hymn about wisdom. The wisdom literature within the Bible was a fundamental building block of belief in the God of Abraham, Issac and Jacob. The weighty book of Proverbs underlines the importance of wisdom in the life of men like Job.

This chapter marks the extent and diversity of creation; a portrayal of God's wisdom without borders, placing each person at the mercy of His providence. It is a hymn to God which illustrates the enormous gulf between things human and divine. The writer draws upon ancient philosophy – the love of wisdom – to illuminate the meaning and purpose of life, regardless of time, nation or gender. This unique wisdom encompasses knowledge, understanding and kindness, which calls for a response of righteousness and reverence to the faithful care and guidance of God. To aspire for wisdom gave structure and fulfilment to the lives of ancient readers as much as our lives today.

Gold, silver, lapis lazuli, coral, jasper, topaz – each person of that time knew the extreme labour and hardship entailed to gather such precious items. Yet the writer stressed not even earth's most fabulous riches could buy wisdom, nor could anything be exchanged for wisdom. So, is wisdom beyond human reach? Yes and no. Wisdom comes from God. It is God's gift of grace to those who, like Job, remain faithful and 'shun evil' (28:28). Job is *twice* described as someone who 'fears God and shuns evil' (1:1,8). By this endorsement, the writer portrayed Job as a man of wisdom – greater wisdom than his friends who felt so full of wisdom. It is this wisdom that is important and essential to cling to especially in times of struggle.

To glimpse the importance of wisdom in the ancient world we take a look at the words of Moses addressing the Israelites: 'Observe them [the decrees and laws] carefully, for this will show your wisdom' (Deut. 4:6). Further on in the Bible, many of the Psalms extol wisdom and we can also trace the thread in Proverbs – a book full of the moral benefits of wisdom and its importance above all else.

Within Paul's letter to the multicultural citizens of Corinth and Rome, he appears to have echoed themes from Job. He portrayed Jesus as the fulfilment of God's wisdom and power. True wisdom for the follower of Jesus is therefore a reverent relationship with Him, an acknowledgement of human limitation and dependence on His saving grace. Our Lord Jesus *is* God's wisdom. Jesus is not some kind of replacement for wisdom, but His divine person equates to wisdom. He is above and beyond, transcendent, in the same way as God. Yet in the mystery and miracle of the power of the Holy Spirit, Jesus our redeemer is intimate and involved.

Today, the incredible human brain has mastered the ability to photograph creatures living miles below the surface of the ocean and to travel into space. However, in an age of medical and technological advances there remains a gaping void of wisdom.

The last verse of chapter 28 could be said to sum up the whole message of the Old Testament: 'The fear of the Lord – that is wisdom, and to shun evil is understanding.' Is this the ultimate key to endurance?

Discussion Starters

1. The early verses in Job 28 catalogue the wonders of creation. Which aspects of creation fill you with awe and wonder? How does this help you to worship?

2. God said there was no one on earth like Job. How would you describe him and how he bore his suffering?

3. How can we hold on to our faith when faced with personal suffering?

4. Chapter 28 makes plain that wisdom cannot be measured, controlled, fully comprehended or bought. Discuss the difference, if any, between our attitude to suffering and Job's.

5. In the Beatitudes (Matt. 5:1–12), Jesus turns the world's values upside down. In the context of today's world, would you consider this teaching to be wise or foolish?

_____

_____

_____

_____

_____

6. The Apostle Paul carried the concept of wisdom by calling Jesus Christ 'the power of God and the wisdom of God' (1 Cor. 1:24). What do you think this means?

_____

_____

_____

_____

_____

7. How would you respond to Job's statement in 12:12: 'Is not wisdom found among the aged? Does not long life bring understanding?'

_____

_____

_____

_____

_____

Personal Application

T.S. Eliot, in his poem *The Rock*, wrote, 'Where is the Life we have lost in living? Where is the wisdom we have lost in knowledge?' These are challenging questions to ask ourselves in the rush of modern life. In any personal experience of suffering we need to learn, through prayer, how to apply our experience of God's loving care to our ability to cope with a situation we cannot change. Job was overcome with understandable self-pity, which clouded his trust in God. Although we do not have the full knowledge of our own story, we have the knowledge of Job's story. Therefore, we can trust that as God was with Job so God is also with us, whatever our situation.

Seeing Jesus in the Scriptures

Jesus is the personification of wisdom, as inter-culturally respected as it was. We see this in the importance given in the introductions in Luke's Gospel, written for the Greek-speaking world, and in John's Gospel, written for the predominantly Hebrew speakers. Luke twice mentions the wisdom of the young Jesus: 'he was filled with wisdom, and the grace of God was on him' (Luke 2:40), and again, 'Jesus grew in wisdom' (Luke 2:52). The prologue of John's Gospel begins with 'the Word': in Greek, the *logos*. Jesus is God's Word, God's divine reason, plan and purpose.

For Reflection

Heavenly Father, I know the wisdom that comes from You 'is first of all pure; then peace-loving, considerate, submissive, full of mercy and good fruit, impartial and sincere' (James 3:17). I ask for Your gifts of grace and wisdom. Amen.

WEEK SEVEN

Divine intervention

Opening Icebreaker

In what in the world do you see miracles of God's creation?
What do you consider to be the greatest human achievement?

Bible Readings

- Job 29:1–25
- Job 30:1–15
- Job 31:1–6
- Job 38:1–7,31–33
- Job 40:1–8
- Job 42:1–6,10–16

Opening Our Eyes

Job began his final defence by recounting his past youth and virtuous way of life. In his own eyes and the eyes of those in the town, he had been a model citizen. Eliphaz, Bildad, Zophar and Elihu, however, deduced that Job could not possibly have been as perfect as he maintained.

Finally, God enters 'out of the storm' (38:1). However we imagine the tone of the voice of God in chapter 38 – whether loud and booming, or gentle and inquisitive – He presents Himself clearly as an unequalled power. God poses these unanswerable questions at Job. Rather than a feisty inquisition by God to a chastened and vulnerable Job, we need to see this episode as a dramatic method to spotlight God's supremacy. God is not human but divine. He is beyond all human limitations and understanding. Job demonstrates his acceptance of the divide between human and divine by admitting there were things 'too wonderful for me to know' (42:3). Yet far from being crushed into the abyss, something wonderful has happened to Job. He had heard of God, but suddenly God becomes real to him (42:5).

Has the author provided us with an answer to innocent suffering? It's not that simple. Maybe we ask the wrong questions. In this book, the writer has forged an emotive, unforgettable story over which all generations have struggled. The purpose seems to have been twofold. First: to elevate the Lord God beyond human understanding. Second: to oppose the rigidity of the retribution dogma – the idea that God brings prosperity to the righteous and takes delight in punishing the wicked. This prompts us to realign basic attitudes towards reward and punishment. It's common for children to be threatened with the consequences of bad behaviour, such as, 'If you're naughty you'll be sent to your room.' From our earliest years we become programmed to understand that good behaviour works to our advantage, although good behaviour is not necessarily our primary desire. Breaking any of the Ten Commandments can land us in trouble, impacting not only on our own mental, physical and spiritual wellbeing but also that of others. It is for this reason that we do our best to live within certain norms of behaviour. However, this Old Testament book is the prime example of when inexplicable suffering strikes the most moral and spiritual people.

At the very beginning of the book, Satan pushed his theory – true goodness is not self-serving. Likewise, true faith in God is not an insurance policy adopted in case of problems. Would Job, this upright and blameless man, crack when everybody and everything he loved was gone? Would he retain his faith no matter what? That was the essence of Satan's question. Though it wasn't at all easy and there were times of complete despair, Job held on to his faith in God.

In the face of random, undeserved suffering does our faith crack and crumble? Can we acknowledge that suffering does not come from God?

The epilogue confronts us with more questions. How can this scale of tragedy suddenly evaporate into a happy-ever-after ending? Is this a regression to the very philosophy the author had been at pains to contradict? Why does the innocent suffering we see and read about daily not have the same cheerful resolution? These are legitimate questions from our contemporary viewpoint. However, we need to look through the biblical lens in order to pan for the nuggets of God's golden truth. God is ever present, whatever our storm, and we are promised ultimate victory through our redeemer, Jesus Christ (1 Cor. 15:57).

Discussion Starters

1. In what ways do you think Job was a different man by the
    end of the story?

2. What words would you use to describe Job's
    spiritual journey?

3. How do you feel when you know a friend has
    prayed for you?

4. Use this question in conjunction with Question 5.
    Compare the different ways God is represented in the
    Old Testament. For example, a storm (Job 38:1), a pillar of
    cloud (Exod. 13:21) and a gentle whisper (1 Kings 19:12).

5. Now compare how the Holy Spirit is represented in the New Testament, in particular in John 20:22 and Acts 2:2–3.

6. Looking back over the portions of Job in these seven studies, which of Job's words have resonated with your own experience?

7. At the end of these sessions, what are your feelings towards the book of Job?

Personal Application

We often get so caught up in our own hurts and injustices that it is hard to move beyond how *we* feel. In the Hebrew text of 42:6, there is no word for 'myself'. And what has been translated as 'despise' could also be read as 'ashamed of', allowing for a reading of: 'I'm ashamed of my previous attitude', or 'I reject all I've previously said against God'. We are not alone in suffering, in calling out to God or in demanding answers. But beware: Job looked back with nostalgia and pride on his previous life and status. There are occasions when we need to reject concentration on our own laments and problems and move in faith to the future. Here especially, a meeting with God, an experience of the presence of Jesus, makes all the difference.

Seeing Jesus in the Scriptures

Job's restoration into a right relationship with God brought about great blessings: family, material prosperity and long life. It was the best happy ending for pre-Christian thought. But for us, faced with evil in the world and traumas within our own lives or the lives of those around us, Jesus offers not an ending but a new beginning. A relationship in this life that gives us courage and lasts eternally (John 14:15–20). This is God's richest blessing. Hallelujah!

For Reflection

'He lives, all glory to his name; he lives, my Saviour, still the same; what joy the blest assurance gives, I know that my Redeemer lives!' (Samuel Medley, *I Know That My Redeemer Lives*, 1738–1799)

Leader's Notes

Bible Readings
Due to the length of the book of Job, you'll notice that the readings are extensive. You might find it helpful to ask the group to read them beforehand. Or you may prefer to read through them all before the session and decide which ones you think will be key for your group.

Discussion Starters
There is no obligation to plough through all of the Discussion Starters. They are, as the heading suggests, 'starters'. Often the text will bring out other topics to discuss. If there is one eager participant with a lot to say, encourage different people to speak, while avoiding embarrassment to those who are reticent. It is always much easier if the leader knows his/her group members.

Week One: The prologue

Opening Our Eyes
Such a deep and emotive subject as suffering cannot be adequately covered in seven short sessions, but I hope that members of the group will be motivated to delve deeper into this book. Whether the minimum verses are read or some readers plough through the whole book, it is an unsettling read. What is the original author getting at? Underline for the group how difficult it is to open a window into such a different world to our own. This was a basic world. A flat world. A world which accepted the governance of rulers and powers and unseen forces. Therefore, the idea grew that Yahweh, the living God, would order His heavenly court in a similar manner. In parallel to earthly rulers, Yahweh would protect and prosper those who were obedient to Him, while those who rebelled would be severely punished.

Unmatched in his upright life, Job worshipped God and, within his family, acted as a priest in making sacrifices and praying for his children. This is one of the facts that prompts many scholars to place the dating of this story to well before Moses, the Exodus and Levitical laws.

The imagery evoked by the conversation in heaven represents the conflict between good and evil. The dramatic dialogue borders on pantomime yet out of this bizarre opening sequence we take vital truth: God does not *cause* tragedy. Whatever happens in our life, God our creator knows and cares.

With jaw-dropping rapidity, Job receives news of catastrophe after catastrophe. Yet even as a broken man, his response was to worship God. The tearing of clothes and sprinkling of ashes was a common sign of deepest mourning, remorse and despair (compare Josh. 7:6). It was a dramatic way to demonstrate his feelings to the world. We tend to hide our feelings, but Job blurted out his misery without restraint, as we will look at further in the next session.

In your group there may be people wrestling with the same question that we will see throughout the book of Job: 'Why?' It is helpful to see what the apostle Paul wrote to encourage new believers in Rome: whatever happens, nothing will separate us from the love of God in Jesus (Rom. 8:35–39). Job longed to find that truth; the same truth for us to grasp today.

There is no hint here that Eliphaz, Bildad and Zophar were anything but close friends. They went to considerable trouble leaving their homes to go and support Job. The men came across a shaven, broken man covered in sores, reduced to sitting outside the city gate like a leper. A social and religious outcast. In sincere support they mourned with him for seven days. In Hebrew, seven was considered the complete number.

'The patience of Job' has become a well-worn cliché, but if the reader had assumed Job was a demure, mild and patient sufferer, a shock awaits.

To end you may like to share the Peace or say the Grace together.

Week Two: 'If I were you...'

Opening Our Eyes

People's experiences vary and some in the group may feel the book opens old or unresolved wounds. Job's plight confronts us with inescapable, raw misery. But as we dig deeper into these scriptures it is fascinating to recognise the core themes that take hold.

Whatever our place in history and wherever we live in the world, each one of us at some point in time has to face the tension between the existence of the horrendous suffering of innocent people, and the God of love, incarnate in the person Jesus. The leader should seek to help the group differentiate between man-made tragedies (caused by things like violence, corruption, inequality and greed) and the life-changing effects of physical and mental illness, crushing bereavements and losses of many kinds. In other words, something like war obviously causes suffering, but a child can suffer from a life-limiting illness which has no attributable cause or reason.

Stress the point that through the speeches and replies, the biblical author seeks to demonstrate that God does *not* inflict suffering. It is vital for this to be said.

Throughout the Bible we find an acceptance of evil in the world, but also the unshakeable belief in the eternal and almighty God having the ultimate victory. Compare Peter's

reference to the devil prowling around looking for someone to devour (1 Pet. 5:8) with the similar idea of Satan 'roaming throughout the earth' mentioned in Job 1:7. The Bible underlines the universal fact that evil can be found anywhere and everywhere, but the power of God in Jesus transcends all suffering with ultimate victory.

It's salutary to recognise the theme of 'good advice' and the temptation to think we know best, that we have the answers. Well-meaning advice can ring trite and hollow to someone whose suffering we can never imagine. Eliphaz had acknowledged Job's godliness but made it plain that no human was more pure than God, even moving to contradict his acknowledgement with accusation.

We also meet another of the great biblical themes: darkness versus light. Through symbolism we track Job in the dark night of his soul, but even so we catch tiny pin-pricks of light reflected from his indomitable spirit. Words such as integrity and perseverance spring to mind as we wait for Job to falter and curse God. He gets close to it, but such is his faith and his historically close relationship with God that he is able to approach Him with honesty and with his protestations such as, 'Why?' and, 'It's unfair!' In 23:11 he argues, 'I have kept to his way without turning aside'. It may be helpful at this point to notice distinct echoes of 23:8–10 in Psalm 139:7–12.

In the face of all his suffering and loss, Job cannot curse God. References to Job's specific suffering are scattered through the chapters but here is the full picture: head-to-toe painful sores (2:7), broken skin and scabs (7:5), reduced to skin and bones (19:20), gnawing pains (30:17), blackened, peeling skin and his body burning with fever (30:30).

Often those who bear the greatest burdens are the most courageous and inspirational, and there are times when we may need to put our own situation into perspective. In the light of the resurrection, we have a 'living hope' (1 Pet. 1:3) that all our trials will be a distant memory in eternity. In the life to come we will know the light, peace and presence of our Saviour.

Week Three: 'In my opinion...'

Opening Our Eyes

Bildad had begun by assuring Job that if he was truly pure and upright then God would restore him. But chapter 18 is harsh indeed. His speech is a description of a 'wicked man', one 'who does not know God'. He is definitely pointing the finger at Job. The final mention of this second friend comes in chapter 25. Frustrated that Job rejected his advice, Bildad had no more to say.

In Old Testament times, family relationships added credence and authority to any narrative. Could this be why Bildad is given the title 'the Shuhite'? If we turn back to Genesis 25:1–2, we read that after Sarah's death, Abraham married Keturah, and one of their sons was called Shuah.

Considering Bildad's arguments, we see that he was neither wholly right, nor was he wholly wrong. He did his best to try to show Job ways to extricate himself from his predicament, but there is little compassion and even less empathy.

Job's retort to Bildad in chapter 19 lays bare the heat of his anger. There is anger towards Bildad and anger towards God, and he even accused God of turning a burning anger against him. Poor Job was crumbling under his suffering and it seems things could not become more hopeless. But what a dramatic

use of contrast between his anger and isolation and his declaration of faith.

There are three glorious subjects to draw from this session. First, a question which can be asked to the group: who do they think Job was addressing, Bildad or God? Second, introducing the theme of a mediator between God and the individual. Third, Job's declaration in 19:25–27 and its role as the central jewel of the book.

Although Job had accused God of causing his distress, he couldn't stop himself from talking as though God was listening. This underlines the human longing to know a power beyond ourselves.

Job longed for a mediator – a go-between, intercessor or bridge – between himself and God. He may not have had any specific messianic thoughts or even hope of resurrection, but he longed for someone who would ease his burden. We are blessed to *know* we have a mediator in God's Son, our Lord Jesus.

Job, a man who had been very much in control of his life, now found himself in emotional turmoil, out of control, gripped by the depression of spiralling helplessness. Such turmoil from so long ago packs a surprisingly powerful impact on today's reader. Job's plight brings out our sympathy and our own bewilderment in the randomness of innocent suffering. Strange as it may seem to secular minds, for all Job's suffering, his greatest need was not to regain his health but to find God, speak to Him and be vindicated.

If nothing else is remembered from these sessions, let it be 19:23–27. This was a heartfelt outpouring of the deepest faith. Crushed by circumstance, Job nevertheless believed this life was not all. One day, somehow, he would see God.

He had longed for a mediator to speak on his behalf, and in these verses Job had full confidence that somewhere he had a redeemer. The tradition of the redeemer ran deep in the people's history. The *goel*, the kinsman-redeemer, was like a relative who could buy a person out of debt, redeem a slave, restore their rights and even avenge their wrongs. In light of how God's relationship with His people developed, there can be no better sentiment for the Christian to utter than: 'I know that my redeemer lives!'

Week Four: 'It's because of...'

Opening Our Eyes

It may be helpful to remind the group of when the friends had sat in silent sympathy with Job. Their companionable silence was preferable to their subsequent tirade of 'good advice'. Within these slices of sharp counsel Job swung from the depths of depression, wishing he had never been born, to the highest of hopes for a redeemer and a longing to see God face to face. His outpourings were directed both to God and to his friends. In one breath he groaned at being crushed by God's severe injustice and in the next moment he admitted that wisdom, power and understanding belong to God. Anyone who has suffered will find the extremes of Job's experiences heartfelt and deeply moving.

Take a moment to recap the horror of Job's situation to the group. His sons and daughters had been murdered. The entirety of his livestock, oxen, donkeys and camels stolen and sheep destroyed. He was covered head to toe in painful sores, his skin broken, his breath offensive, and his friends and remaining family had turned against him.

Together with the other two friends, Zophar, held to the rigid tradition of prosperity for the righteous and punishment

for the wicked. This too had been Job's understanding, until catastrophe struck him. The structure of these dramatic speeches show us Job's inner struggle with these received beliefs and how, out of his despair and furious accusations against God, he discovered his own ignorance and vulnerability. Job cried out to God in anger and frustration, accusing God of being vengeful. He cried out to his friends in pitiful, bitter, resentful and even sarcastic words (12:2). He bristled at being patronised.

Zophar had no doubt Job had sinned. In his eyes, Job's protestations were blasphemous and arrogant. What could Job know about the ways of God? (See 11:8.) To the zealous Zophar it was simple: God only punished the wicked, so Job needed to admit his sin and seek forgiveness. However, as we progress through this drama, we become aware of just how much Job's faith was maturing and how he was moving closer to regain his relationship with God, while the three friends held to their original dogma.

The problem of evil has exercised the finest minds in every century and country. The flourishing of people who have committed great wrong confounds and shocks us. We will have all heard the question, often an accusation, 'Why does God allow such tragedy?' Sadly, many people have lost all faith through unexplainable, crushing circumstances. Job even wondered if there was any point in being born at all (3:11). Rather than words of comfort, Zophar talked about a far-removed God of power and might, occupied with his creation and unmoved by human need.

Did Zophar attribute to his God the fierce revenge for sin that he himself would like to inflict? His final contribution was a stylised and colourful vision of how he felt God should deal with the wicked.

Before we leave Zophar, we must give him credit for offering hope, even if it was in a veiled way. Zophar's simplistic remedy was for Job to devote his heart to God (11:13), then all would be well. This friend was on the right track but more focussed on the Law than on love. Even though this leaves us with the same questions, we have the promise given to Paul when he wrestled with his thorn in the flesh (whatever that was): 'My grace is sufficient for you, for my power is made perfect in weakness' (2 Cor. 12:8). The presence of Jesus Christ in our lives will give us strength.

Week Five: 'Listen to me...'

Opening Our Eyes

Elihu's tirade flows uninterrupted for six chapters. He is truly excited by his superior insight and understanding of God. He says: 'my heart pounds and leaps' (37:1). Compare what the founder of Methodism, John Wesley, said on his conversion: 'I felt my heart strangely warmed'. Elihu's spiritual experience was real enough but was perhaps clouded by self-righteousness.

Job's abject misery had driven him to make a radical reappraisal both of life and God. This brings us to another major theme: the God of our preconceptions. We need more than a handed-down God from other people. The God of all creation is the God who offers a personal relationship through His Son, Jesus Christ. For each one of us, the pathway to inner healing and deeper faith comes by confronting our doubts, by being open and honest before God. Within the core of our being, our very soul, there is a need to find this God – a God for the here and now – *our* God.

Elihu fully believed he spoke on God's behalf, so his speech was filled with explanations to justify God's perceived action

or non-action. He condemned Job as ignorant, rebellious and scornful (34:34–37) and his self-righteous enthusiasm led to barbed comments (35:14–16). However, we have been told from the very beginning that Job is blameless and upright. He had no sin of which to repent. Or had he? Job's anguish and frustration boiled through the speeches offered by the four men. How much had pride, anger and defiance caused a barrier between himself and God? Suffering can be harmful when it makes us resentful and bitter or when we become so self-absorbed we reject God. Elihu, having run out of theological arguments, declared that awesome power and might belonged to God alone, the God of all creation who is great and 'beyond our understanding' (36:26). He believed Job's agony and protestations did not affect God in any way.

Having made a few caustic comments, Elihu ended his contribution with kinder words. Nevertheless, they appear contradictory words. After saying that God 'shatters the mighty' (34:24) and 'punishes them for their wickedness' (34:26), he ended by saying that God does not oppress (37:23). He then makes the point that in the face of God's 'awesome majesty' (37:22), mere mortals can do nothing but worship in humble reverence.

The Hebrew word for fear (*yir'ah*), as in 'the fear of God', has a modern definition similar to respect, reverence and awe. In the Old Testament there were two types of fear. One was the fear of punishment and the other a fear of divine glory. Job felt both of these fears, he felt he was being punished but he also retained his awe and reverence of God.

In writing to the small group of believers in Rome, the apostle Paul, quoting from Psalm 36, echoed many of the same ideas as Elihu. Paul's message was that problems occur because we have lost our fear (respect, awe, reverence) of God (Rom. 3:11–18). For a right relationship with the living

God, and therefore a moral and upright life, we need to recognise, as David Atkinson says, 'The living God is one who is not so much to be debated as encountered, not so much to be discussed as to be known.'* Job's friends delighted in their debate but Job was desperate to have that personal relationship restored. He longed to rekindle the relationship he had once had with his God. For everyone, that relationship with God begins with a new perspective on life.

*David Atkinson, *The Bible Speaks Today: The Message of Job* (Inter-Varsity Press: Nottingham, 1991) p154

Week Six: Words of wisdom

Opening Our Eyes

Whether this was originally Job's speech, or the linking thoughts of the unknown author, chapter 28 stands like a literary aid for the time in which it was written. Modern plays and concerts have their intervals, television programmes their commercial breaks, and in the same way the author uses this chapter as a dramatic 'pause'. After the spiral of misery, the rising tempo of Job's accusations against God and his friends, and the friends' repetitive monologues, this chapter gives space for calm reappraisal of the situation. And it will be helpful to use this space to take a step back, digest the story so far and consider how we, with our modern minds, deal with our preconceptions of Job and, more importantly, God.

Ask members of the group if they have been surprised by Job's attacks on God. The old phrase 'the patience of Job' has been shown to be misleading. His temper has raged at the injustice of his trauma; he has fluctuated wildly between accusing God of pursuing and crushing him, and being desperate to speak face to face and to plead his innocence. In despair Job

had previously wanted to die, only to then acknowledge that God's wisdom is profound (28:23). He had begged God to leave him alone, then cried out for God to show Himself. These mercurial swings have the ring of authenticity. Few readers will not have experienced a harrowing situation where a loved one has suffered from cancer, dementia or other significant illness that cannot be cured. In these situations, our faith often mirrors that of Job. Although we believe in the power of almighty God, we can accuse Him of not answering our fervent prayers. We too fluctuate wildly into anger and despair, with our unanswerable questions. None of us can remain steadfast 100% of the time. We all know what it is to waiver, wobble and lose heart. This is when we need to cling to Scripture, God's inspired Word. Direct the group to look at Colossians 2:2–3,6–7. Our focus must be on Christ Himself, the human face of God.

Chapter 28 literally brings us down to earth. The catalogue of material riches, the inclusion of all the birds and animals who, imbued with innate instinct, cannot match the wisdom of the almighty God of creation. This is what the chapter is about and indeed what the whole book is about – wisdom and the beyond human comprehension of the almighty, creator God. In the shadow of this awesome power, the human mind can only respond by worship. This human response is demonstrated by the pantheon of gods in various ancient and modern cultures, even in the most remote areas of the world.

You may find it helpful to encourage the group to look at the Beatitudes. In these especially, we see the overturning of the world's values, and an illustration of God's wisdom which the world finds foolish. Jesus gave us a window into the kingdom of God and the way to deal with life with all its complexities. This teaching brings us to realise our own need to trust; 'trust in the LORD with all your heart and lean not on your own understanding' (Prov. 3:5). Neither the story of Job nor the teaching of our Lord Jesus can be dismissed as dusty words unrelated to us. They are timeless words of wisdom, connecting with all those searching for meaning and purpose for life.

Week Seven: Divine intervention

Opening Our Eyes

Job had shouted out to God throughout the book, and in the epilogue, Yahweh, the covenant God of the first chapter, comes to Job. It's interesting that in the intervening chapters the name used for God is El Shaddai, God Almighty. This is not to imply there are two types of God, rather Job's perception of God was changed by his suffering. At first Job was at ease with God as both friend and focus of worship, but his suffering left him feeling deserted. Job's faith was shaken by thinking God had become distant, vindictive, unjust and uncaring. Using the name for the covenant God was the way of expressing Job's restored relationship with Him.

If not already used in the Discussion Starters, point out the different ways that God is depicted in the Old Testament.

Encourage the group to not let this unrealistic, happy little ending tempt them to walk away from Job's story in the same way we walk out of a cinema, having delved into a tale which temporarily grips but ultimately has little effect on our day-to-day lives. Job's restoration with a new family does not in any way erase or negate the pain of losing his first family. It is the poet's way of making the point that life continues and there is hope.

The end of the book of Job leaves us with an overwhelming lesson: relentless accusations, heated arguments or wonderful theories do not bring us into a personal encounter with God.

The theme of redemption filters through the Old Testament in preparation for God's Word and wisdom in the human form of Jesus. This then is the lens by which the happy ending in Job needs to be seen.

Job's story is never total gloom; there are many 'cracks' through which the light of hope, endurance and redemption flickers until the final blaze of his encounter with God. We may find similar 'cracks' when we face suffering.

In any situation, we can be sure of the hope of eternity. This is something picked up on in the Old Testament and made explicit in the New Testament in the teaching of our Lord Jesus and in the light of His death and resurrection. King David wrote, 'I will dwell in the house of the LORD for ever' (Psalm 23:6). To be in God's presence forever is to be restored and renewed.

When human answers fail us, we can only place our hope and faith in the suffering and resurrection of Jesus Christ, our Saviour and Lord. Through Him, we can have the strength to endure life's difficulties.

For prayer, you might like to place a table in the centre of the room. On the table, place a cross, a candle and either some smaller crosses or a selection of stones for people to hold. Give one to each person and while they hold their cross or stone, take a few moments for silent prayer. The Leader could then read from Ephesians 1:17–18: 'I keep asking that the God of our Lord Jesus Christ, the glorious Father, may give you the Spirit of wisdom and revelation, so that you may know him better. I pray that the eyes of your heart may be enlightened in order that you may know the hope to which he has called you.'

Saying the Lord's Prayer together and sharing the words of the Grace may be a fitting way to draw this challenging study to a close.

Notes...

The *Cover to Cover* Bible Study Series

1 Corinthians
Growing a Spirit-filled church
ISBN: 978-1-85345-374-8

2 Corinthians
Restoring harmony
ISBN: 978-1-85345-551-3

1,2,3 John
Walking in the truth
ISBN: 978-1-78259-763-6

1 Peter
Good reasons for hope
ISBN: 978-1-78259-088-0

2 Peter
Living in the light of God's promises
ISBN: 978-1-78259-403-1

23rd Psalm
The Lord is my shepherd
ISBN: 978-1-85345-449-3

1 Timothy
Healthy churches – effective Christians
ISBN: 978-1-85345-291-8

2 Timothy and Titus
Vital Christianity
ISBN: 978-1-85345-338-0

Abraham
Adventures of faith
ISBN: 978-1-78259-089-7

Acts 1–12
Church on the move
ISBN: 978-1-85345-574-2

Acts 13–28
To the ends of the earth
ISBN: 978-1-85345-592-6

Barnabas
Son of encouragement
ISBN: 978-1-85345-911-5

Bible Genres
Hearing what the Bible really says
ISBN: 978-1-85345-987-0

Daniel
Living boldly for God
ISBN: 978-1-85345-986-3

David
A man after God's own heart
ISBN: 978-1-78259-444-4

Ecclesiastes
Hard questions and spiritual answers
ISBN: 978-1-85345-371-7

Elijah
A man and his God
ISBN: 978-1-85345-575-9

Elisha
A lesson in faithfulness
ISBN: 978-1-78259-494-9

Ephesians
Claiming your inheritance
ISBN: 978-1-85345-229-1

Esther
For such a time as this
ISBN: 978-1-85345-511-7

Ezekiel
A prophet for all times
ISBN: 978-1-78259-836-7

Fruit of the Spirit
Growing more like Jesus
ISBN: 978-1-85345-375-5

Galatians
Freedom in Christ
ISBN: 978-1-85345-648-0

Genesis 1–11
Foundations of reality
ISBN: 978-1-85345-404-2

Genesis 12–50
Founding fathers of faith
ISBN: 978-1-78259-960-9

God's Rescue Plan
Finding God's fingerprints on human history
ISBN: 978-1-85345-294-9

Great Prayers of the Bible
Applying them to our lives today
ISBN: 978-1-85345-253-6

Habakkuk
Choosing God's way
ISBN: 978-1-78259-843-5

Haggai
Motivating God's people
ISBN: 978-1-78259-686-8

Hebrews
Jesus – simply the best
ISBN: 978-1-85345-337-3

Isaiah 1–39
Prophet to the nations
ISBN: 978-1-85345-510-0

Isaiah 40–66
Prophet of restoration
ISBN: 978-1-85345-550-6

Jacob
Taking hold of God's blessing
ISBN: 978-1-78259-685-1

James
Faith in action
ISBN: 978-1-85345-293-2

Jeremiah
The passionate prophet
ISBN: 978-1-85345-372-4

Job
The source of wisdom
ISBN: 978-1-78259-992-0

Joel
Getting real with God
ISBN: 978-1-78951-927-2

John's Gospel
Exploring the seven miraculous signs
ISBN: 978-1-85345-295-6

Jonah
Rescued from the depths
ISBN: 978-1-78259-762-9

Joseph
The power of forgiveness and reconciliation
ISBN: 978-1-85345-252-9

Joshua 1–10
Hand in hand with God
ISBN: 978-1-85345-542-7

Joshua 11–24
Called to service
ISBN: 978-1-78951-138-3

Judges 1–8
The spiral of faith
ISBN: 978-1-85345-681-7

Judges 9–21
Learning to live God's way
ISBN: 978-1-85345-910-8

Luke
A prescription for living
ISBN: 978-1-78259-270-9

Mark
Life as it is meant to be lived
ISBN: 978-1-85345-233-8

Mary
The mother of Jesus
ISBN: 978-1-78259-402-4

Moses
Face to face with God
ISBN: 978-1-85345-336-6

Names of God
Exploring the depths of God's character
ISBN: 978-1-85345-680-0

Nehemiah
Principles for life
ISBN: 978-1-85345-335-9

Parables
Communicating God on earth
ISBN: 978-1-85345-340-3

Philemon
From slavery to freedom
ISBN: 978-1-85345-453-0

Philippians
Living for the sake of the gospel
ISBN: 978-1-85345-421-9

Prayers of Jesus
Hearing His heartbeat
ISBN: 978-1-85345-647-3

Proverbs
Living a life of wisdom
ISBN: 978-1-85345-373-1

Psalms
Songs of life
ISBN: 978-1-78951-240-3

Revelation 1–3
Christ's call to the Church
ISBN: 978-1-85345-461-5

Revelation 4–22
The Lamb wins! Christ's final victory
ISBN: 978-1-85345-411-0

Rivers of Justice
Responding to God's call to righteousness today
ISBN: 978-1-85345-339-7

Ruth
Loving kindness in action
ISBN: 978-1-85345-231-4

Song of Songs
A celebration of love
ISBN: 978-1-78259-959-3

The Armour of God
Living in His strength
ISBN: 978-1-78259-583-0

The Beatitudes
Immersed in the grace of Christ
ISBN: 978-1-78259-495-6

The Creed
Belief in action
ISBN: 978-1-78259-202-0

The Divine Blueprint
God's extraordinary power in ordinary lives
ISBN: 978-1-85345-292-5

The Holy Spirit
Understanding and experiencing Him
ISBN: 978-1-85345-254-3

The Image of God
His attributes and character
ISBN: 978-1-85345-228-4

The Kingdom
Studies from Matthew's Gospel
ISBN: 978-1-85345-251-2

The Letter to the Colossians
In Christ alone
ISBN: 978-1-855345-405-9

The Letter to the Romans
Good news for everyone
ISBN: 978-1-85345-250-5

The Lord's Prayer
Praying Jesus' way
ISBN: 978-1-85345-460-8

The Prodigal Son
Amazing grace
ISBN: 978-1-85345-412-7

The Second Coming
Living in the light of Jesus' return
ISBN: 978-1-85345-422-6

The Sermon on the Mount
Life within the new covenant
ISBN: 978-1-85345-370-0

Thessalonians
Building Church in changing times
ISBN: 978-1-78259-443-7

The Ten Commandments
Living God's Way
ISBN: 978-1-85345-593-3

The Uniqueness of our Faith
What makes Christianity distinctive?
ISBN: 978-1-85345-232-1

Be inspired by God.
Every day.

Confidently face life's challenges by equipping yourself daily with God's Word. There is something for everyone...

Every Day with Jesus

Selwyn Hughes' renowned writing is updated by Mick Brooks into these trusted and popular notes.

Life Every Day

Jeff Lucas helps apply the Bible to daily life with his trademark humour and insight.

Inspiring Women Every Day

Encouragement, uplifting scriptures and insightful daily thoughts for women.

The Manual

Straight-talking guides to help men walk daily with God. Written by Carl Beech.

To find out more about all our daily Bible reading notes, or to take out a subscription, visit **cwr.org.uk/biblenotes** or call 01252 784700.
Also available in Christian bookshops.

 Printed format Large print format Email format Ebook format

SmallGroup central

All of our small group ideas and resources in one place

Online:

smallgroupcentral.org.uk
is filled with free video teaching, tools, articles and a whole host of ideas.

On the road:

A range of seminars themed for small groups can be brought to your local community. Contact us at **hello@smallgroupcentral.org.uk**

In print:

Books, study guides and DVDs covering an extensive list of themes, Bible books and life issues.

Find out more at:
smallgroupcentral.org.uk

Courses and events

Waverley Abbey College

Publishing and media

Conference facilities

Transforming lives

CWR's vision is to enable people to experience personal transformation through applying God's Word to their lives and relationships.

Our Bible-based training and resources help people around the world to:
• Grow in their walk with God
• Understand and apply Scripture to their lives
• Resource themselves and their church
• Develop pastoral care and counselling skills
• Train for leadership
• Strengthen relationships, marriage and family life and much more.

Our insightful writers provide daily Bible reading notes and other resources for all ages, and our experienced course designers and presenters have gained an international reputation for excellence and effectiveness.

CWR's Training and Conference Centre in Surrey, England, provides excellent facilities in an idyllic setting – ideal for both learning and spiritual refreshment.

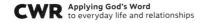

CWR Applying God's Word
to everyday life and relationships

CWR, Waverley Abbey House,
Waverley Lane, Farnham,
Surrey GU9 8EP, UK

Telephone: **+44 (0)1252 784700**
Email: **info@cwr.org.uk**
Website: **cwr.org.uk**

Registered Charity No. 294387
Company Registration No. 1990308